Introductory statistics
with applications in
general insurance

Introductory statistics with applications in general insurance

I. B. HOSSACK
Senior Lecturer in Statistics, Macquarie University

J. H. POLLARD
Professor of Actuarial Studies, Macquarie University

B. ZEHNWIRTH
Senior Lecturer in Statistics, Macquarie University

CAMBRIDGE
UNIVERSITY PRESS

Published by the Press Syndicate of the University of Cambridge
The Pitt Building, Trumpington Street, Cambridge CB2 1RP
40 West 20th Street, New York, NY 10011–4211, USA
10 Stamford Road, Oakleigh, Victoria 3166, Australia

First published 1983
Reprinted 1987, 1988, 1989, 1990, 1992

Printed in Great Britain at the University Press, Cambridge

Library of Congress catalogue card number: 82–4421

British Library cataloguing in publication data
Hossack, I. B.
Introductory statistics with applications in general insurance.
1. Insurance–Statistical methods
I. Title   II. Pollard, J. H.
III. Zehnwirth, B.
519.5'024368   HA29

ISBN 0 521 24781 0 hardback
ISBN 0 521 28957 2 paperback

MU

CONTENTS

Contents

Contents

PREFACE

The success of the general insurance industry over several hundred years is a tribute to the judgement and skill of generations of underwriters who were able to assess diverse risks and underwrite them without extensive statistical data. The business was profitable because the premiums were more than adequate and included substantial margins for contingencies.

The twentieth century brought risks of previously unimagined magnitude, and saw the development of fierce competition between insurers in markets which were better informed, severe rate-cutting, consumerism, government control of premium rates in certain classes of business, and other factors, all of which combined to make the underwriting of insurance in modern conditions extremely difficult. Bouts of high inflation have led to claim settlements considerably higher than those allowed for in the premiums. The rapid development of new technologies has meant that new risks, for which there is insufficient experience upon which to base rates, now comprise a larger proportion of all risks. Clients have become accustomed to change, and now expect to change their insurers whenever they can see an advantage in doing so. It is no longer possible, therefore, for an insurer to charge a premium which is obviously more than adequate, and remain in business.

The twentieth century has also seen the growth of statistical theory and practice from infancy to full maturity, and the development of sophisticated computers with huge storage capacities. In the modern environment the use of these tools by insurers is essential. It needs to be emphasised, however, that in assessing premium rates, contingency margins, retention limits, provisions for outstanding claims, provisions for incurred but not reported claims, etc., *statistical methods and computer technology are tools to aid the professional; they are not substitutes for professional judgement.*

The aim of this book (which evolved from a set of lecture notes prepared for a Macquarie University Continuing Education Course with the same title) is to provide practitioners in the general insurance industry with basic statistical tools, which are of immediate application in the industry, and to demonstrate that the methods are both practical and useful.

Preface

While our primary objective is to introduce readers with little or no statistical background to a variety of statistical methods with applications in general insurance (and we hope that they will be stimulated to pursue some of the topics in greater depth through the references), we also include a limited number of more difficult topics for the more advanced reader. *Sections and examples marked with single asterisks may be omitted at a first reading* without impairing the reader's understanding of subsequent sections and chapters. *More difficult topics for the more advanced reader are indicated by double asterisks.* Exercises are given at the end of each chapter and, in solving these problems, the reader should learn a great deal more about the methods involved. Answers to these exercises are given on pages 257–268.

We would like to record our indebtedness to colleagues in the general insurance industry and at the University for their helpful comments and discussions. In particular, we would like to thank Robert Buchanan, who read the draft manuscript critically, drew certain errors and ambiguities to our attention, and offered much useful advice. We also thank Miss Betty Thorn, who drew the diagrams.

Macquarie University,   I.B.H.
Sydney, Australia.   J.H.P.
December 1982   —   B.Z.

1 INTRODUCTION AND MATHEMATICAL PRELIMINARIES

Summary. In this chapter we outline some of the topics treated in later chapters. We then review a number of basic mathematical results required from time to time in the theoretical development of subsequent chapters: summation notation; factorial and combinatorial notation; power notation; differentiation to find the slope of a curve; maxima and minima; and the exponential and natural logarithmic functions. It must be emphasised, however, that the reader does not have to have a detailed knowledge of these results to be able to appreciate the statistical theory of insurance as described in the remainder of this book.

1.1   Introduction

The title of this book is *Introductory statistics with applications in general insurance.* It is introductory in the sense that it presents fundamental statistical ideas and explains their application in general insurance. It does not give the last word on any of the topics treated, but leaves it to the reader to pursue in depth, through the references given at the end of each section, those matters which interest him most.

The early chapters form a general introduction to the study of probability and statistics. A chapter on statistical distributions, useful in general insurance, follows and thereafter the emphasis is on applications — inferences from general insurance data; exposure and the estimation of claim frequency rates; calculation of risk premium and risk premium for excess of loss reinsurance; experience rating and credibility; no claim discount systems; simulation of general insurance problems; methods for estimating outstanding claim provisions; risk theory and its application to retention levels.

Quantitative methods always involve mathematical formulae and computation, and statistics is no exception. What is remarkable, however, is the extent to which problems in an area as complex as general insurance can be analysed and solved using little more than basic school mathematics.

The remainder of this chapter is devoted to a review of selected mathematical topics required in subsequent chapters. The main purpose is to refresh the memory of the reader who has been away from mathematical studies longer than he cares to remember. The reader familiar with all of these topics should move directly to chapter 2.

1.2   Summation notation

In statistical work, we often need to calculate the sum of a number of quantities $x_1, x_2, \ldots x_n$. We can of course write the sum out longhand as

$$x_1 + x_2 + x_3 + \ldots + x_n. \tag{1.2.1}$$

A standard shorthand notation has been developed, however, which makes use of the upper case Greek letter sigma (for sum):

$$\sum_{i=1}^{n} x_i \tag{1.2.2}$$

In essence, this formula says 'sum all the x_i values from $i = 1$ to $i = n$'. Thus

■ $$\sum_{i=1}^{n} x_i = x_1 + x_2 + \ldots + x_n. \tag{1.2.3}$$

Often, an alternative 'dummy' subscript will be used instead of i.

Example 1.2.1. Evaluate $\sum_{i=1}^{5} i^2$.

We need to sum all the values of i^2 from $i = 1$ to $i = 5$. In other words,

$$\sum_{i=1}^{5} i^2 = 1^2 + 2^2 + 3^2 + 4^2 + 5^2 = 55.$$

Example 1.2.2. Evaluate $\sum_{r=1}^{4} x_r^2$ where $x_1 = 1.2$ $x_2 = 1.3, x_3 = 1.5,$ $x_4 = 1.8$.

We need to sum all the values of x_r^2 from $r = 1$ to $r = 4$. In other words,

$$\sum_{r=1}^{4} x_r^2 = (1.2)^2 + (1.3)^2 + (1.5)^2 + (1.8)^2 = 8.62 .$$

Further reading: Dolciani *et al.* [8] 76–9.

1.3   Factorial notation $n!$

The product of the first n natural numbers is frequently required in mathematical and statistical work. A convenient shorthand has therefore been devised for this product and is referred to as *factorial n* :

■ $$n! = 1 \times 2 \times 3 \times \ldots \times n. \tag{1.3.1}$$

By convention 0! is set equal to 1. Clearly, factorial n satisfies the recurrence equation

■ $n! = n \times (n-1)!$ (1.3.2)

Using this recurrence equation, we see that the factorials of 0, 1, 2, 3, 4, 5 and 6 are, respectively, 1, 1, 2, 6, 24, 120 and 720.

       Further reading: Dolciani *et al.* [8] 89; Mode [22] 102.

1.4   Combinatorial notation $\binom{n}{r}$

     A committee consists of five men. How many ways can we select a sub-committee of two from among them?

     Let us denote the members of the committee by the letters A, B, C, D and E. The possible sub-committees are then as follows:

     AB AC AD AE BC
     BD BE CD CE DE .

Ten different sub-committees are possible.

     Generally, the number of different ways of selecting r objects from n is denoted[1] by $\binom{n}{r}$ and

■ $\binom{n}{r} = \dfrac{n!}{r!\,(n-r)!} = \dfrac{n(n-1)\ldots(n-r+1)}{1 \times 2 \times \ldots \times r}$.   (1.4.1)

In our numerical example $n = 5, r = 2$, and

$$\binom{5}{2} = \frac{5 \times 4 \times 3 \times 2 \times 1}{(2 \times 1) \times (3 \times 2 \times 1)} = \frac{5 \times 4}{1 \times 2} = 10 .$$

     Situations also arise where we need to evaluate $[x(x-1)\ldots(x-r+1)]/r!$ for non-integer values of x. The definition of $\binom{n}{r}$ can be generalised to cover all possible values of x (integer, non-integer, positive, or negative) as follows:

■ $\binom{x}{r} = \dfrac{x(x-1)\ldots(x-r+1)}{1 \times 2 \times \ldots \times r}$.   (1.4.2)

This formula, however, only has a combinatorial meaning when x is a non-negative integer.

     Example 1.4.1. Evaluate $\binom{n}{r}$ for all possible values of r and values of n from 0 to 7 inclusive. Use formula (1.4.1).

---

[1]   Some textbooks denote the number of different ways of selecting r objects from n by $^{n}C_{r}$.

Sample calculations are as follows:

$$\binom{0}{0} = \frac{0!}{0!\,0!} = \frac{1}{1 \times 1} = 1 \; ;$$

$$\binom{1}{0} = \frac{1!}{0!\,1!} = \frac{1}{1 \times 1} = 1 \; ;$$

$$\binom{1}{1} = \frac{1!}{1!\,0!} = \frac{1}{1 \times 1} = 1 \; ;$$

$$\binom{2}{0} = \frac{2!}{0!\,2!} = \frac{2}{1 \times 2} = 1 \; ;$$

$$\binom{2}{1} = \frac{2!}{1!\,1!} = \frac{2}{1 \times 1} = 2 \; ;$$

$$\binom{2}{2} = \frac{2!}{2!\,0!} = \frac{2}{2 \times 1} = 1 \; ;$$

$$\binom{6}{3} = \frac{6!}{3!\,3!} = \frac{6 \times 5 \times 4 \times 3 \times 2 \times 1}{(3 \times 2 \times 1) \times (3 \times 2 \times 1)} = 20 \; .$$

The full set of results is shown as table 1.4.1 in the form of a *Pascal triangle*. Note that each entry is equal to the sum of two other entries: the entry immediately above, and the entry above but one place to the left.

Table 1.4.1. *The Pascal triangle – a table of values of* $\binom{n}{r}$

n \\ r	0	1	2	3	4	5	6	7
0	1							
1	1	1						
2	1	2	1					
3	1	3	3	1				
4	1	4	6	4	1			
5	1	5	10	10	5	1		
6	1	6	15	20	15	6	1	
7	1	7	21	35	35	21	7	1

Example 1.4.2. Evaluate $\binom{1.5}{3}$.

$$\binom{1.5}{3} = \frac{1.5 \times (1.5-1) \times (1.5-2)}{1 \times 2 \times 3} = \frac{1.5 \times 0.5 \times (-0.5)}{1 \times 2 \times 3} = -0.0625 \; .$$

Further reading: Feller [9] 26–37; Hoel [14] 23; Mode [22] 102–4; Mood & Graybill [23] 19–24; Tranter & Lambe [28] 50.

1.5 **Power notation**

The sixth power of a number x is x^6, and

$$
\begin{aligned}
x^6 &= x \times x \times x \times x \times x \times x \times x \times x \\
&= (x \times x \times x \times x \times x) \times (x \times x) \\
&= (x \times x) \times (x \times x) \times (x \times x) \\
&= (x \times x \times x) \times (x \times x \times x).
\end{aligned}
\tag{1.5.1}
$$

We see, therefore, that

$$
x^6 = x^4 \times x^2 = (x^2)^3 = (x^3)^2,
\tag{1.5.2}
$$

and

$$
x^6/x^4 = x^2.
\tag{1.5.3}
$$

These equations are of course particular examples of the following general relationships connecting powers:

- $x^a \times x^b = x^{a+b}$; $\tag{1.5.4}$
- $x^a/x^b = x^{a-b}$; $\tag{1.5.5}$
- $(x^a)^b = x^{ab} = (x^b)^a$. $\tag{1.5.6}$

It is clear that these relationships hold whenever a, b and $a - b$ are positive integers. They are, in fact, valid for *all a* and *b,* positive or negative, integral or fractional, provided the following conventions are adopted:

- $x^0 = 1$; $\tag{1.5.7}$
- $x^{-a} = 1/x^a$; $\tag{1.5.8}$
- $x^{\frac{1}{a}} = a$th root of x. $\tag{1.5.9}$

Modern pocket calculators often have x^y keys which allow the rapid calculation of any power y (positive, negative or zero; fractional or integral) of any positive number x. If such a key is not available, the following relationship can be used:[2]

- $x^y = e^{y \ln x}$. $\tag{1.5.10}$

Example 1.5.1. Evaluate
(a) 2^{-3} .
(b) $3^{\frac{1}{2}}$.

---

[2] The exponential function e^x and the natural logarithmic function $\ln x$ are described below in sections 1.9 and 1.10 respectively.

(c) $3^{-\frac{1}{2}}$.

(d) $27^{\frac{2}{3}}$.

(e) $27^{-\frac{2}{3}}$.

(f) $(5^2)^{\frac{1}{2}} \times 5^2 \times 5^{-3}$.

Solution:

(a) $2^{-3} = \left(\frac{1}{2}\right)^3 = \frac{1}{8} = 0.125$.

(b) $3^{\frac{1}{2}} = \sqrt{3} = 1.7321$.

(c) $3^{-\frac{1}{2}} = \left(\frac{1}{3}\right)^{\frac{1}{2}} = \frac{1}{\sqrt{3}} = 0.577\ 35$.

(d) $(27)^{\frac{2}{3}} = [(27)^{\frac{1}{3}}]^2 = 3^2 = 9$.

(e) $(27)^{-\frac{2}{3}} = 1/(27)^{\frac{2}{3}} = \frac{1}{9} = 0.111\ 11$.

(f) $(5^2)^{\frac{1}{2}} \times 5^2 \times 5^{-3} = 5^1 \times 5^2 \times 5^{-3} = 5^0 = 1$.

Example 1.5.2. Evaluate $(10.8673)^{0.45}$.

The evaluation may be performed directly using the x^y key on a pocket calculator. The answer is 2.925 87.

Alternatively, we can use (1.5.10):

$$x = 10.8673\ ;$$
$$\ln x = 2.385\ 758\ ;$$
$$0.45\ \ln x = 1.073\ 591\ 1\ ;$$
$$(10.8673)^{0.45} = e^{0.45\ \ln x} = 2.925\ 87\ .$$

A calculator with an x^y key actually follows this procedure automatically.

Further reading: Dolciani *et al.* [8] 70–3; Green [11] 285–7; Tranter & Lambe [28] 13–15.

1.6   Differentiation; the slope of a curve

Fig. 1.6.1 shows a straight line which rises with increasing values of x. When $x = 2$, the height of the line is 2.0 and when $x = 4$, the height is 3.0. It is clear, therefore, that as we move along horizontally 2 units, the line rises vertically 1 unit. We may say that the line has a slope of 1 in 2 or 0.5.

Alternatively, we may note that between $x = 2$ and $x = 5$, the line rises 1.5 units from 2 to 3.5. The slope is, therefore, 1.5 in 3 or 0.5. The answer is the same as that obtained previously, because the slope of a straight line is constant. It does not become more steep; nor does it become less steep.

A line *falling* 1 unit between $x = 2$ and $x = 4$ would have a slope of -1 in 2 or -0.5.

Fig. 1.6.2 shows a curve which is initially fairly flat, but which becomes progressively steeper and steeper. An estimate of the slope of the curve at the point x may be obtained as follows.

　　1. Note the height $f(x)$ of the curve at the point x.

　　2. Move along the curve to the right and note the height $f(x + H)$ at the point $x + H$.

The rise over horizontal distance H is $f(x + H) - f(x)$, and we deduce that the slope at the point x is approximately $f(x + H) - f(x)$ in H or

$$\frac{f(x + H) - f(x)}{H} .$$

(1.6.1)

Fig. 1.6.1. A straight line.

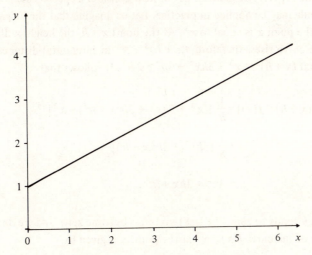

Fig. 1.6.2. Estimating the slope of a curve.

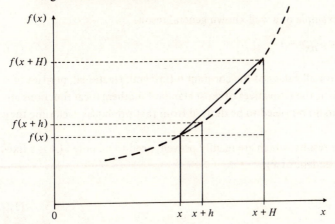

The curve, however, is rising more and more steeply, and it is apparent that if we select a large value of *H,* a poor estimate of the slope at the point *x* will be obtained. A better estimate will result from using a smaller horizontal distance *h* (fig. 1.6.2). The best estimate is obtained by making *h* as small as possible (i.e. close to zero) and calculating the limit, as *h* gets closer and closer to zero, of $[f(x + h) - f(x)]/h$. The slope we have defined in this manner is often referred to as the *derivative* of the $f(x)$ curve at the point *x* and denoted by $df(x)/dx$ or df/dx. We may write

■
$$\frac{df}{dx} = \frac{d}{dx} f(x) = \lim_{h \to 0} \frac{f(x + h) - f(x)}{h} .$$
(1.6.2)

This formula is perfectly general. Let us now consider a special case and show how the formula may be applied in practice. Let us imagine that the height $f(x)$ of a curve at the point *x* is equal to x^3. At the point $x + h$, the height will be $(x + h)^3$. The curve rises, therefore, $(x + h)^3 - x^3$ in horizontal distance *h*. We note that $(x + h)^3 = x^3 + 3hx^2 + 3h^2x + h^3$. It follows that

$$\frac{1}{h} [f(x + h) - f(x)] = \frac{1}{h} [(x^3 + 3hx^2 + 3h^2x + h^3) - x^3]$$

$$= \frac{1}{h} [3hx^2 + 3h^2x + h^3]$$

$$= 3x^2 + 3hx + h^2 .$$

In the limit as *h* tends to zero, the last two terms become zero, and we deduce that the slope of the curve $f(x) = x^3$ at the point *x* is given by

$$\frac{d}{dx} x^3 = 3x^2 .$$
(1.6.3)

This is an example of a well-known general result

■
$$\frac{d}{dx} x^n = nx^{n-1} ,$$
(1.6.4)

which is valid for all values of the constant *n* (integral, fractional, positive or negative). In fact, the derivatives of most standard mathematical functions are well known and do not need to be derived from first principles each time they are required.

Three other results, which are readily proven, need to be noted (*A* is a fixed constant independent of *x*):

■
$$\frac{d}{dx} A = 0 ;$$
(1.6.5)

■ $\dfrac{d}{dx} Af(x) = A \dfrac{d}{dx} f(x);$ (1.6.6)

■ $\dfrac{d}{dx}\left[f(x) + g(x)\right] = \dfrac{d}{dx} f(x) + \dfrac{d}{dx} g(x).$ (1.6.7)

Sometimes the slope $d(df/dx)/dx$ of the slope curve df/dx is required. This *second derivative* is usually denoted by d^2f/dx^2. Third and higher derivatives are also encountered.

Example 1.6.1. What is the function $F(x)$ which when differentiated is equal to $3x^2$?

We might be inclined (in view of (1.6.3)) to answer immediately: x^3. It is indeed true that the derivative of x^3 is $3x^2$, but so is the derivative of $x^3 + 37$ and the derivative of $x^3 + A$, for any constant A whatsoever, because the derivative of a constant A is zero (equation (1.6.5)) and the derivative of a sum is the sum of the derivatives (equation (1.6.7)).

The function $F(x)$ which when differentiated yields $3x^2$ is

$$F(x) = x^3 + A$$ (1.6.8)

and the constant A cannot be determined without further information. This may at first seem surprising. It is not really so surprising when we observe that, by knowing the slope of a line at all points on it, we can work out the relative heights of various points on the line, but we cannot determine the absolute height of any point on it without knowing the absolute height of some base point on that line. The three curves in fig. 1.6.3 have the same slopes as each other, but they are located at different altitudes.

Fig. 1.6.3. Three curves with the same slopes.

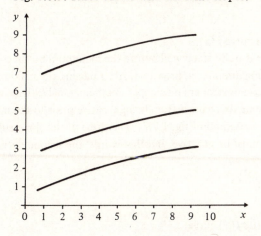

Example 1.6.2. Find the first, second and third derivatives of the function $f(x) = x^5$ at the point $x = 2$.

According to (1.6.4) the first derivative or slope of the curve $f(x) = x^5$ at the point x is

$$\frac{df}{dx} = 5x^4 .$$

At the point $x = 2$, therefore, the first derivative or slope is $5 \times 2^4 = 80$.

Using (1.6.4) again and (1.6.6) as well, we see that the second derivative, or slope of the slope curve at the point x is

$$\frac{d^2f}{dx^2} = \frac{d}{dx}(5x^4) = 20x^3 .$$

At the point $x = 2$, therefore, the second derivative is $20 \times 2^3 = 160$.

In a similar manner, the third derivative, or slope of the slope of the slope curve of $f(x)$ at the point x is

$$\frac{d^3f}{dx^3} = \frac{d}{dx}(20x^3) = 60x^2 .$$

At the point $x = 2$, therefore, the third derivative is $60 \times 2^2 = 240$.

Further reading: Green [11] 428–56; Reichmann [27] 36–65; Tranter & Lambe [28] 166–95.

1.7   Maxima and minima

Fig. 1.7.1 depicts a curve $f(x)$ which rises to a maximum and then falls away. The slope of the curve is positive before the maximum and negative afterwards. At the maximum itself, the slope is zero. In other words,

$$\frac{df}{dx} = 0 \qquad (1.7.1)$$

at a maximum point on a curve $f(x)$.

The slope of the curve is quite steep well before the maximum but becomes flatter and flatter as the maximum is approached. After passing the maximum, the slope downwards becomes steeper and steeper. Mathematically, therefore, we see that the derivative df/dx changes from being positive prior to the maximum to negative after the maximum (fig. 1.7.2). The slope of the slope curve at the maximum of $f(x)$ must be negative. In other words, the second derivative (section 1.6).

$$\frac{d^2f}{dx^2} < 0 \qquad (1.7.2)$$

at a maximum point on the $f(x)$ curve.

The same type of reasoning leads us to conclude that, at a minimum point on a curve $f(x)$,

- $$\frac{df}{dx} = 0 \; ;$$ (1.7.3)

- $$\frac{d^2f}{dx^2} > 0 \; .$$ (1.7.4)

Maximum and minimum points are sometimes referred to as *stationary points,* because the rate of change (or slope) is zero.

Fig. 1.7.1. A curve with a maximum point.

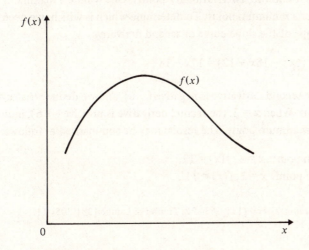

Fig. 1.7.2. Slope curve of the curve in Fig. 1.7.1.

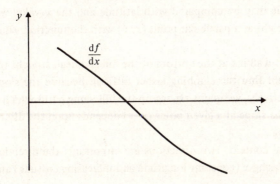

Example 1.7.1. Find the stationary points of the function

$$f(x) = 2x^3 - 9x^2 + 12x + 7 .$$

What are the values of $f(x)$ at these points?

At a stationary point, the slope must be zero. In other words,

$$\frac{df}{dx} = 6x^2 - 18x + 12 = 0 ,$$

or

$$x^2 - 3x + 2 = 0 .$$

There are two possible solutions to this quadratic equation: $x = 1$ and $x = 2$. The $f(x)$ curve has, therefore, two stationary points. One will be a maximum point and the other a minimum point. To determine which is which, we need to examine the slope of the slope curve or second derivative

$$\frac{d^2 f}{dx^2} = \frac{d}{dx} (6x^2 - 18x + 12) = 12x - 18 .$$

When $x = 1$, the second derivative is negative (-6), and we deduce that $x = 1$ is a maximum point. When $x = 2$, the second derivative is positive ($+6$), indicating that $x = 2$ is a minimum point. The results may be summarised as follows:

maximum point: $x = 1$, $f(x) = 12$;
minimum point: $x = 2$, $f(x) = 11$.

Further reading: Green [11] 463–72; Tranter & Lambe [28] 205–11.

*1.8   Functions of more than one variable; maxima and minima

The slope of a function $f(x)$ in one dimension is the rate of increase of that function as x increases. A function of two variables x and y can be likened to a hill. The x-value may be compared with latitude and the y-value with longitude and the height at a particular point (x, y) with the function value $f(x, y)$.

If we were to start walking at the bottom of the hill and head straight towards the summit, we might find the climbing rather difficult because the slope is rather steep. Alternatively, we might zig-zag up the hill along paths which are less steep. Clearly, the slope at a given point (x, y) depends upon the direction in which we are heading.

In a mathematical context, two directions are important: the direction of constant y and increasing x (constant longitude and increasing latitude) and the direction of constant x and increasing y (constant latitude and increasing longitude). These two directions are at right angles.

The slope in the direction of constant y and increasing x is referred to as the partial derivative of $f(x,y)$ with respect to x and is denoted by $\partial f/\partial x$. It is obtained by treating y as a constant and differentiating $f(x, y)$ with respect to x in the usual way. Likewise, the slope in the direction of constant x and increasing y is referred to as the partial derivative of $f(x, y)$ with respect to y and is denoted by $\partial f/\partial y$. It is obtained by treating x as a constant and differentiating $f(x, y)$ with respect to y.

At the top of the hill, the slope in any direction is zero, including the direction (y constant, x increasing) and the direction (x constant, y increasing). At a *maximum point* of the function $f(x, y)$ (or *minimum point,* for that matter), $\partial f/\partial x$ and $\partial f/\partial y$ are both zero.

These results generalise to functions of three or more variables (example 1.8.2).

Example 1.8.1. Find the minimum values of

$$f(x, y) = x^2 + y^2 - x + y + xy - 3 .$$

Using the above definitions of the partial derivatives of $f(x, y)$ with respect to x and y, and (1.6.4), we see that in this particular case the partial derivatives are, respectively,

$$\frac{\partial f}{\partial x} = 2x - 1 + y ;$$

$$\frac{\partial f}{\partial y} = 2y + 1 + x .$$

At the minimum point, both these derivatives (or slopes) must be zero. That is,

$$2x - 1 + y = 0 ;$$
$$2y + 1 + x = 0 .$$

We solve these two simultaneous equations in two unknowns and find that the minimum is $- 4$ at the point $(1, - 1)$ i.e. when $x = 1$ and $y = - 1$. This *stationary point* is a minimum point, because f increases as x and y move away from the point $x = 1, y = -1$.

Example 1.8.2. Find the minimum value of

$$f(x, y, z) = x^2 + y^2 + z^2 + (x + y + z - 3)^2 .$$

Expanding[3] f, we obtain

$$f(x, y, z) = 2x^2 + 2y^2 + 2z^2 + 2xy + 2yz + 2zx - 6x - 6y - 6z + 9 \ .$$

The partial derivatives with respect to x, y and z are as follows:

$$\frac{\partial f}{\partial x} = 4x + 2y + 2z - 6 \ ;$$

$$\frac{\partial f}{\partial y} = 4y + 2x + 2z - 6 \ ; \cdot$$

$$\frac{\partial f}{\partial z} = 4z + 2y + 2x - 6 \ .$$

To obtain the minimum point of $f(x, y, z)$, we equate these three partial derivatives to zero. We then have

$$4x + 2y + 2z = 6 \ ;$$
$$2x + 4y + 2z = 6 \ ;$$
$$2x + 2y + 4z = 6 \ .$$

The solution to these three simultaneous equations in three unknowns turns out to be

$$x = y = z = \frac{3}{4} \ .$$

The minimum value of $f(x, y, z)$ is, therefore,

$$f\left(\frac{3}{4}, \frac{3}{4}, \frac{3}{4}\right) = \left(\frac{3}{4}\right)^2 + \left(\frac{3}{4}\right)^2 + \left(\frac{3}{4}\right)^2 + \left(\frac{3}{4} + \frac{3}{4} + \frac{3}{4} - 3\right)^2 = 2.25 \ .$$

Further reading: Green [11] 626–31; Pollard [26] 5.

1.9   The exponential function e^x

The exponential function e^x occupies an important position in mathematical and statistical theory, and we make considerable use of it in this book. The function may be defined in terms of the infinite series

■ $$e^x = 1 + \frac{x}{1!} + \frac{x^2}{2!} + \frac{x^3}{3!} + \cdots \ . \qquad (1.9.1)$$

Sometimes $\exp(x)$ is written instead of e^x. The modern pocket calculator often has an e^x key which causes the value of e^x to be computed rapidly (almost instantaneously) by this formula.

---

[3]   The reader familiar with the 'function of a function' rule for differentiation can write down the partial derivatives directly without expanding f.

The exponential function e^x is in fact the xth power of a number $e = 2.718\ 28 \ldots$. It follows (section 1.5) that if we set $x = 1$ in (1.9.1) we should obtain $2.718\ 28 \ldots$; if we set $x = 1/2$, we should obtain $\sqrt{(2.718\ 28 \ldots)}$ $= 1.648\ 72$, and if we set $x = 2$, we should obtain $(2.718\ 28 \ldots)^2 = 7.389\ 06$. These results are confirmed in examples 1.9.1 and 1.9.2. The graph of e^x is given in fig. 1.9.1.

We frequently need to know the slope of the exponential function e^{kx}, where k is a given constant. The slope is

■
$$\frac{\mathrm{d}}{\mathrm{d}x} e^{kx} = k e^{kx} .$$
(1.9.2)

The proof is given in example 1.9.3. It follows from (1.9.2) that the function which, when differentiated yields e^{kx}, must be $(e^{kx}/k) + C$, where C is an arbitrary constant.

Fig. 1.9.1. The graph of the exponential function e^x.

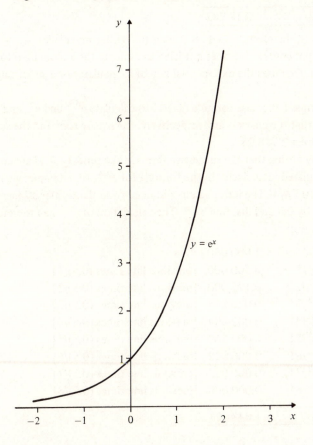

Example 1.9.1. Use the series (1.9.1) to compute the exponential
number e correct to five decimal places.

We set $x = 1$ in (1.9.1) and recall the factorials in section 1.3. The arithmetic
may be set out as follows:

1	1.000 000
1/1!	1.000 000
1/2!	0.500 000
1/3!	0.166 667
1/4!	0.041 667
1/5!	0.008 333
1/6!	0.001 389
1/7!	0.000 198
1/8!	0.000 025
1/9!	0.000 003
1/10!	0.000 000
Total	2.718 282

The number e is, therefore, 2.718 28 correct to five decimal places.

In practice, of course, one does not have to evaluate the exponential function
in this manner. One uses the exponential key of a calculator or a set of tables.

Example 1.9.2. Use formula (1.9.1) to calculate $e^{0.5}$ and e^2, and confirm that the answers are, respectively, the square root and the square
of the number e = 2.718 28.

We begin by noting that the successive terms in the series (1.9.1) are con-
veniently calculated recursively. In the formula for $e^{0.5}$, for example, we require
$(0.5)^3/3!$ and $(0.5)^4/4!$ The latter can be obtained from the former by merely
multiplying it by 0.5 and dividing by 4. The calculation of $e^{0.5}$ can therefore be
set out as follows:

1	1.000 000	
$(0.5)/1!$	0.500 000	[previous line times (0.5)/1]
$(0.5)^2/2!$	0.125 000	[previous line times (0.5)/2]
$(0.5)^3/3!$	0.020 833	[previous line times (0.5)/3]
$(0.5)^4/4!$	0.002 604	[previous line times (0.5)/4]
$(0.5)^5/5!$	0.000 260	[previous line times (0.5)/5]
$(0.5)^6/6!$	0.000 022	[previous line times (0.5)/6]
$(0.5)^7/7!$	0.000 002	[previous line times (0.5)/7]
$(0.5)^8/8!$	0.000 000	[previous line times (0.5)/8]
Total	1.648 721	

The value of $e^{0.5}$ is, therefore, 1.648 72 correct to five decimal places, and this is the square root of 2.718 28.

The calculations for e^2 are as follows:

1	1.000 000	
2/1!	2.000 000	[previous line times 2/1]
$2^2/2!$	2.000 000	[previous line times 2/2]
$2^3/3!$	1.333 333	[previous line times 2/3]
$2^4/4!$	0.666 667	etc.
$2^5/5!$	0.266 667	
$\vdots$	$\vdots$	
$2^{11}/11!$	0.000 051	
$2^{12}/12!$	0.000 009	
$2^{13}/13!$	0.000 001	
$2^{14}/14!$	0.000 000	
Total	7.389 055	

The value of e^2 is, therefore, 7.389 06 correct to five decimal places, and this is the square of 2.718 28.

The reader should note that the recursive approach to the calculation of successive terms in the series could also have been used in example 1.9.1.

Example 1.9.3. Prove that the derivative (slope) of e^{kx} at the point x is ke^{kx}.

According to (1.9.1)

$$e^{kx} = 1 + kx + \frac{k^2x^2}{2!} + \frac{k^3x^3}{3!} + \dots .$$

From section 1.6 we know the derivatives of $1, x, x^2, x^3$, are, respectively, $0, 1, 2x, 3x^2, \dots$. The derivative of e^{kx} is, therefore,

$$\frac{\mathrm{d}}{\mathrm{d}x}e^{kx} = 0 + k(1) + \frac{k^2 \, (2x)}{2!} + \frac{k^3 \, (3x^2)}{3!} + \dots$$

$$= k + \frac{k^2x}{1!} + \frac{k^3x^2}{2!} + \dots$$

$$= k \left(1 + \frac{kx}{1!} + \frac{k^2x^2}{2!} + \dots \right)$$

$$= ke^{kx}.$$

Example 1.9.4. The slope of a function $F(x)$ at the point x is $0.5\, e^{-0.5x}$, and the value of the function $F(x)$ at the point $x = 0$ is zero. Find the formula for $F(x)$, and its value at $x = 2$.

According to (1.9.2) and the text beneath it, the function $F(x)$ which when differentiated yields $0.5\, e^{-0.5x}$ is

$$C - e^{-0.5x},$$

where C is a constant yet to be determined. We know, however, that when $x = 0$, $F(x) = 0$. In other words,

$$C - e^0 = 0.$$

But $e^0 = 1$, so that $C = 1$. We deduce that

$$F(x) = 1 - e^{-0.5x}.$$

When $x = 2$, $F(x) = 1 - e^{-1.0} = 0.632$.

Further reading: Backhouse *et al.* [1] 211–15; Green [11] 413–16.

1.10   The natural logarithm function ln *x*

The logarithm to base 10 of a number x, denoted by $\log_{10} x$, is the power to which 10 must be raised to obtain the number in question. In other words,

$$10^{\log_{10} x} = x. \tag{1.10.1}$$

It follows, therefore, that $\log_{10} 1 = 0$, $\log_{10} 10 = 1$, $\log_{10} 100 = 2$, $\log_{10} 1000 = 3$, etc.,

Base 10 is very convenient for arithmetical purposes. It is not, however, the most useful base for mathematical and statistical purposes. Base e is much more convenient.[4]

The *logarithm to base* e or *natural logarithm* of a number x, denoted by ln x, is the power to which e = 2.718 28 . . . must be raised to obtain the number in question. In other words,

■ $$e^{\ln x} = x. \tag{1.10.2}$$

---

[4]   The exponential number e is defined in section 1.9.

It follows, for example, that

$$
\left.
\begin{aligned}
\ln 1 &= 0 ; \\
\ln e &= \ln 2.718\ 28\ \ldots\ = 1 ; \\
\ln e^2 &= \ln 7.389\ 05\ \ldots\ = 2 ; \\
\ln e^3 &= \ln 20.085\ 53\ \ldots = 3 ; \\
\ln \sqrt{e} &= \ln 1.648\ 72\ \ldots = 0.5 .
\end{aligned}
\right\}
\qquad (1.10.3)
$$

The modern pocket calculator often has a $\ln x$ key, in which case there is no problem obtaining the natural logarithm of any positive number. Tables are also available. In the absence of a calculator with a $\ln x$ key and $\ln x$ tables, the natural logarithm of a number x can be obtained from its logarithm to base 10 by the so-called *change of base theorem*:

■ $\ln x = (\ln 10) \times \log_{10} x \doteq 2.3026 \log_{10} x.$ $\qquad (1.10.4)$

Fig. 1.10.1 shows the graph of $\ln x$ for positive values of x. Note that the curve approaches $-\infty$ as x drops towards zero, and approaches $+\infty$ as x becomes larger and larger.

From the definition of $\ln x$ in (1.10.2), it follows that

■ $\ln xz = \ln x + \ln z ;$ $\qquad (1.10.5)$

Fig. 1.10.1. The graph of the natural logarithm function $\ln x$.

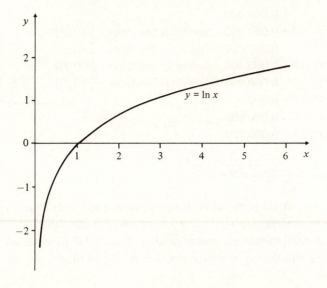

■ $\ln (x/z) = \ln x - \ln z$; (1.10.6)

■ $\ln x^a = a \ln x$. (1.10.7)

In these formulae, x and z must be positive; a, on the other hand, may be positive or negative. Similar results are true for logarithms to base 10.

The following series for $\ln (1 + y)$ is valid for all values of y greater than $- 1$ and less than $+ 1$, and is often useful:

■ $\ln (1 + y) = y - \frac{1}{2}y^2 + \frac{1}{3}y^3 - \ldots$. (1.10.8)

This series can in fact be used in the calculation of the natural logarithm of any positive number whatsoever (examples 1.10.2 and 1.10.3), and the $\ln x$ key on the pocket calculator makes use of it.

The final result we need to note is the derivative (or slope) of $\ln x$, which we derive in example 1.10.4:

■ $\dfrac{\mathrm{d}}{\mathrm{d}x} \ln x = \dfrac{1}{x}$. (1.10.9)

Example 1.10.1. Use formula (1.10.8) to compute the natural logarithm of 1.2 correct to five decimal places. Confirm that your answer satisfies (1.10.2).

The calculation of $\ln 1.2$ may be set out as follows:

0.2	0.200 000	
$-\frac{1}{2}(0.2)^2$	$-$ 0.020 000	[previous line times $-\frac{1}{2}(0.2)$]
$\frac{1}{3}(0.2)^3$	0.002 667	[previous line times $-\frac{2}{3}(0.2)$]
$-\frac{1}{4}(0.2)^4$	$-$ 0.000 400	[previous line times $-\frac{3}{4}(0.2)$]
$\frac{1}{5}(0.2)^5$	0.000 064	[previous line times $-\frac{4}{5}(0.2)$]
$-\frac{1}{6}(0.2)^6$	$-$ 0.000 011	etc.
$\frac{1}{7}(0.2)^7$	0.000 002	
$-\frac{1}{8}(0.2)^8$	$-$ 0.000 000	
Total	0.182 322	

The natural logarithm of 1.2 is, therefore, 0.182 32 correct to five decimal places. This may be confirmed using the $\ln x$ key on a pocket calculator.

We are asked to confirm that our answer satisfies (1.10.2). Let us therefore substitute 0.182 32 into the exponential series (1.9.1). The arithmetic may be set out as follows:

1	1.000 000	
$(0.182\ 32)/1!$	0.182 320	[previous line times 0.182 320/1]
$(0.182\ 32)^2/2!$	0.016 620	[previous line times 0.182 320/2]
$(0.182\ 32)^3/3!$	0.001 010	[previous line times 0.182 320/3]
$(0.182\ 32)^4/4!$	0.000 046	etc.
$(0.182\ 32)^5/5!$	0.000 002	
$(0.182\ 32)^6/6!$	0.000 000	

Total	1.199 998

Thus $e^{0.182\ 32} = 1.200\ 00$ correct to five decimal places. Our answer satisfies (1.10.2).

In practice, of course, we do not need to evaluate natural logarithms and exponentials using the infinite series (1.10.8) and (1.9.1). We merely press the ln x or e^x key on our calculator, or look up tables.

*Example 1.10.2. In formula (1.10.8) the value of y must lie between – 1 and 1. The formula cannot therefore be used *directly* to calculate the logarithm of a number greater than 2. Use the fact that 1.5 divided by 0.5 is 3.0, and that the logarithm of the ratio of two numbers is equal to the difference between their logarithms, to obtain the natural logarithm of 3, correct to five decimal places, via (1.10.8).

Formula (1.10.8) can be used directly to evaluate both ln 1.5 and ln 0.5. The calculation is set out in table 1.10.1. We find that ln 1.5 = 0.405 465 and ln 0.5 = – 0.693 145. It follows that

$$\ln 3 = \ln \left(\frac{1.5}{0.5}\right)$$
$$= \ln 1.5 - \ln 0.5$$
$$= 0.405\ 465 + 0.693\ 145$$
$$= 1.098\ 610 .$$

The natural logarithm of 3 is, therefore, 1.098 61 correct to five decimal places.

*Example 1.10.3. Obtain the natural logarithm of 24.102 64 correct to five decimal places.

One approach to the solution of this problem would be to find y such that

$$\frac{1+y}{1-y} = 24.102\ 64$$

and continue in the manner of example 1.10.2. The value of y required, however, is 0.920 327, and the logarithmic series will converge extremely slowly (much more slowly even than those in table 1.10.1). Another approach is called for.

Dividing 24.102 64 repeatedly by e = 2.718 28, we find that

$$24.102\ 64 = 1.200\ 00\ e^3\ .$$

The natural logarithm of 1.200 00 is readily obtained via the logarithmic series (1.10.8) (we calculated it in example 1.10.1), and the natural logarithm of e^3 is 3. From (1.10.5) we conclude that

$$
\begin{aligned}
\ln 24.102\ 64 &= \ln 1.200\ 00 + \ln e^3 \\
&= 0.182\ 32 + 3.000\ 00 \\
&= 3.182\ 32\ .
\end{aligned}
$$

Table 1.10.1 *Calculation of ln 1.5 and ln 0.5 in example 1.10.2*

Numerical value of term in ln series		Contribution of term to	
		ln 1.5	ln 0.5
0.5	0.500 000	0.500 000	− 0.500 000
$(0.5)^2/2$	0.125 000	− 0.125 000	− 0.125 000
$(0.5)^3/3$	0.041 667	0.041 667	− 0.041 667
$(0.5)^4/4$	0.015 625	− 0.015 625	− 0.015 625
$(0.5)^5/5$	0.006 250	0.006 250	− 0.006 250
$(0.5)^6/6$	0.002 604	− 0.002 604	− 0.002 604
$(0.5)^7/7$	0.001 116	0.001 116	− 0.001 116
$(0.5)^8/8$	0.000 488	− 0.000 488	− 0.000 488
$(0.5)^9/9$	0.000 217	0.000 217	− 0.000 217
$(0.5)^{10}/10$	0.000 098	− 0.000 098	− 0.000 098
$(0.5)^{11}/11$	0.000 044	0.000 044	− 0.000 044
$(0.5)^{12}/12$	0.000 020	− 0.000 020	− 0.000 020
$(0.5)^{13}/13$	0.000 009	0.000 009	− 0.000 009
$(0.5)^{14}/14$	0.000 004	− 0.000 004	− 0.000 004
$(0.5)^{15}/15$	0.000 002	0.000 002	− 0.000 002
$(0.5)^{16}/16$	0.000 001	− 0.000 001	− 0.000 001
$(0.5)^{17}/17$	0.000 000	0.000 000	− 0.000 000
Total	−	0.405 465	− 0.693 145

*Example 1.10.4. Show that the slope of the curve $y = \ln x$ at the point x is $1/x$.

According to section 1.6 the slope of the curve $y = \ln x$ is the limit as h becomes very small of

$$\frac{1}{h}\left[\ln(x+h) - \ln x\right]$$

$$= \frac{1}{h}\ln\left(\frac{x+h}{x}\right) \quad \text{using (1.10.6)}$$

$$= \frac{1}{h}\ln\left(1 + \frac{h}{x}\right)$$

$$= \frac{1}{h}\left[\frac{h}{x} - \frac{1}{2}\left(\frac{h}{x}\right)^2 + \frac{1}{3}\left(\frac{h}{x}\right)^3 - \right].. \quad \text{according to (1.10.8)}$$

$$= \frac{1}{x} - \frac{1}{2}\frac{h}{x^2} + \frac{1}{3}\frac{h^2}{x^3} - \cdots.$$

In the limit as h approaches zero, all the terms except the first vanish and we deduce that the slope is $1/x$.

Further reading: Backhouse *et al.* [1] 211–24; Reichmann [27] 135–52; Tranter & Lambe [28] 300–1.

1.11   Exercises

1. Evaluate $\Sigma_{j=1}^{10} j$.

2. Evaluate $\Sigma_{j=1}^{10} j^2$.

3. Evaluate $\Sigma_{r=1}^{\infty} [-1(-0.1)^r/r]$.

4. How many different sub-committees of three are possible from among the members of a committee of six?

5. Evaluate $\binom{-3}{2}$.

6. Evaluate $2^{\frac{1}{2}}; 2^{\frac{1}{3}}; 2^{\frac{1}{4}}; 2^{\frac{1}{10}}$ and $2^{\frac{1}{100}}$.

7. Evaluate $(0.7)^{\frac{1}{2}}; (0.7)^{\frac{1}{3}}; (0.7)^{\frac{1}{4}}; (0.7)^{\frac{1}{10}}$ and $(0.7)^{\frac{1}{100}}$.

8. Comment on your answers to questions 6 and 7.

9. Use the e^x key on your calculator to evaluate $e^{-0.1x}$ for $x = 1, 2, 3, 4, 5, 6, 7, 8, 9$ and 10. Plot the curve over this range on graph paper.

10. Draw a tangent to the $e^{-0.1x}$ curve of question 9 at the point $x = 5$, and use it to estimate the slope of the curve at that point.

11. Calculate the slope of the $e^{-0.1x}$ curve at $x = 5$, and compare the answer with your answer to question 10.

12. Confirm the value of $\ln 3$ obtained in example 1.10.2 by substitution in (1.9.1).

13. Use the fact that $3 = 1.103\ 639\ e$ to obtain $\ln 3$ correct to five decimal places.

14. Show numerically that $x^x e^{-x} \sqrt{(2\pi/x)}$ provides an accurate estimate of $(x-1)!$ and that the percentage error decreases as x increases.[5]

---

[5] This is Stirling's approximation to $(x-1)!$ It may be substituted into $\binom{n}{r}$ to derive the normal approximation to the binomial distribution (section 5.8). The $\sqrt{(2\pi)}$ in Stirling's formula and in the normal probability-density function (section 5.1) are thus not unrelated.

2 ELEMENTARY PROBABILITY

Summary. The basis of statistics is probability, and in this chapter we outline the fundamental concepts of probability theory. The terms 'experiment', 'random variable', 'event', 'joint events' and 'disjoint events' are defined and explained. The chapter concludes with a discussion of conditional probability and independence.

2.1   Introduction; concept of probability

Probability theory finds application in almost every area of human endeavour. Most practical applications, however, require a lengthy description of the mathematical model of the process being studied. Games of chance, on the other hand, are usually easy to describe and readily understood. They are convenient, therefore, for introducing and demonstrating the basic concepts of probability, and we shall make use of them for this purpose in this chapter. Intuitively, at least, there is great similarity between insurance and a game of chance!

A gambler tosses a coin four times. This process may be referred to as an *experiment* or *random experiment* (to emphasise the fact that the outcome is uncertain). At each toss, the gambler will obtain either a 'head' (H) or a 'tail' (T). The particular sequence of 'heads' and 'tails' he obtains is called the *outcome* of the experiment, and it is clear that the experiment we have described has $2^4 = 16$ possible outcomes. The sequence $H\,H\,T\,H$ is one possible outcome. The performance of an experiment is called a *trial*.

The gambler may count the number of 'heads' he obtains in a trial. This number is a *random variable* which may take any one of the non-negative integer values $0, 1, 2, 3, 4$.

Let us imagine that the gambler obtains a sequence containing three 'heads' and one 'tail'. Then we can say that the *event* 'three "heads" and one "tail" ' has occurred, or, for example, the event 'an odd number of "heads" ' has occurred, or the event 'more "heads" than "tails" ' has occurred.

If a random experiment is performed n times under identical conditions, and a particular event is observed to occur in m of the n trials, then an *estimate* of the probability that the particular event will occur at any one trial is given by the proportion m/n, which must lie in the range 0 to 1. Clearly, the reliability of this estimate of probability depends on the number of times the experiment is performed. A perfectly symmetrical coin tossed three times, for example, might turn up 'heads' twice giving as an estimate of the probability of a 'head' the fraction $\frac{2}{3}$, when intuitively one might regard $\frac{1}{2}$ as a better measure. If, however, the coin were tossed 1000 times and it had no physical bias, a fraction much closer to $\frac{1}{2}$ would emerge. To allow for this, we shall adopt the following definition of probability.

If a random experiment is performed n times under identical conditions,[1] and a particular event E is observed to occur in m of the n trials, then the probability of the event occurring is $P(E)$ where

■ $$P(E) = \lim_{n \to \infty} m/n. \tag{2.1.1}$$

The limit notation on the right-hand side indicates that (theoretically) an infinite number of identical random experiments were performed. In practice, of course, only a finite number of such experiments can be performed, and as a result m/n (n finite) provides an estimate only of the underlying probability. The accuracy of the estimate increases the larger n becomes. We return to this problem briefly in section 6.4 in the discussion of confidence intervals.

By defining $P(E)$ as we do in (2.1.1), we emphasise the fact that probability involves a long-run concept. This is important in the general insurance context. Suppose that a casino offered a gambler the chance of receiving $5 for an outlay of $1 if with one throw of two dice he threw a total of 7; then it would be possible for the casino to lose money over a short operating period (the first gambler might, for example, obtain 7 at his first attempt) but in the long run the casino could expect to make a substantial profit (one attempt in six should total 7). The analogy with general insurance is apparent.

It is clear from (2.1.1) that

■ $$0 \leqslant P(E) \leqslant 1. \tag{2.1.2}$$

Further reading: Hoel [13] 33–42; Hoel [14] 92–4; Mendenhall & Scheaffer [21] 17–32; Mode [22] 92–4.

2.2   Joint and disjoint events; intersection and union

An unbiased coin is tossed four times and the numbers of 'heads' and 'tails' noted. Event E_1 occurs if the number of 'heads' exceeds the number of

---

[1]   In certain practical situations (including some areas of general insurance) it is very difficult to repeat an experiment under *identical* conditions. Nevertheless, the probability concept is most useful.

'tails', event E_2 if the number of 'heads' is even, and event E_3 if the number of 'tails' is odd and exceeds the number of 'heads'.

The possible outcomes are enumerated in table 2.2.1, and it is immediately apparent that events E_2 and E_3 cannot occur simultaneously. Nor can E_1 and E_3. Events E_2 and E_3 are said to be *disjoint* (or *mutually exclusive*) and so are E_1 and E_3.

Events E_1 and E_2, on the other hand, can occur simultaneously and the *joint event* of E_1 and E_2 is denoted by $E_1 \cap E_2$ (E_1 *intersection* E_2).

The possible outcomes can also be usefully represented diagrammatically as in fig. 2.2.1. Using symmetry arguments, it is easy to see that all the possible outcomes are equally likely, so that

$$P(E_1) = \tfrac{5}{16} ;$$
$$P(E_2) = \tfrac{8}{16} ;$$
$$P(E_3) = \tfrac{4}{16} ;$$
$$P(E_1 \cap E_2) = \tfrac{1}{16} ;$$
$$P(E_1 \cap E_3) = 0 ;$$
$$P(E_2 \cap E_3) = 0 .$$

Table 2.2.1. *Possible outcomes for the experiment described in section 2.2*

Outcome	Event E_1	Event E_2	Event E_3
$HHHH$	✓	✓	
$HHHT$	✓		
$HHTH$	✓		
$HHTT$		✓	
$HTHH$	✓		
$HTHT$		✓	
$HTTH$		✓	
$HTTT$			✓
$THHH$	✓		
$THHT$		✓	
$THTH$		✓	
$THTT$			✓
$TTHH$		✓	
$TTHT$			✓
$TTTH$			✓
$TTTT$		✓	

The event which occurs whenever E_1 or E_2 or both occur is denoted by $E_1 \cup E_2$ (E_1 *union* E_2). We can see from fig. 2.2.1 that, in our numerical example,

$$P(E_1 \cup E_2) = \tfrac{12}{16}.$$

It is important to note that, for *any* two events E_1 and E_2,

$\blacksquare$ $P(E_1 \cup E_2) = P(E_1) + P(E_2) - P(E_1 \cap E_2)$.   (2.2.1)

The negative term is required to avoid double counting (fig. 2.2.1). When E_1 and E_2 are disjoint, $P(E_1 \cap E_2)$ is zero and can be omitted from the formula.

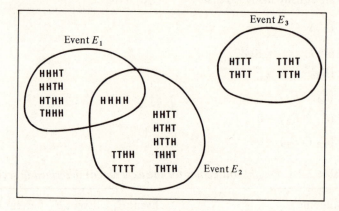

Fig. 2.2.1. Possible outcomes and events E_1, E_2 and E_3 for the experiment described in section 2.2. This type of diagram is sometimes referred to as a 'Venn diagram'.

Example 2.2.1. According to a recent market research survey conducted on behalf of a general insurance group, 40% of males over the age of 30 own both a car and a house, 60% own a house and 70% own a car. What is the probability that a man over age 30, chosen at random, owns a house, or a car, or both?

Let us denote the event that he owns a house by E_H and the event that he owns a car by E_C. We are told that $P(E_H \cap E_C) = 0.4$, $P(E_H) = 0.6$ and $P(E_C) = 0.7$, and we need to compute $P(E_H \cup E_C)$. According to (2.2.1),

$$P(E_H \cup E_C) = P(E_H) + P(E_C) - P(E_H \cap E_C)$$

$$= 0.6 + 0.7 - 0.4$$

$$= 0.9.$$

The reader should confirm that 20% of males over 30 own a house but no car, 30% own a car but no house, 40% own both, and 10% neither.

Example 2.2.2. The data in table 2.2.2 relate to 1083 claims on a general insurer in respect of 9872 vehicle-damage-only motor policies issued in 1979. Denote by E_1 the event 'no claim', E_2 'a single claim', E_3 'two or more claims', E_4 'total claim amount below \$2000', and E_5 'total claim amount above or equal to \$2000'.

(a) How many times did each of the following events occur?
$E_1, E_2, E_3, E_4, E_5, E_1 \cap E_3, E_1 \cup E_3, E_3 \cap E_5, E_3 \cup E_5$.

(b) Estimate the probability of each of the events enumerated under (a).

(c) What does $E_3 \cup E_5$ represent (in words)?

(d) Represent the data diagrammatically, indicating the number of times each event occurred. Shade $E_3 \cup E_5$.

Table 2.2.2. *Policies issued in 1979 making at least one claim*

	Total claim amount	
	Under \$2000	\$2000 or over
	Number of policies	
One claim only	937	28
More than one claim	103	15

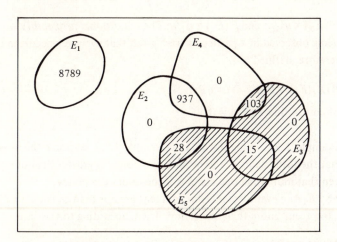

Fig. 2.2.2. Diagrammatic representation of the data of example 2.2.2 $E_3 \cup E_5$ is shaded.

(a) The number of times the various events occurred are, respectively, 8789, 965, 118, 1040, 43, 0, 8907, 15, 146.

(b) We divide each of the figures in (a) by 9872 and obtain: 0.890, 0.098, 0.012, 0.105, 0.004, 0, 0.902, 0.002, 0.015.

(c) The event of a policy incurring two or more claims, or total claims in excess of $2000 during the year, or both.

(d) See fig. 2.2.2.

Further reading: Feller [9] 98–101**; Hoel [14] 10–18; Mode [22] 94–7.

2.3   Conditional probability

Suppose a random experiment is performed n times under identical conditions and that n is large. Suppose also that the events E_2 and $E_1 \cap E_2$ are observed, respectively, n_2 and n_{12} times. The number of trials n is large, so that

$$P(E_2) \doteqdot n_2/n \text{ and } P(E_1 \cap E_2) \doteqdot n_{12}/n.$$

Of the n_2 trials which result in event E_2, n_{12} result in the simultaneous occurrence of event E_1. In other words, a proportion n_{12}/n_2 of the trials which result in event E_2 also result in the simultaneous occurrence of E_1.

The probability that event E_1 is observed in a particular trial, given that event E_2 is observed in that particular trial, is denoted by $P(E_1|E_2)$. The numbers n, n_2 and n_{12} are large. It is apparent, therefore, from the previous paragraph, that

$$P(E_1|E_2) \doteqdot n_{12}/n_2 = \left(\frac{n_{12}}{n}\right) \bigg/ \left(\frac{n_2}{n}\right). \tag{2.3.1}$$

But $P(E_1 \cap E_2) \doteqdot n_{12}/n$ and $P(E_2) \doteqdot n_2/n$. The *conditional probability* of event E_1 being observed in a particular trial, given that event E_2 occurs in that trial, is, therefore, defined as

■ $$P(E_1|E_2) = P(E_1 \cap E_2)/P(E_2), \tag{2.3.2}$$

provided of course that $P(E_2) \neq 0$.

Example 2.3.1. Using the data of example 2.2.2, estimate the probability that the total claim size in respect of a policy is greater than or equal to $2000, given that more than one claim is made under the policy.

Denote by E_1 the event 'total claim payment greater than or equal to $2000', and by E_2 the event 'more than one claim'. Then, according to the data,

$$P(E_2) = (103 + 15)/9872 = 118/9872 \; ;$$

$$P(E_1 \cap E_2) = 15/9872.$$

The probability that the total claim amount in respect of a policy chosen at random is greater than or equal to $2000, given that more than one claim is made under the policy, is

$$P(E_1|E_2) = P(E_1 \cap E_2)/P(E_2)$$
$$= (15/9872)/(118/9872)$$
$$= 15/118$$
$$= 0.127 \ .$$

Example 2.3.2. The general insurance group described in example 2.2.1 has only written motor vehicle insurances in the past and, because of its marketing strategy, the vast majority of its policyholders are males over the age of 30. Apart from the fact that they all own cars, the policyholders are typical of males over age 30 in the wider community. The insurance group is about to enter the householders insurance class of business, and plans to market its new product initially by direct mailing to its existing policyholders. What is the probability that an existing policyholder, chosen at random, owns a house?

Using the notation of example 2.2.1, the probability that a male over 30 years of age, chosen at random from the wider community, owns a house, given that he owns a car, is

$$P(E_H|E_C) = P(E_H \cap E_C)/P(E_C)$$
$$= 0.4/0.7$$
$$= 0.57 \ .$$

Since existing policyholders are typical of males over 30 in the wider community, other than the fact that they own cars, the probability that an existing policyholder owns a house must also be 0.57.

This is slightly *less* than $P(E_H)$, the probability that a male over age 30, chosen at random, owns a house (0.6), and the group might well reconsider the plan to market directly to existing policyholders. The decision will probably depend on the management's view on the extent to which the goodwill of existing policyholders will lead them to buy the new product.

Further reading: Feller [9] 114–18**; Hoel [13] 45–6; Hoel [14] 18–20; Mode [22] 96–7; Mood & Graybill [23] 33–5.

2.4 Independence of two events

Two events E_1 and E_2 are said to be *independent* if $P(E_1|E_2) = P(E_1)$. This is logical because the equality implies that the probability of event E_1 occurring is unaffected by the occurrence of event E_2. Using (2.3.2) and stipulating that $P(E_2) \neq 0$, we see that, *for two independent events E_1 and E_2,*

■ $P(E_1 \cap E_2) = P(E_1) \times P(E_2)$.   (2.4.1)

The presence of independent events usually simplifies statistical work considerably. It is customary, therefore, to make use of independence whenever possible. In general insurance, we often assume that claims are independent. Sometimes, however, it is not safe to make such an assumption. For example, a fire engulfing a factory might spread to a neighbouring factory covered by the same insurer. (There are ways of getting round the problem. One might, for example, define as a single risk all risks in close proximity to one another.)

Example 2.4.1. If the probability of a house being burgled is 1 in 100 and the probability of it being struck by lightning is 1 in 10 000, find the probability that a house is burgled or struck by lightning or is both burgled and struck by lightning.

Denoting the event 'burglary' by B and the event 'being struck by lightning' by L, and assuming that the two are independent, we have from (2.4.1),

$$
\begin{aligned}
P(B \cap L) &= P(B) \times P(L) \\
&= 0.01 \times 0.0001 \\
&= 0.000\ 001 \ .
\end{aligned}
$$

The probability that a house is burgled or struck by lightning, or is both burgled and struck by lightning, is, according to (2.2.1),

$$
\begin{aligned}
P(B \cup L) &= P(B) + P(L) - P(B \cap L) \\
&= 0.01 + 0.0001 - 0.000\ 001 \\
&= 0.010\ 099 \ .
\end{aligned}
$$

Further reading: Feller [9] 125−32**; Hoel [13] 46−55; Hoel [14] 15; Mendenhall & Scheaffer [21] 32−54; Mode [22] 97; Mood & Graybill [23] 43.

2.5   Exercises

1. Two good dice are rolled simultaneously. Let A denote the event 'the sum shown is 8' and B the event 'the two dice show the same number'. Find $P(A)$, $P(B)$, $P(A \cap B)$, $P(A \cup B)$, $P(A|B)$, $P(B|A)$.

2. Let A represent the event that a man chosen at random from a certain population is overweight and B the event that he is over 50. Write down symbols for the probabilities of the following events:

   (a) the man is not overweight;
   (b) if he is overweight, he is also over 50;
   (c) if he is over 50, he is not also overweight.

3. If in question 2, $P(A) = \frac{1}{3}$ and $P(B) = \frac{1}{4}$, and A and B are independent events, calculate $P(A \cup B)$.

4.[2] A perfectly symmetrical coin is tossed four times. Prove that the probabilities of obtaining 0, 1, 2, 3 and 4 'heads' are respectively $\frac{1}{16}, \frac{4}{16}, \frac{6}{16}, \frac{4}{16}$ and $\frac{1}{16}$.
(*Hint*: $(1/2)^4 = 1/16$.)

5. The experiment of question 4 is performed. Let A denote the event '4 "heads" ', B the event 'an odd number of "heads" ' and C the event 'more "heads" than "tails" '. Use the results of question 4 to calculate

   (a) $P(A)$;
   (b) $P(B)$;
   (c) $P(C)$;
   (d) $P(A \mid B)$;
   (e) $P(B \mid A)$;
   (f) $P(A \mid C)$;
   (g) $P(C \mid A)$;
   (h) $P(B \mid C)$;
   (i) $P(C \mid B)$.

[2]   This is an example of the binomial distribution of section 5.8.

3 RANDOM VARIABLES AND THEIR DISTRIBUTIONS

Summary In this chapter, the concept of a statistical distribution is introduced for both discrete and continuous random variables. The distribution function $F(x)$ is defined and its use demonstrated. The probability-density function $f(x)$ of a continuous random variable is also defined and its relationship to the distribution function $F(x)$ explained. Numerous general insurance examples are given.

3.1   Discrete random variables and their distributions

In section 2.1, we described a gambler tossing a coin four times and counting the number of 'heads' he obtains. The number is a *random variable* which may take any one of the non-negative integer values 0, 1, 2, 3 or 4. The random variable is *discrete* because it is restricted to particular point values; it cannot assume all values in any interval (for example, all values between 3 and 4). The number of claims incurred by an insurance company is always a discrete random variable.

We shall denote the probability that the above random variable takes the value 0 by p_0, the probability that it takes the value 1 by p_1, and so on. From exercise 4 of section 2.5, we know that $p_0 = \frac{1}{16}, p_1 = \frac{4}{16}, p_2 = \frac{6}{16}, p_3 = \frac{4}{16}$ and $p_4 = \frac{1}{16}$. These probabilities define the *statistical distribution* of the random variable, which may be represented graphically as a series of spikes, as shown in fig. 3.1.1. The heights of the spikes represent the probabilities and must, of

Fig. 3.1.1 The distribution of the number of 'heads' obtained when an unbiased coin is tossed four times.

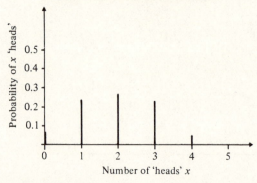

Number of 'heads' x

course, sum to 1.0. A general insurance example of a statistical distribution is given below as example 3.1.1.

Another useful concept is that of the *distribution function F(x)*, defined as the probability that a random variable X (say) takes a value less than or equal to x. In our coin-tossing example; $F(x) = 0$ for $x < 0$ because the probability of obtaining less than zero 'heads' is zero. $F(x)$ jumps to $\frac{1}{16}$ when $x = 0$, because the probability of zero or less 'heads' is $\frac{1}{16}$. $F(x)$ then remains level at $\frac{1}{16}$ until $x = 1$, because it is not possible to obtain a number of 'heads' between 0 and 1. At $x = 1$, $F(x)$ jumps to $\frac{5}{16}$, because the probability of obtaining 1 or less 'heads' is $\frac{5}{16}$. And so on. The complete distribution function is shown as fig. 3.1.2.

We note that $F(x)$ always starts at zero when $x = -\infty$. It must remain constant or increase as x increases, and it becomes 1.0 at (or before) $x = \infty$. It cannot exceed 1.0.

A gambler performs the above coin-tossing experiment 100 times, and obtains the results shown in table 3.1.1. The results of his labours may be summarised in a *relative frequency distribution* showing the proportion of experiments yielding 0 'heads', the proportion yielding 1 'head', and so on, and represented graphically as a series of spikes as shown in fig. 3.1.3. The relative frequency distribution in fig. 3.1.3 is clearly an *estimate* of the true underlying distribution of the random variable. An *observed distribution function* can also be plotted to summarise the gambler's results (fig. 3.1.4). This observed distribution function is an estimate of the true underlying distribution function, based on the results of the gambler's 100 experiments.

Fig. 3.1.2. The distribution function $F(x)$ of the number of 'heads' obtained when an unbiased coin is tossed four times.

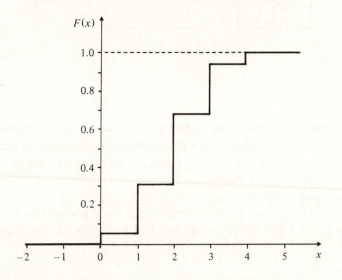

Table 3.1.1. *Observed frequency distribution in a coin-tossing experiment*

Number of 'heads' j	Number of experiments producing j 'heads'
0	6
1	27
2	39
3	21
4	7
Total	100

Fig. 3.1.3. The observed relative frequency distribution in a coin-tossing experiment. The heights of the spikes (0.06, 0.27, 0.39, 0.21 and 0.07) estimate the true underlying probabilities shown in fig. 3.1.1.

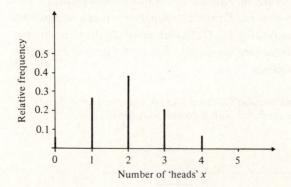

Example 3.1.1. The figures in table 3.1.2 are taken from a paper by Johnson & Hey [15] and show the numbers of policyholders in a certain insurance portfolio making 0, 1, 2, 3, . . . claims in a year. Plot the relative frequencies and the observed distribution function.

These are shown as figs. 3.1.5 and 3.1.6.

Further reading: Feller [9] 212–20**; Hoel [13] 73–8; Hoel [14] 26–30, 39–44; Mendenhall & Scheaffer [21] 67–8; Mode [22] 40–64; Mood & Graybill [23] 44–5; Pollard [26] 75–7; Yamane [30] 112.

Table 3.1.2. *Numbers of policyholders making 0, 1, 2, 3, 4, 5 claims in a year (data of Johnson & Hey [15])*

Number of claims in year	Frequency
0	370 412
1	46 545
2	3 935
3	317
4	28
5	3
$\geqslant 6$	0

Fig. 3.1.4. Observed distribution function in a coin-tossing experiment. The *increments* in height at $x=0, 1, 2, 3$ and 4 are equal to the heights of the corresponding spikes in fig. 3.1.3. This observed distribution function estimates the true underlying distribution function shown in fig. 3.1.2.

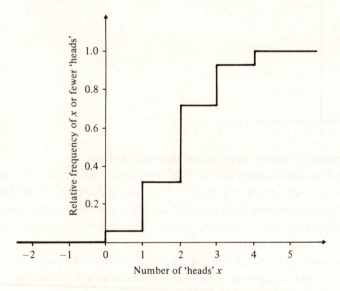

Fig. 3.1.5. The relative frequencies of policies making 0, 1, 2 . . . claims in a year. The spikes at $x = 2, 3, 4$ and 5 are too small to be visible on the graph.

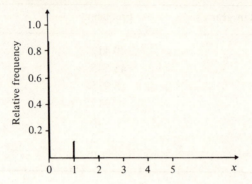

Fig. 3.1.6. The observed distribution function of Johnson & Hey. From $x = 2$ onwards, the function is so close to 1.0 as to be indistinguishable from it.

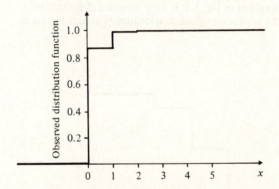

3.2   Continuous random variables and their distributions

Some random variables are, by their very nature, continuous and may assume any value over a continuous interval. Examples include the height of an adult male chosen at random, the amount of rainfall in a certain location during a given period, and the size of an insurance claim (ignoring the complication that fractions of cents cannot be paid!).

For a continuous random variable it is meaningless to seek the probability that the variable takes a particular value because there is an infinite number of values that the variable may take within its range, and the probability that it takes a particular value is, therefore, zero. It *is* meaningful, however, to seek the probability that the random variable lies in a particular interval. Thus, in the case of an insurance claim, it would not be very meaningful to ask for the probability of obtaining a claim of \$374.13, but it *would* be meaningful to seek the probability that the claim amount fell between \$250 and \$500.

More often than not, frequency data for continuous variables have a discrete quality, for, whatever measurements are taken, whether it is to be to the nearest centimetre or nearest cent, observations have to be grouped in finite bands. As an example, consider the claim size frequency distribution in table 3.2.1. We might depict this frequency distribution by plotting spikes equal to the relative frequency of claims in the interval at the central points of the various intervals, as in fig. 3.2.1. A more productive approach, however, is to plot a *histogram* as in fig. 3.2.2, where the *area under the histogram* in each interval is equal to the relative frequency of claims in that interval.

This latter approach provides us with a method for dealing with continuous data. We consider a function $f(x)$ which is non-negative. This function is called a *probability-density function,* and the area under it, between $x = a$ and $x = b$ (say) is the probability that the random variable lies between a and b. An example is provided in fig. 3.2.3. Note that the total area under the curve between $x = -\infty$ and $x = +\infty$ must always be 1.0, because the random variable must lie between $-\infty$ and $+\infty$.

The distribution function $F(x)$ of a continuous random variable X is defined in exactly the same manner as it was in the discrete case, namely, as the probability that the random variable X takes a value less than or equal to x. It follows that $F(x)$ must always start at zero when $x = -\infty$. It must remain constant or increase as x increases, and it becomes 1.0 at (or before) $x = \infty$. It

Table 3.2.1. *A claim size frequency distribution*

Claim size (\$)	Number of claims
0– 2 000	488
2 000– 4 000	115
4 000– 6 000	92
6 000– 8 000	54
8 000–10 000	33
10 000–12 000	19
12 000–14 000	15
14 000– 16 000	15
16 000–18 000	7
18 000–20 000	4
Total	842

cannot exceed 1.0. Furthermore, because of the way in which we have defined the probability-density function $f(x)$, $F(a)$ is the area under the $f(x)$ curve and to the left of the vertical line at $x = a$.

Since the total area under the probability-density curve must be 1.0, the shaded area in fig. 3.2.3 is $1 - F(2000)$.

Fig. 3.2.1. Spike representation of the grouped claim size frequency data in table 3.2.1. The height of the first spike is $488/842 = 0.580$.

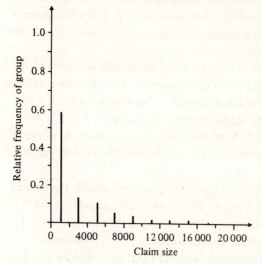

Fig. 3.2.2. Histogram representation of the grouped claim size frequency data in table 3.2.1. The area under the histogram between $x = 0$ and $x = 2000$ must be 0.580 to be consistent with fig. 3.2.1. The width of the interval is 2000; the height of this section of the histogram must, therefore, be $0.580/2000 = 0.000\,290$. The shaded area under the histogram between $x = 8000$ and $x = 16\,000$ estimates the probability that a claim will lie in the range \$8000–\$16\,000.

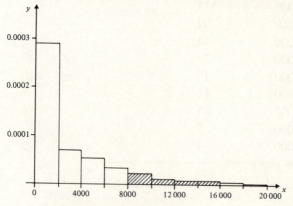

Example 3.2.1. Table 3.2.1 shows the distribution of claim sizes in an insurance portfolio. Treating the claim size X as a continuous random variable with range \$0–\$20 000, sketch the graph of the observed distribution function $F(x)$ and hence estimate the probability that a particular claim exceeds \$5000.

The probability that the claim size is less than zero is of course zero, and an estimate of the probability that it is less than \$2000 is 488/842 = 0.58. These are the first two values plotted in fig. 3.2.4. The next point, estimating the

Fig. 3.2.3. The probability-density function of a claim size distribution. Negative claims are not possible, so $f(x)$ is zero for $x < 0$. The total area under the curve must be 1.0 (text), and the shaded area is the probability that the claim size exceeds \$2000.

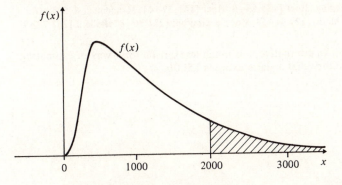

Fig. 3.2.4. Estimated distribution function $F(x)$ for the claim size data in table 3.2.1. The probability that a claim is less than or equal to \$5000 is estimated by the height of the vertical line at $x = 5000$ (0.8 approximately).

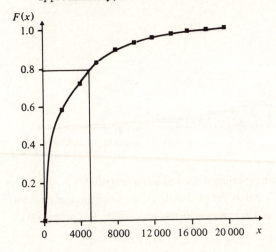

probability that a claim is less than or equal to $4000, is calculated as (488 + 115)/842 = 0.72. The remaining values are calculated similarly and a curve drawn to represent the observed distribution function $F(x)$.

The height of the curve at $x = 5000$ (0.8 approximately) estimates the probability that a claim is less than or equal to $5000. We deduce that the probability that a claim exceeds $5000 is approximately 0.2 (one in five).

An alternative, but generally *much less accurate method* for estimating this probability, would be to redraw fig. 3.2.2 on graph paper and sketch a smooth $f(x)$ curve like the one in fig. 3.2.5. (Note: the total area under this $f(x)$ curve should be 1.0, and the areas under sections of its length should approximate the areas under the corresponding sections of the histogram.) One can then estimate the probability by determining the area under the smooth $f(x)$ curve to the right of $x = 5000$ (counting the small squares on the graph paper).

Further reading: Hoel [13] 83–6; Hoel [14] 39–44; Mendenhall & Scheaffer [21] 115; Mode [22] 44–54; Mood & Graybill [23] 76–82; Pollard [26] 77–9.

Fig. 3.2.5. An alternative, but much less satisfactory, way of estimating the probability that a claim exceeds $5000.

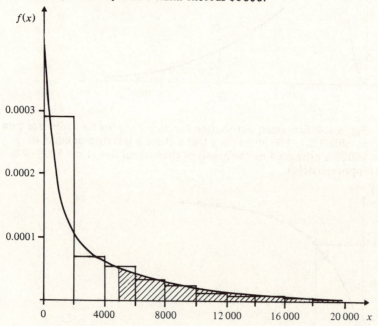

3.3   The area under a curve; integration and differentiation

We saw in section 3.2 that the probability that a continuous random variable X falls between a and b is equal to the area under the probability-density curve $f(x)$ between $x = a$ and $x = b$. Let us divide this area into narrow strips, each of width δx, as in fig. 3.3.1. The strip immediately to the right of the point x has height $f(x)$ and width δx, so that its area is (approximately) $f(x)\,\delta x$. If we were to sum all the strip areas for x going from a in steps of δx to b, we would have the area under the $f(x)$ curve between a and b, at least approximately, and this total area might be written as

$$\underset{\substack{x = a \text{ to } b \\ \text{in steps} \\ \text{of } \delta x}}{\text{Sum}} \quad f(x)\,\delta x.$$

Obviously, the calculation of the area becomes more and more accurate the narrower the strips become. When δx becomes infinitesimally small, mathematicians write $\mathrm{d}x$ instead of δx and replace the word 'Sum' by the shorter symbol $\int$. The *exact* area is then written

$$\int_a^b f(x)\,\mathrm{d}x. \tag{3.3.1}$$

This area is also referred to as 'the integral of $f(x)$ with respect to x between the limits $x = a$ and $x = b$'.

Formula (3.3.1) may look complicated to readers unfamiliar with the integral calculus but, as we have shown, it does have a very simple explanation. Such readers are advised to concentrate on fundamental principles by treating each integral as an area under a curve and forgetting about formal integration. Readers familiar with the integral calculus should have no difficulty performing the integrations in the examples.

When $f(x)$ has an explicit mathematical form, it may be (and often is) possible to perform the integration in a simple manner and hence obtain the required area. We give several examples below.

$F(u)$ is the probability that the random variable X is less than or equal to u, which is the area under the $f(x)$ curve between $x = -\infty$ and $x = u$. In other words,

∎ $$F(u) = \int_{-\infty}^u f(x)\,\mathrm{d}x. \tag{3.3.2}$$

Fig. 3.3.1. The area under the curve $f(x)$ between the points x and $x + \delta x$.

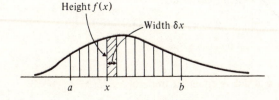

The area to the left of $x = u$ in fig. 3.3.2 is $F(u)$ and the area to the left of $x = u + \delta u$ is $F(u + \delta u)$, which of course exceeds $F(u)$. It is clear from the diagram that the difference $F(u + \delta u) - F(u)$ must be approximately equal to $f(u)\,\delta u$. In other words,

$$f(u) \doteqdot [F(u + \delta u) - F(u)]/\delta u.$$

Again, the approximation becomes more and more accurate the smaller δu becomes, and exact when δu becomes infinitesimally small. In the limit, mathematicians write du instead of δu, and represent the difference $F(u + \mathrm{d}u) - F(u)$ by dF. We then have

■ $$f(u) = \frac{\mathrm{d}F}{\mathrm{d}u} = \frac{\mathrm{d}}{\mathrm{d}u}\,F(u). \tag{3.3.3}$$

In other words, the probability-density function $f(u)$ is the derivative or slope of the distribution function $F(x)$ at the point $x = u$ (fig. 3.3.3 and section 1.6).

In summary, therefore, the F-function is the integral of the f-function and $f(u)$ is the derivative of $F(u)$. To evaluate $F(u)$ from $f(u)$ we must either plot $f(x)$, and obtain the area under $f(x)$ to the left of $x = u$ numerically, or find a function which when differentiated is equal to $f(x)$. We now give some examples of how these results can be applied.

Fig. 3.3.2. The area representing the difference between $F(u + \delta u)$ and $F(u)$.

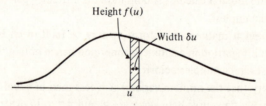

Fig. 3.3.3. The slope of the $F(x)$ curve at the point x = u is approximately $[F(u + \delta u) - F(u)]/\delta u$. The exact slope is given by the limit dF/du.

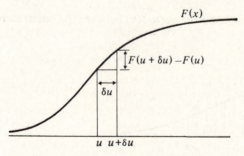

Example 3.3.1. A continuous random variable X can take any value between 0 and 1, and it cannot lie outside this interval. Find the probability that X is less than 0.5 if its probability-density function $f(x)$ is $3x^2$ in the interval $0 \leqslant x \leqslant 1$.

We require $F(0.5)$. Since the random variable X is restricted to the interval $(0, 1)$, the probability-density function $f(x)$ must be zero for $x < 0$ and $x > 1$ (fig. 3.3.4). In this particular case, therefore,

$$F(0.5) = \int_{-\infty}^{0.5} f(x)\, dx = \int_{0}^{0.5} f(x)\, dx = \int_{0}^{0.5} 3x^2 \, dx.$$

Integration is the inverse process of differentiation. We require, therefore, the function $F(x)$ which when differentiated yields $3x^2$, and according to example 1.6.1,

$$F(x) = x^3 + A.$$

A is a constant to be determined.

The random variable X cannot lie in the interval $(-\infty, 0)$ and it is continuous over the interval $(0, 1)$. Thus $F(0)$ must be zero, whence $A = 0$.

The probability that X is less than 0.5 is, therefore,

$$F(0.5) = (0.5)^3 = 0.125.$$

Note that $F(1) = 1$, as it should, since X cannot exceed 1.0.

Fig. 3.3.4. The graph of $f(x)$ for example 3.3.1.

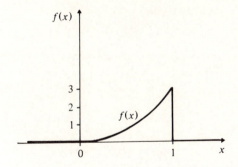

Example 3.3.2. A continuous random variable X taking only non-negative values has the probability-density function

$$f(x) = 0.5\, e^{-0.5x} \quad (x \geqslant 0).$$

Such a random variable is said to have the (negative) exponential distribution. Find its distribution function $F(x)$, and the probability that X exceeds 5.0.

As in the previous example, $f(x) = 0$ for $x < 0$, and

$$F(u) = \int_{0}^{u} f(x)\, dx = \int_{0}^{u} 0.5\, e^{-0.5x} \, dx,$$

for u greater than 0. The distribution function $F(u)$ will be zero for all u less than or equal to zero.

Integration is the inverse process of differentiation and we require therefore the function $F(x)$ which when differentiated yields $0.5 \, e^{-0.5x}$. According to example 1.9.4 this function is

$$F(x) = C - e^{-0.5x},$$

where C is a constant yet to be determined.

When $x = 0$, $e^{-0.5x}$ is 1.0 and $F(x)$ must be zero (the random variable cannot assume values less than 0). We deduce that $C = 1$ and

$$F(x) = 1 - e^{-0.5x}.$$

The probability that X exceeds 5.0 is the area under the $f(x)$ curve to the right of $x = 5.0$ or

$$1 - F(5.0) = 0.082.$$

The graphs of $f(x)$ and $F(x)$ are shown in fig. 3.3.5.

Fig. 3.3.5. Graphs of $f(x)$ and $F(x)$ for example 3.3.2. The shape of the $f(x)$ curve might usefully be compared with the claim size $f(x)$ curve in fig. 3.2.5.

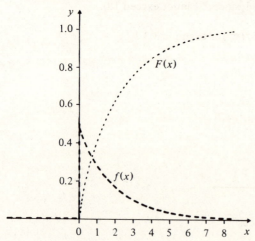

Example 3.3.3. A random variable X may assume any value between 0 and 100. All values (including fractional values such as $33.870\,65\dot{3}$) are equally likely.

(a) What is the probability that the random variable is less than 37.5?

(b) What is the probability that the random variable is less than x, where $0 < x < 100$?

(c) Use the answer to (b) to deduce the probability-density function of the random variable.

(a) Probability = 37.5/100 = 0.375.
(b) Probability = $x/100$.
(c) From (b) we know that $F(x) = x/100$. It follows, therefore from (3.3.3), that

$$f(x) = \frac{d}{dx} F(x) = \frac{d}{dx} \frac{x}{100} = \frac{1}{100} \cdot$$

In other words, the probability-density function $f(x)$ is constant and equal to 1/100 in the interval $0 \leqslant x \leqslant 100$; it is zero elsewhere (fig. 3.3.6). A random variable which has a probability-density function equal to a constant, as this one has, is said to be uniformly distributed, the constant being the reciprocal of the range of values it may take.

Fig. 3.3.6. The probability-density function in example 3.3.3.

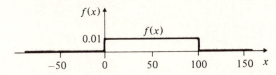

Example 3.3.4. It is observed that a particular claim size distribution may be represented by the distribution function

$$F(x) = 1 - e^{-0.01x}.$$

Sketch the curve $y = F(x)$, and calculate the probability that a particular claim lies between $50 and $100.

The sketch of the curve is shown as fig. 3.3.7. The probability that a

Fig. 3.3.7. The negative exponential claim size distribution function of example 3.3.4.

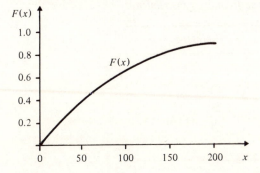

particular claim lies between $50 and $100 is given by

$$F(100) - F(50) = 0.632 - 0.393$$
$$= 0.239,$$

or almost one in four.

It is worth noting that the probability-density function of the claim size distribution is

$$f(x) = \frac{d}{dx} F(x) = 0.01 \ e^{-0.01x}.$$

The required probability is also equal to the area under this curve between $x = 50$ and $x = 100$ (fig. 3.3.8).

Fig. 3.3.8. The negative exponential claim size probability-density function of example 3.3.4. The shaded area is the probability that a particular claim lies between $50 and $100.

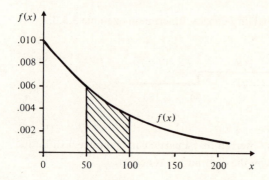

Example 3.3.5. A survey of claims reveals the distribution shown in table 3.3.1. Sketch the observed distribution function and use it to estimate the probability that a particular claim lies between $150 and $250. The total frequency is 86. An estimate of $F(100)$, the probability that a

Table 3.3.1. *Claim size frequency distribution*

Claim size ($)	Frequency
0– 100	15
100– 200	40
200– 500	23
500–1000	8
over 1000	0

particular claim is less than $100, is given by $15/86 = 0.17$. Estimates of $F(200)$, $F(500)$ and $F(1000)$ are obtained similarly:

$$F(200) = (15 + 40)/86 = 0.64;$$
$$F(500) = (15 + 40 + 23)/86 = 0.91;$$
$$F(1000) = (15 + 40 + 23 + 8)/86 = 1.00.$$

These points are then sketched and joined by a smooth curve as in fig. 3.3.9.

An estimate of the required probability $F(250) - F(150)$ is given by the difference between the heights of the observed $F(x)$ curve at $x = 250$ and $x = 150$, namely $0.71 - 0.50 = 0.21$ (fig. 3.3.9).

Example 3.3.6. The cumulative distribution function in example 3.3.5 rose very steeply and, as a result, it was difficult to read the required probabilities from the graph. In this situation, a transformation is sometimes helpful. Use the transformation $Y = \ln X$, where X is the claim size, to estimate the probability that X lies between $150 and $250.

The required probability is the same as the probability that Y lies between 5.01 and 5.52. The observed distribution function for Y takes the following values:

$y = \ln x$	Distribution function $F(y)$
4.61	0.17
5.30	0.64
6.21	0.91
6.91	1.00

Fig. 3.3.9. The observed distribution function $F(x)$ for example 3.3.5.

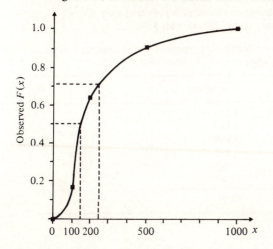

and is depicted in fig. 3.3.10. From the graph, the required probability is
0.71 - 0.49 = 0.22.

Further reading: Hoel [14] 42–4; Mendenhall & Scheaffer [21] 115–22; Pollard
[26] 37–43*; Reichmann [27] 251–9.

Fig. 3.3.10. The observed distribution function of $Y = \ln X$ for
example 3.3.6.

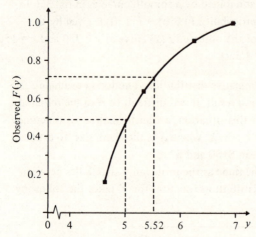

3.4   Exercises

1. Two good dice are rolled and the sum of the uppermost faces noted. Calculate the
probabilities of the various possible outcomes and plot the relative frequency
distribution. Plot also the distribution function $F(x)$.

2. Using the data of table 3.2.1, estimate the probability that a particular claim is
less than $16 000, given that the claim is greater than $10 000.

3. Table 3.4.1 is a summary of the claim sizes of 7821 householders' claims during
1980. Using graph paper,
(a) plot the observed distribution function $F(x)$ of claim size;
(b) estimate the probability that a claim exceeds $500.

Table 3.4.1. *The claim size distribution experienced by an insurer in respect
of 7821 householders' claims*

Size of claim ($)	Frequency
0– 50	1728
50–100	1346
100–200	1869
200–400	1822
400–800	907
over 800	149
Total	7821

4. Two householders' claims are received. Estimate the probability that at least one exceeds $500. (Use the data in table 3.4.1.)

5. Table 3.2.1 shows the distribution of claim sizes in an insurance portfolio. Use graph paper, and the alternative approach outlined in the last paragraph of example 3.2.1, to estimate the probability that a particular claim exceeds $5000. Compare your answer with that obtained by the simpler, and generally more accurate, method of the example.

6. A random fraction is equally likely to lie anywhere between 0 and 1. Draw the graphs of $f(x)$ and $F(x)$.

7. An observed claim size distribution is given as table 3.2.1. Use the logarithmic transformation method of example 3.3.6 to estimate the proportion of losses which would receive no claim settlement payment if an excess of $500 were introduced (i.e. if the insured has to meet the first $500 of any loss himself).

4 LOCATION AND DISPERSION

Summary: The mean is introduced as a measure of the location of a statistical distribution and the variance as a measure of dispersion around that mean. These concepts are essential to the understanding of much of the material in later chapters. Expectations, moments and skewness are also discussed. More advanced topics treated include conditional means and variances.

4.1 Measures of location – mean, median and mode

A distribution of claim frequency is given in table 4.1.1 and depicted in fig. 4.1.1. It is immediately apparent that the probability that the number of claims will lie between 5 and 15, inclusive, is very high (over 90%). In other words, we would expect the number of claims to be somewhere near a central value of about 10 with a high probability. Three different statistics or measures

Table 4.1.1. *A distribution of claim frequency*

Number of claims j	Probability that j claims occur	Number of claims j	Probability that j claims occur
0	0.000	11	0.116
1	0.000	12	0.100
2	0.002	13	0.079
3	0.006	14	0.058
4	0.016	15	0.040
5	0.032	16	0.026
6	0.056	17	0.016
7	0.082	18	0.009
8	0.106	19	0.005
9	0.121	20	0.002
10	0.124	>20	0.004

are commonly used to describe the centre of such a distribution. These are the *mode*, the *median* and the *mean*.

The mode[1] is the value most likely to occur (10 in our example). The median[2] is the value which divides the distribution in half. In other words, it is just as likely that the random variable will take a value less than the median as it is for it to take a value greater than the median. In our example $F(9) = 0.421$ and $F(10) = 0.545$, and, by convention, we take 10 as the median.

The mean, however, is the most commonly used measure of central tendency in general insurance work, and the only one we use in this book.

If we were able to examine 1000 independent insurance portfolios, each having the claim frequency distribution in table 4.1.1, we would expect two to experience 2 claims, six to experience 3 claims, sixteen to experience 4 claims, and so on. The mean (or average) number of claims would be

$$(0 \times 0 + 1 \times 0 + 2 \times 2 + 3 \times 6 + 4 \times 16 + \ldots)/1000,$$

or

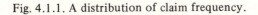

$$0 \times 0.000 + 1 \times 0.000 + 2 \times 0.002 + 3 \times 0.006 + 4 \times 0.016 + \ldots.$$

Fig. 4.1.1. A distribution of claim frequency.

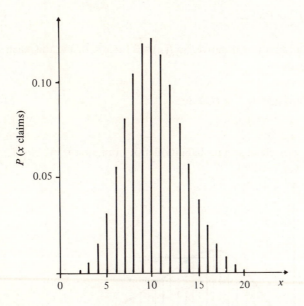

---

[1] The mode of a continuous distribution is the value of x for which $f(x)$ is largest.
[2] The median of a continuous distribution is the value of x for which $F(x) = 1/2$.

In other words, the mean of the distribution of a discrete random variable X is given by

∎ $$\text{mean} = \sum_{\substack{\text{all} \\ \text{possible} \\ x}} x\, P\,(X = x).$$ (4.1.1)

To obtain a formula for the mean of a continuous random variable, consider the claim size probability-density function in fig. 4.1.2 with its area divided into a series of strips, each of width δx. The probability that the random variable (X say) lies between x and $x + \delta x$ is equal to the shaded area, namely $f(x)\,\delta x$. According to (4.1.1), the mean of the distribution will be approximately equal to

$$\underset{\substack{x \text{ goes from} \\ -\infty \text{ to } \infty \\ \text{in steps of} \\ \delta x}}{\text{Sum}} \quad x\, f(x)\, \delta x.$$

The calculation becomes more and more accurate the narrower the strips become. In the limit, δx becomes infinitesimally small and is replaced by dx, and the word 'Sum' is replaced by the integral sign $\int$ (section 3.3). For a continuous distribution, therefore, the

∎ $$\text{mean} = \int_{-\infty}^{\infty} x\, f(x)\, dx.$$ (4.1.2)

Claim amounts cannot be negative. So $f(x) = 0$ for $x < 0$, and the mean size of a claim is given by

∎ $$\text{mean claim size} = \int_{0}^{\infty} x\, f(x)\, dx.$$ (4.1.3)

Fig. 4.1.2. A claim size probability-density function $f(x)$.

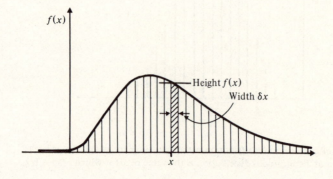

The following properties of means are often useful and should be noted.

1. If X is a random variable and k is a fixed constant, then the mean of the random variable kX is given by

■   mean $(kX) = k$ mean (X). (4.1.4)

2. The mean of the sum of a number of random variables is equal to the sum of their means. Thus, for example, if X and Y are random variables and $Z = X + Y$, then

■   mean $(Z) =$ mean $(X) +$ mean (Y). (4.1.5)

3. If X and Y are *independent* random variables, and a random variable Z is defined as the product of X and Y, then the mean of Z is given by

■   mean $(Z) =$ mean $(X) \times$ mean (Y). (4.1.6)

A mean calculated using observed data, rather than an underlying statistical distribution, is often referred to as a *sample mean*. The sample mean in fact estimates the mean of the underlying distribution.

Example 4.1.1. Calculate the sample mean of the number of claims under a policy during its year in force using the data in table 4.1.2.

We estimate the unknown probabilities by the relative frequencies and substitute these into (4.1.1) to obtain the mean number of claims

$$0 \times \frac{17\,353}{19\,412} + 1 \times \frac{1414}{19\,412} + 2 \times \frac{620}{19\,412} + 3 \times \frac{25}{19\,412} = 0.1406.$$

Table 4.1.2. *Observed numbers of policyholders making 0, 1, 2 and 3 claims during their year in force*

Number of claims j	Number of policyholders making j claims in year
0	17 353
1	1 414
2	620
3	25
Total	19 412

Example 4.1.2. The claim size distribution function in respect of a particular risk is

$$F(x) = 1 - e^{-0.001x} \quad (x \geqslant 0).$$

Obtain the mean claim size by a graphical method.

Using the fact that the derivative of a constant is zero and the derivative of e^{kx} is ke^{kx}, we deduce from (3.3.3) that the probability-density function of the claim size is

$$f(x) = \frac{d}{dx} F(x) = 0.001\, e^{-0.001x} \quad (x \geqslant 0).$$

According to (4.1.3), therefore, the mean claim size is

$$\int_0^\infty 0.001xe^{-0.001x}\, dx, \tag{4.1.7}$$

which is the area under the curve $g(x) = 0.001xe^{-0.001x}$ to the right of the origin (fig. 4.1.3). The $g(x)$ curve was carefully plotted on graph paper and, by counting the number of small squares under the curve (including fractions of squares), an area of 1040 was estimated. We conclude that the mean claim size is about $1040.

The area (4.1.7) can in fact be obtained by formal integration, producing an exact mean claim size of $1000.

Fig. 4.1.3. The mean claim size in respect of a risk with claim size distribution function $F(x) = 1 - e^{-0.001x}$ is obtained by calculating the area under the $g(x)$ curve. rve.

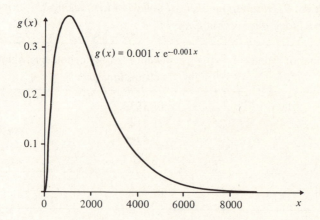

Example 4.1.3. An insurance portfolio consists of 100 independent policies of the type described in example 4.1.1. Estimate the mean number (or expected number[3]) of claims which will need to be processed for a portfolio of this size.

The total number of claims requiring processing will be equal to the sum of the number of claims for the 100 individual policies. According to example 4.1.1, an estimate of the mean number of claims for an individual policy is 0.1406. We conclude, by property (2) above, that an estimate of the mean or expected number of claims for the portfolio of 100 policies is 100 × 0.1406, or 14.06 claims.

Further reading: Hoel [13] 15–25; Hoel [14] 102–5; Mendenhall & Scheaffer [21] 85–95, 175–8; Mode [22] 18–25; Pollard [26] 79–81; Yamane [30] 35–58.

4.2 Dispersion – variance and standard deviation

The probability-density functions of two continuous random variables are shown in fig. 4.2.1. It is clear that they have the same mean. The first random variable, however, is much more likely to assume a value near that mean than the second, which has a much more widely dispersed distribution.

The *variance* of the distribution provides a measure of the spread of the distribution. In the case of a random variable X with a discrete distribution, the variance is

$$\blacksquare \qquad \sigma^2 = \sum_{\substack{\text{all} \\ \text{possible} \\ x}} (x - \text{mean})^2 \, P(X = x). \qquad (4.2.1)$$

Fig. 4.2.1. The probability-density functions of two continuous random variables. Both have the same mean (10).

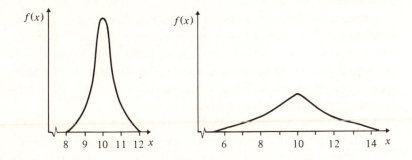

---

[3] Section 4.3.

For a continuous distribution over the range $(-\infty, \infty)$

■ $$\sigma^2 = \int_{-\infty}^{\infty} (x - \text{mean})^2 \, f(x) \, dx. \qquad (4.2.2)$$

When all the likely outcomes are concentrated near the mean, the variance σ^2 will be small.

The following alternative (but mathematically equivalent) formulae for the variance tend to be more useful in practice:

■ $$\sigma^2 = \sum_x x^2 \, P\,(X = x) - (\text{mean})^2 \, ; \qquad (4.2.3)$$

■ $$\sigma^2 = \int_{-\infty}^{\infty} x^2 \, f(x) \, dx - (\text{mean})^2. \qquad (4.2.4)$$

The sum on the right-hand side of (4.2.3) (or the integral on the right-hand side of (4.2.4) for a continuous variable) is often referred to as the *second moment of the distribution about the origin* (section 4.3) and will be denoted by α_2.

Variances have the following important properties.

1. If X is a random variable and k is a fixed constant, then

■ $$\text{Var}\,(k\,X) = k^2 \, \text{Var}\,X. \qquad (4.2.5)$$

2. If X and Y are *independent* random variables, a and b are fixed constants and $Z = aX + bY$, then

■ $$\text{Var}\,Z = a^2 \, \text{Var}\,X + b^2 \, \text{Var}\,Y. \qquad (4.2.6)$$

Two special cases of this latter rule should be noted:

■ $$\text{Var}\,(X + Y) = \text{Var}\,X + \text{Var}\,Y; \qquad (4.2.7)$$

■ $$\text{Var}\,(X - Y) = \text{Var}\,X + \text{Var}\,Y. \qquad (4.2.8)$$

In both these formulae, X and Y *must* be independent. We also deduce, as an extension of (4.2.7), that the variance of the sum of a number of *independent* random variables is equal to the sum of the individual variances.

The square root of the variance of a random variable is called the *standard deviation* and is denoted by σ.

A variance calculated using observed data rather than an underlying statistical distribution is often referred to as a *sample variance* and denoted by s^2. The sample variance in fact estimates the variance of the underlying statistical distribution, which in most cases is unknown. The *sample standard deviation s* is equal to the square root of the sample variance, and estimates the standard deviation of the underlying distribution.

Example 4.2.1. Calculate the sample variance and standard deviation of the number of claims under a policy, during its year in force, using the data in table 4.1.2.

From example 4.1.1, we know that the (sample) mean number of claims is 0.1406. Estimates of the probabilities of 0, 1, 2, and 3 claims are provided by 17 353/19 412, 1414/19 412, 620/19 412 and 25/19 412 respectively. According to (4.2.3), therefore, the sample variance is

$$s^2 = 0^2 \times \frac{17\,353}{19\,412} + 1^2 \times \frac{1\,414}{19\,412} + 2^2 \times \frac{620}{19\,412} + 3^2 \times \frac{25}{19\,412} - (0.1406)^2$$
$$= 0.2122 - 0.0198$$
$$= 0.1924.$$

The sample standard deviation is $s = \sqrt{(0.1924)} = 0.4386$.

Example 4.2.2. An insurance portfolio consists of 100 independent policies of the type described in example 4.2.1. Estimate the variance and standard deviation of the total number of claims from these policies.

The variance of the sum of a number of independent random variables is equal to the sum of their individual variances. We have 100 independent policies and, for each of these, the variance of the number of claims under the policy is σ^2, which is unknown but estimated by the sample variance s^2, to be 0.1924. An estimate of the variance of the number of claims in respect of the whole portfolio is, therefore, $100 \times 0.1924 = 19.24$. An estimate of the standard deviation of the underlying distribution is given by

$$s = \sqrt{(19.24)} = 4.39.$$

Example 4.2.3. A gambling casino offers two games, each requiring a stake of $8. In the first game, the player tosses two dice simultaneously and receives as many dollars as the sum of the two numbers thrown. In the second game, the player tosses two dice simultaneously; if both show 'sixes', the player receives $252; otherwise he receives nothing.

Which of the two games is preferred by the casino

(a) in the short run?

(b) in the long run?

Suppose that the dice are unbiased so that the probabilities of the various payouts are those shown in table 4.2.2. The mean payout is obtained by multiplying the payout column in table 4.2.2 by the corresponding probability column and summing the products. We obtain

mean payout for game (1) = $7;

mean payout for game (2) = $7.

The variances of the payouts under the two games can be obtained by multiplying the square of the payout figure in table 4.2.2 by the corresponding probability, summing the products, and subtracting the square of the mean (formula (4.2.3)). The variance for the first game is

$$2^2 \times \tfrac{1}{36} + 3^2 \times \tfrac{2}{36} + \ldots + 12^2 \times \tfrac{1}{36} - 7^2 = 5.8\dot{3},$$

and for the second

$$\left(252^2 \times \tfrac{1}{36} + 0^2 \times \tfrac{35}{36}\right) - 7^2 = 1715.$$

In each game the casino operator receives $1 more than he expects to have to pay out so in the long run he should make the same profit with each game. In the short run, however, there is much greater chance of a heavy payout with the second game than with the first, and this is reflected in the considerably larger variance of the payout for the second game.

An early payment of $252 would hardly bankrupt the casino. If the stakes were much higher, however, the consequences could be serious. In a comparable situation, a general insurer would seek reinsurance.

Further reading: Hoel [13] 18–25; Mode [22] 25–30; Pollard [26] 79–80; Yamane [30] 59–77.

Table 4.2.2. *Possible payouts and their probabilities for the two games described in example 4.2.3*

First game		Second game	
Payout	Probability	Payout	Probability
2	1/36	0	35/36
3	2/36	252	1/36
4	3/36		
5	4/36		
6	5/36		
7	6/36		
8	5/36		
9	4/36		
10	3/36		
11	2/36		
12	1/36		

**4.3 Expectations and moments

The expected value of a random variable is a weighted average of the values the random variable can take, the weights being the probabilities with which the random variable takes these values. The expected value of a variable X is written $E(X)$ and is defined in the case of a discrete distribution by

$$E(X) = \sum_x x\, P\,(X = x). \qquad (4.3.1)$$

That is, $E(X)$ is simply the mean value of X. In the case of a continuous random variable,

$$E(X) = \int_{-\infty}^{\infty} x\, f(x)\,\mathrm{d}x, \qquad (4.3.2)$$

which is also the mean.

The following properties of expected values are useful and should be noted.

1. The expected value of a constant is that constant.
2. If X is a random variable and k is a constant, then

$$E(kX) = kE(X). \qquad (4.3.3)$$

3. If a random variable Z is equal to the sum of two random variables X and Y, then

$$E(Z) = E(X) + E(Y). \qquad (4.3.4)$$

4. If a random variable Z is equal to the product of two *independent* random variables $X,\ Y$ then

$$E(Z) = E(X)\,E(Y). \qquad (4.3.5)$$

The important properties of means and variances, quoted in sections 4.1 and 4.2 respectively, are direct consequences of these expectation results.

The square of a random variable is also a random variable and has an expectation. In the case of a discrete random variable X,

$$E(X^2) = \sum_{x^2} x^2\, P(X^2 = x^2)$$
$$= \sum_x x^2\, P(X = x). \qquad (4.3.6)$$

Similarly, for a continuous random variable,

$$E(X^2) = \int_{-\infty}^{\infty} x^2\, f(x)\,\mathrm{d}x. \qquad (4.3.7)$$

The expected value of the square of a random variable is often referred to as

the *second moment of that random variable about the origin* and denoted by α_2.
More generally,

■ $$\alpha_r = E(X^r) = \begin{cases} \sum_x x^r P(X = x) & \text{(discrete case)} \\[2mm] \int_{-\infty}^{\infty} x^r f(x)\, dx & \text{(continuous case)} \end{cases} \qquad (4.3.8)$$

is the *rth moment about the origin* of the random variable X.

It is worth noting that the variance of a random variable is also an expected value; for if we consider the related random variable $Y = (X - \mu)^2$, where μ is the mean of X,

$$E(Y) = \sum (x - \mu)^2 \, P[(X - \mu)^2 = (x - \mu)^2]$$
$$= \sum_x (x - \mu)^2 \, P(X = x)$$
$$= \text{Var } X. \qquad (4.3.9)$$

The proof is similar when X is a continuous random variable.

The variance of X is also sometimes referred to as the second central moment of X. Generally, the *rth central moment* of a random variable X with mean μ is defined by

■ $$\mu_r = E(X - \mu)^r = \begin{cases} \sum_x (x - \mu)^r P(X = x) & \text{(discrete case)} \\[2mm] \int_{-\infty}^{\infty} (x - \mu)^r f(x)\, dx & \text{(continuous case)} \end{cases} \qquad (4.3.10)$$

Formulae (4.3.10) should be compared with (4.3.8).

When the underlying distribution is unknown, *sample moments* may be calculated using the distribution observed in a sample. A sample moment provides an estimate of the corresponding moment of the underlying distribution.

Example 4.3.1. Prove that the second central moment of a random variable X with mean μ is equal to the second moment about the origin minus the square of the mean (i.e. prove (4.2.3) and (4.2.4)).

$$E(X - \mu)^2 = E(X^2 - 2\mu X + \mu^2)$$
$$= E(X^2) - 2\mu E(X) + E(\mu^2)$$
$$= E(X^2) - 2\mu \times \mu + \mu^2$$
$$= E(X^2) - \mu^2.$$

Example 4.3.2. If the rth moment about the origin of a random variable X with mean μ is denoted by α_r, and the rth central moment is denoted by μ_r, prove that

$$\mu_3 = \alpha_3 - 3\alpha_2\alpha_1 + 2\alpha_1^3. \qquad (4.3.11)$$

The third central moment is

$$\mu_3 = E(X - \mu)^3$$
$$= E(X^3 - 3\mu X^2 + 3\mu^2 X - \mu^3)$$
$$= E(X^3) - 3\mu E(X^2) + 3\mu^2 E(X) - E(\mu^3)$$
$$= \alpha_3 - 3\mu\alpha_2 + 3\mu^2\alpha_1 - \mu^3.$$

But the mean μ is really the first moment about the origin α_1. Formula (4.3.11) follows.

> *Further reading*: Hoel [13] 80–6; Hoel [14] 54–7; Mode [22] 97–9; Mood & Graybill [23] 103–16**; Pollard [26] 81–3; Yamane [30] 110–12.

**4.4   Conditional means

Conditional probability was defined in section 2.3. We now define a conditional mean.

The *conditional mean* (or *conditional expectation*) of *a discrete variable X, given that another random variable Y is equal to y*, is

■ $$E(X \mid Y = y) = \sum_x x P(X = x \mid Y = y).$$ (4.4.1)

This is the same as the definition of $E(X)$ except that conditional probabilities are used for the weights in the summation. An analogous formula can be written down when X has a continuous distribution.

It is possible to prove that the expected value of X (i.e. the *unconditional mean* of X) is equal to the expectation over all possible values of the variable Y of the conditional expectation of X given Y. That is,

$$E(X) = \sum_y E(X \mid Y = y) P(Y = y),$$ (4.4.2)

or, more concisely,

■ $$E(X) = \underset{Y}{E}[E(X \mid Y)].$$ (4.4.3)

This result finds frequent application.

> **Example 4.4.1**. A policy is of the type described in example 4.1.1 and table 4.1.2. The distribution function of the size of an individual claim is
> $$F(x) = 1 - e^{-0.001x}.$$

Estimate the expected claim cost arising from 100 policies in force for 12 months.

From example 4.1.2 we know that the expected cost of a single claim is $1000. We deduce, using (4.1.5), that the expected cost of two claims is $2000 and the expected cost of three claims is $3000. These figures are the conditional mean costs *given* one, two and three claims respectively.

According to table 4.1.2, in respect of a single policy,

the estimated probability of one claim is 1414/19 412 = 0.0728;
the estimated probability of two claims is 620/19 412 = 0.0319;
the estimated probability of three claims is 25/19 412 = 0.0013.

It follows from (4.4.2) that the estimated unconditional mean payout in respect of an individual policy is

1000 × 0.0728 + 2000 × 0.0319 + 3000 × 0.0013 = 140.5.

The total payout in respect of the 100 policies is the sum of the payments in respect of the 100 individual policies. Since the 100 means are additive (section 4.1), the estimated expected total claim cost will be \$14 050.

Further reading: Mood & Graybill [23] 117–18**; Parzen [24] 51–4**.

**4.5 Conditional variances

In the case of a discrete random variable X, the conditional variance of X, given that the random variable Y has the value y, is

■ $$\text{Var}\,(X \mid Y = y) = \sum_x x^2\, P(X = x \mid Y = y) - [E(X \mid Y = y)]^2. \qquad (4.5.1)$$

This is the usual variance formula (4.2.3) with the unconditional probability $P(X = x)$ replaced by the conditional probability $P(X = x \mid Y = y)$ and the unconditional mean $E(X)$ replaced by the conditional mean $E(X \mid Y = y)$. An analogous formula exists when X is continuous.

It is possible to prove the following relationship between the unconditional variance of X and the conditional variance of X given Y:

■ $$\text{Var}\,(X) = \underset{Y}{E}[\text{Var}\,(X \mid Y)] + \underset{Y}{\text{Var}}\,[E(X \mid Y)]. \qquad (4.5.2)$$

Example 4.5.1. Estimate the standard deviation of the total payout in respect of the 100 policies in example 4.4.1.

The claim size distribution has mean 1000 (example 4.1.2) and its variance can be calculated to be 1 000 000. We know that the distribution of the number of claims under a policy has an estimated mean 0.1406 and estimated variance 0.1924 (example 4.2.1).

Let us denote the number of claims under a particular policy by the random variable Y and the total payout in respect of that policy by X. The variance of the payout under a single claim is 1 000 000 and, using the additive property of the variances of independent random variances (section 4.2), we conclude that the variance of the total payout in respect of Y independent claims on a particular policy is 1 000 000 Y. That is,

$$\text{Var}\,(X \mid Y) = 1\,000\,000\,Y.$$

We also deduce, using the additive property of means (section 4.1), that

$$E(X \mid Y) = 1000 \ Y.$$

The unconditional variance of X is then given by (4.5.2) as

$$\text{Var} \ (X) = E \ (1\ 000\ 000 \ Y) + \text{Var} \ (1000 \ Y).$$

Using (4.1.4) and (4.2.5), we deduce that

$$\text{Var} \ (X) = 1\ 000\ 000 \ E(Y) + (1000)^2 \ \text{Var} \ Y.$$

The expected value and variance of Y are unknown. We have already obtained estimates of them in examples 4.1.1 and 4.2.1, however, namely 0.1406 and 0.1924. An estimate of the variance of X is, therefore, given by

$$1\ 000\ 000 \times 0.1406 + (1000)^2 \times 0.1924 = 333\ 000.$$

This is the estimated variance of the total payout in respect of a single policy.

The portfolio consists of 100 such policies, which are independent. According to the additive rule of variances for sums of independent variables (section 4.2), an estimate of the variance of the total payout for the whole portfolio is

$$100 \times 333\ 000 = 33\ 300\ 000.$$

The required estimate of the standard deviation of the total payout in respect of the portfolio is, therefore,

$$\sqrt{(33\ 300\ 000)} = \$5771.$$

Further reading: Parzen [24] 54–5**.

**4.6 Skewness

The probability-density functions of two continuous random variables are depicted in fig. 4.6.1. The first distribution is symmetric, but the second is very skew, having a long 'tail' to the right. Many of the distributions encountered in general insurance (both continuous and discrete) are skew with long 'tails' to the right.

Fig. 4.6.1. The probability-density functions of two continuous random variables. The first is symmetric and the second positively skew.

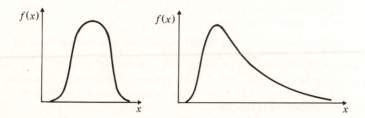

A measure of skewness has been devised. It is usually written as $\sqrt{\beta_1}$ and is defined as the third central moment of the distribution (section 4.3) divided by the cube of the standard deviation (section 4.2). This measure is zero for a symmetric distribution, positive for distributions with long tails to the right (*positively skew distributions*), and negative for distributions with long tails to the left.

Example 4.6.1. Calculate the sample third central moment for the claim frequency data in table 4.1.2 and deduce an estimate of the skewness of the underlying distribution.

From examples 4.1.1 and 4.2.1, we already know that the sample first and second moments about the origin, in respect of these data, are 0.1406 and 0.2122 respectively. The sample third moment about the origin is

$$0^3 \times \frac{17\,353}{19\,412} + 1^3 \times \frac{1414}{19\,412} + 2^3 \times \frac{620}{19\,412} + 3^3 \times \frac{25}{19\,412} = 0.3631.$$

It follows from (4.3.11) that the sample third central moment is

$$0.3631 - 3 \times 0.2122 \times 0.1406 + 2 \times (0.1406)^3 = 0.2792.$$

According to example 4.2.1, the sample standard deviation of the distribution is 0.4386. The sample measure of skewness is, therefore,

$$(0.2792) / (0.4386)^3 = 3.31.$$

Further reading: Mendenhall & Scheaffer [21] 195; Mode [22] 80–1; Mood & Graybill [23] 109–10; Pollard [26] 81–3.

4.7   Exercises

1. The following claims on an insurer arose out of policies in force during July 1980:

   $250, $280, $50, $314, $250, $90, $450, $180, $150, $250, $309, $2100, $206, $150, $146, $220, $300, $50, $220, $688.

   Calculate the sample mean and the sample standard deviation.

2. Table 3.4.1 is a summary of the claim sizes of 7821 householders' claims during 1980. Estimate

   (a) the mean claim size; and
   (b) the variance of the claim size.

3. Confirm the variance of 1 000 000 quoted in the solution to example 4.5.1.

*4. You are told that $\int_0^\infty e^{-x} x^n \, dx = n\,!$ for n a non-negative integer.

   (a) Confirm that $f(x) = e^{-x} x^r / r\,!$ is a proper probability-density function.
   (b) Find the mean and variance of the continuous distribution having this probability-density function.

**5. Use the fact that $P(X = x) = \sum\limits_{y} P[(X = x) \cap (Y = y)]$ and $P[(X = x) \cap (Y = y)] =$

$P(X = x \mid Y = y) P(Y = y)$ to derive (4.4.3).

**6. Estimate the skewness $\sqrt{\beta_1}$ of the claim size distribution in table 3.4.1.

5 STATISTICAL DISTRIBUTIONS USEFUL IN GENERAL INSURANCE WORK

Summary. In this chapter the normal, log-normal, Pareto, gamma, Poisson, binomial and negative binomial distributions are examined. It is shown that their shapes are determined by their *parameters*. The *standardising* of a random variable is explained and the usefulness of the Central Limit Theorem is shown. The importance of these distributions in general insurance work is also emphasised.

5.1   The normal distribution

The normal distribution occupies a central position in statistical theory, and although we give only one insurance example in this section, the importance of this distribution in the statistical analysis of insurance problems will become evident as this chapter progresses and in subsequent chapters.

The distribution is continuous and has two parameters, its mean μ and its standard deviation σ. These determine the location and dispersion respectively (sections 4.1, 4.2). The probability-density function is bell-shaped and symmetrical about the mean (fig. 5.1.1). The formula is rather complicated:

$$f(x) = \frac{1}{\sigma\sqrt{(2\pi)}} \exp \left\{ -\tfrac{1}{2} \left[(x-\mu)/\sigma\right]^2 \right\} \quad (-\infty < x < \infty). \qquad (5.1.1)$$

Fortunately, we rarely have to make use of it.

Although the range of a normal random variable X is from $-\infty$ to ∞, the probability that X takes very small or very large values is small. Put another way,

Fig. 5.1.1. The probability-density function of the normal distribution with mean μ and variance σ^2.

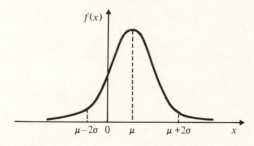

it is 95% certain that X lies between two standard deviations on either side of the mean (fig 5.1.1).

The probability that a normal random variable X with mean μ and standard deviation σ lies between two values a and b is (according to (5.1.1)),

$$\int_a^b \frac{1}{\sigma\sqrt{(2\pi)}} \exp\left\{-\tfrac{1}{2}[(x-\mu)/\sigma]^2\right\} dx . \tag{5.1.2}$$

It is not possible to express this integral (or area) in terms of explicit mathematical functions. Numerical integration is required. Tables could be prepared for this integral, but they would need to be 4-entry tables involving μ, σ, a and b.

To avoid this, the random variable X is transformed into a variable Z having a mean of zero and a standard deviation of 1. The transformation is

$$Z = \frac{X-\mu}{\sigma} \tag{5.1.3}$$

When this transformation, namely,

$$\blacksquare \quad Z = \frac{X - \text{mean of } X}{\text{standard deviation of } X} \tag{5.1.4}$$

is made, X is said to be *standardised*. It can be shown that if X is normally distributed Z is also normally distributed. To reflect the fact that it has a standard deviation of 1, Z is called a *unit normal variable*. It also has a mean of zero.

Because of the importance of the unit normal distribution, we use a special symbol for its probability-density function: $\phi(x)$ instead of the usual $f(x)$, and we denote its distribution function by $\Phi(x)$ instead of the usual $F(x)$. Thus,

$$\phi(x) = \frac{1}{\sqrt{(2\pi)}} e^{-\frac{1}{2}x^2}; \tag{5.1.5}$$

$$\Phi(u) = \int_{-\infty}^{u} \phi(x)\, dx . \tag{5.1.6}$$

The integral $\Phi(u)$ is the area under the $\phi(x)$ curve from $x = -\infty$ to $x = u$ (fig. 5.1.2).

Fig. 5.1.2. The probability-density function $\phi(u)$ and distribution function $\Phi(u)$ (shaded area) of the unit normal distribution.

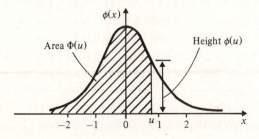

Tables of $\phi(x)$ and $\Phi(x)$ are readily available (for example, table 5.1.1), and we rarely have to have recourse to (5.1.5) or (5.1.6). The probability that a normal random variable X with mean μ and standard deviation σ lies between $\mu + A\sigma$ and $\mu + B\sigma$ is equal to the probability that a unit normal variable Z lies between A and B, which is $\Phi(B) - \Phi(A)$ (the area under the unit normal density

Table 5.1.1. *Normal ordinates and areas*

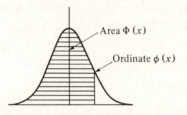

Note: $\phi(-x) = \phi(x)$, $\Phi(-x) = 1 - \Phi(x)$.

x	$\phi(x)$	$\Phi(x)$	x	$\phi(x)$	$\Phi(x)$	x	$\phi(x)$	$\Phi(x)$
0.00	.398 94	.500 00	0.15	.394 48	.559 62	0.30	.381 39	.617 91
0.01	.398 92	.503 99	0.16	.393 87	.563 56	0.31	.380 23	.621 72
0.02	.398 86	.507 98	0.17	.393 22	.567 49	0.32	.379 03	.625 52
0.03	.398 76	.511 97	0.18	.392 53	.571 42	0.33	.377 80	.629 30
0.04	.398 62	.515 95	0.19	.391 81	.575 35	0.34	.376 54	.633 07
0.05	.398 44	.519 94	0.20	.391 04	.579 26	0.35	.375 24	.636 83
0.06	.398 22	.523 92	0.21	.390 24	.583 17	0.36	.373 91	.640 58
0.07	.397 97	.527 90	0.22	.389 40	.587 06	0.37	.372 55	.644 31
0.08	.397 67	.531 88	0.23	.388 53	.590 95	0.38	.371 15	.648 03
0.09	.397 33	.535 86	0.24	.387 62	.594 83	0.39	.369 73	.651 73
0.10	.396 95	.539 83	0.25	.386 67	.598 71	0.40	.368 27	.655 42
0.11	.396 54	.543 80	0.26	.385 68	.602 57	0.41	.366 78	.659 10
0.12	.396 08	.547 76	0.27	.384 66	.606 42	0.42	.365 26	.662 76
0.13	.395 59	.551 72	0.28	.383 61	.610 26	0.43	.363 71	.666 40
0.14	.395 05	.555 67	0.29	.382 51	.614 09	0.44	.362 13	.670 03

Source: Kenney, *Mathematics of Statistics,* part one, 225–7, Van Nostrand, New York. Reprinted with permission of the publisher.

Table 5.1.1 (cont.)

x	φ (x)	Φ (x)	x	φ (x)	Φ (x)	x	φ (x)	Φ (x)
0.45	.360 53	.673 64	0.75	.301 14	.773 37	1.05	.229 88	.853 14
0.46	.358 89	.677 24	0.76	.298 87	.776 37	1.06	.227 47	.855 43
0.47	.357 23	.680 82	0.77	.296 59	.779 35	1.07	.225 06	.857 69
0.48	.355 53	.684 39	0.78	.294 31	.782 30	1.08	.222 65	.859 93
0.49	.353 81	.687 93	0.79	.292 00	.785 24	1.09	.220 25	.862 14
0.50	.352 07	.691 46	0.80	.289 69	.788 14	1.10	.217 85	.864 33
0.51	.350 29	.694 97	0.81	.287 37	.791 03	1.11	.215 46	.866 50
0.52	.348 49	.698 47	0.82	.285 04	.793 89	1.12	.213 07	.868 64
0.53	.346 67	.701 94	0.83	.282 69	.796 73	1.13	.210 69	.870 76
0.54	.344 82	.705 40	0.84	.280 34	.799 55	1.14	.208 31	.872 86
0.55	.342 94	.708 84	0.85	.277 98	.802 34	1.15	.205 94	.874 93
0.56	.341 05	.712 26	0.86	.275 62	.805 11	1.16	.203 57	.876 98
0.57	.339 12	.715 66	0.87	.273 24	.807 85	1.17	.201 21	.879 00
0.58	.337 18	.719 04	0.88	.270 86	.810 57	1.18	.198 86	.881 00
0.59	.335 21	.722 40	0.89	.268 48	.813 27	1.19	.196 52	.882 98
0.60	.333 22	.725 75	0.90	.266 09	.815 94	1.20	.194 19	.884 93
0.61	.331 21	.729 07	0.91	.263 69	.818 59	1.21	.191 86	.886 86
0.62	.329 18	.732 37	0.92	.261 29	.821 21	1.22	.189 54	.888 77
0.63	.327 13	.735 65	0.93	.258 88	.823 81	1.23	.187 24	.890 65
0.64	.325 06	.738 91	0.94	.256 47	.826 39	1.24	.184 94	.892 51
0.65	.322 97	.742 15	0.95	.254 06	.828 94	1.25	.182 65	.894 35
0.66	.320 86	.745 37	0.96	.251 64	.831 47	1.26	.180 37	.896 17
0.67	.318 74	.748 57	0.97	.249 23	.833 98	1.27	.178 10	.897 96
0.68	.316 59	.751 75	0.98	.246 81	.836 46	1.28	.175 85	.899 73
0.69	.314 43	.754 90	0.99	.244 39	.838 91	1.29	.173 60	.901 47
0.70	.312 25	.758 04	1.00	.241 97	.841 34	1.30	.171 37	.903 20
0.71	.310 06	.761 15	1.01	.239 55	.843 75	1.31	.169 15	.904 90
0.72	.307 85	.764 24	1.02	.237 13	.846 14	1.32	.166 94	.906 58
0.73	.305 63	.767 30	1.03	.234 71	.848 50	1.33	.164 74	.908 24
0.74	.303 39	.770 35	1.04	.232 30	.850 83	1.34	.162 56	.909 88

Table 5.1.1 (cont.)

x	$\phi(x)$	$\Phi(x)$	x	$\phi(x)$	$\Phi(x)$	x	$\phi(x)$	$\Phi(x)$
1.35	.160 38	.911 49	1.65	.102 26	.950 53	1.95	.059 59	.974 41
1.36	.158 22	.913 09	1.66	.100 59	.951 54	1.96	.058 44	.975 00
1.37	.156 08	.914 66	1.67	.098 93	.952 54	1.97	.057 30	.975 58
1.38	.153 95	.916 21	1.68	.097 28	.953 52	1.98	.056 18	.976 15
1.39	.151 83	.917 74	1.69	.095 66	.954 49	1.99	.055 08	.976 70
1.40	.149 73	.919 24	1.70	.094 05	.955 43	2.00	.053 99	.977 25
1.41	.147 64	.920 73	1.71	.092 46	.956 37	2.01	.052 92	.977 78
1.42	.145 56	.922 20	1.72	.090 89	.957 28	2.02	.051 86	.978 31
1.43	.143 50	.923 64	1.73	.089 33	.958 18	2.03	.050 82	.978 82
1.44	.141 46	.925 07	1.74	.087 80	.959 07	2.04	.049 80	.979 32
1.45	.139 43	.926 47	1.75	.086 28	.959 94	2.05	.048 79	.979 82
1.46	.137 42	.927 86	1.76	.084 78	.960 80	2.06	.047 80	.980 30
1.47	.135 42	.929 22	1.77	.083 29	.961 64	2.07	.046 82	.980 77
1.48	.133 44	.930 56	1.78	.081 83	.962 46	2.08	.045 86	.981 24
1.49	.131 47	.931 89	1.79	.080 38	.963 27	2.09	.044 91	.981 69
1.50	.129 52	.933 19	1.80	.078 95	.964 07	2.10	.043 98	.982 14
1.51	.127 58	.934 48	1.81	.077 54	.964 85	2.11	.043 07	.982 57
1.52	.125 66	.935 74	1.82	.076 14	.965 62	2.12	.042 17	.983 00
1.53	.123 76	.936 99	1.83	.074 77	.966 38	2.13	.041 28	.983 41
1.54	.121 88	.938 22	1.84	.073 41	.967 12	2.14	.040 41	.983 82
1.55	.120 01	.939 43	1.85	.072 06	.967 84	2.15	.039 55	.984 22
1.56	.118 16	.940 62	1.86	.070 74	.968 56	2.16	.038 71	.984 61
1.57	.116 32	.941 79	1.87	.069 43	.969 26	2.17	.037 88	.985 00
1.58	.114 50	.942 95	1.88	.068 14	.969 95	2.18	.037 06	.985 37
1.59	.112 70	.944 08	1.89	.066 87	.970 62	2.19	.036 26	.985 74
1.60	.110 92	.945 20	1.90	.065 62	.971 28	2.20	.035 47	.986 10
1.61	.109 15	.946 30	1.91	.064 39	.971 93	2.21	.034 70	.986 45
1.62	.107 41	.947 38	1.92	.063 16	.972 57	2.22	.033 94	.986 79
1.63	.105 67	.948 45	1.93	.061 95	.973 20	2.23	.033 19	.987 13
1.64	.103 96	.949 50	1.94	.060 77	.973 81	2.24	.032 46	.987 45

Table 5.1.1 (cont.)

x	$\phi(x)$	$\Phi(x)$	x	$\phi(x)$	$\Phi(x)$	x	$\phi(x)$	$\Phi(x)$
2.25	.031 74	.987 78	2.55	.015 45	.994 61	2.85	.006 87	.997 81
2.26	.031 03	.988 09	2.56	.015 06	.994 77	2.86	.006 68	.997 88
2.27	.030 34	.988 40	2.57	.014 68	.994 92	2.87	.006 49	.997 95
2.28	.029 65	.988 70	2.58	.014 31	.995 06	2.88	.006 31	.998 01
2.29	.028 98	.988 99	2.59	.013 94	.995 20	2.89	.006 13	.998 07
2.30	.028 33	.989 28	2.60	.013 58	.995 34	2.90	.005 95	.998 13
2.31	.027 68	.989 56	2.61	.013 23	.995 47	2.91	.005 78	.998 19
2.32	.027 05	.989 83	2.62	.012 89	.995 60	2.92	.005 62	.998 25
2.33	.026 43	.990 10	2.63	.012 56	.995 73	2.93	.005 45	.998 31
2.34	.025 82	.990 36	2.64	.012 23	.995 85	2.94	.005 30	.998 36
2.35	.025 22	.990 61	2.65	.011 91	.995 98	2.95	.005 14	.998 41
2.36	.024 63	.990 86	2.66	.011 60	.996 09	2.96	.004 99	.998 46
2.37	.024 06	.991 11	2.67	.011 30	.996 21	2.97	.004 85	.998 51
2.38	.023 49	.991 34	2.68	.011 00	.996 32	2.98	.004 71	.998 56
2.39	.022 94	.991 58	2.69	.010 71	.996 43	2.99	.004 57	.998 61
2.40	.022 39	.991 80	2.70	.010 42	.996 53	3.00	.004 43	.998 65
2.41	.021 86	.992 02	2.71	.010 14	.996 64	3.01	.004 30	.998 69
2.42	.021 34	.992 24	2.72	.009 87	.996 74	3.02	.004 17	.998 74
2.43	.020 83	.992 45	2.73	.009 61	.996 83	3.03	.004 05	.998 78
2.44	.020 33	.992 66	2.74	.009 35	.996 93	3.04	.003 93	.998 82
2.45	.019 84	.992 86	2.75	.009 09	.997 02	3.05	.003 81	.998 86
2.46	.019 36	.993 05	2.76	.008 85	.997 11	3.06	.003 70	.998 89
2.47	.018 89	.993 24	2.77	.008 61	.997 20	3.07	.003 58	.998 93
2.48	.018 42	.993 43	2.78	.008 37	.997 28	3.08	.003 48	.998 97
2.49	.017 97	.993 61	2.79	.008 14	.997 36	3.09	.003 37	.999 00
2.50	.017 53	.993 79	2.80	.007 92	.997 44	3.10	.003 27	.999 03
2.51	.017 09	.993 96	2.81	.007 70	.997 52	3.11	.003 17	.999 06
2.52	.016 67	.994 13	2.82	.007 48	.997 60	3.12	.003 07	.999 10
2.53	.016 25	.994 30	2.83	.007 27	.997 67	3.13	.002 98	.999 13
2.54	.015 85	.994 46	2.84	.007 07	.997 74	3.14	.002 88	.999 16

Table 5.1.1 (cont.)

x	$\phi(x)$	$\Phi(x)$	x	$\phi(x)$	$\Phi(x)$	x	$\phi(x)$	$\Phi(x)$
3.15	.002 79	.999 18	3.45	.001 04	.999 72	3.75	.000 35	.999 91
3.16	.002 71	.999 21	3.46	.001 00	.999 73	3.76	.000 34	.999 92
3.17	.002 62	.999 24	3.47	.000 97	.999 74	3.77	.000 33	.999 92
3.18	.002 54	.999 26	3.48	.000 94	.999 75	3.78	.000 31	.999 92
3.19	.002 46	.999 29	3.49	.000 90	.999 76	3.79	.000 30	.999 92
3.20	.002 38	.999 31	3.50	.000 87	.999 77	3.80	.000 29	.999 93
3.21	.002 31	.999 34	3.51	.000 84	.999 78	3.81	.000 28	.999 93
3.22	.002 24	.999 36	3.52	.000 81	.999 78	3.82	.000 27	.999 93
3.23	.002 16	.999 38	3.53	.000 79	.999 79	3.83	.000 26	.999 94
3.24	.002 10	.999 40	3.54	.000 76	.999 80	3.84	.000 25	.999 94
3.25	.002 03	.999 42	3.55	.000 73	.999 81	3.85	.000 24	.999 94
3.26	.001 96	.999 44	3.56	.000 71	.999 81	3.86	.000 23	.999 94
3.27	.001 90	.999 46	3.57	.000 68	.999 82	3.87	.000 22	.999 95
3.28	.001 84	.999 48	3.58	.000 66	.999 83	3.88	.000 21	.999 95
3.29	.001 78	.999 50	3.59	.000 63	.999 83	3.89	.000 21	.999 95
3.30	.001 72	.999 52	3.60	.000 61	.999 84	3.90	.000 20	.999 95
3.31	.001 67	.999 53	3.61	.000 59	.999 85	3.91	.000 19	.999 95
3.32	.001 61	.999 55	3.62	.000 57	.999 85	3.92	.000 18	.999 96
3.33	.001 56	.999 57	3.63	.000 55	.999 86	3.93	.000 18	.999 96
3.34	.001 51	.999 58	3.64	.000 53	.999 86	3.94	.000 17	.999 96
3.35	.001 46	.999 60	3.65	.000 51	.999 87	3.95	.000 16	.999 96
3.36	.001 41	.999 61	3.66	.000 49	.999 87	3.96	.000 16	.999 96
3.37	.001 36	.999 62	3.67	.000 47	.999 88	3.97	.000 15	.999 96
3.38	.001 32	.999 64	3.68	.000 46	.999 88	3.98	.000 14	.999 97
3.39	.001 27	.999 65	3.69	.000 44	.999 89	3.99	.000 14	.999 97
3.40	.001 23	.999 66	3.70	.000 42	.999 89			
3.41	.001 19	.999 68	3.71	.000 41	.999 90			
3.42	.001 15	.999 69	3.72	.000 39	.999 90			
3.43	.001 11	.999 70	3.73	.000 38	.999 90			
3.44	.001 07	.999 71	3.74	.000 37	.999 91			

function between $x = A$ and $x = B$). In other words, writing a instead of $\mu + A\sigma$ and b instead of $\mu + B\sigma$, the probability that a normal random variable X with mean μ and standard deviation σ lies between a and b is

■ $\Phi\,[(b - \mu)/\sigma] - \Phi\,[(a - \mu)/\sigma]$. (5.1.7)

An important property of the normal distribution needs to be noted. Linear combinations of independent normal random variables are also normal, and the mean and variance of a particular linear combination can be found using the additive properties of means and variances noted earlier in sections 4.1 and 4.2 respectively.

Example 5.1.1. A random variable X is normally distributed with mean 3.6 and standard deviation 1.2. What is the probability that X lies between 4.2 and 5.4?

We require the probability that X lies between the mean plus 0.5 standard deviations ($4.2 = 3.6 + 0.5 \times 1.2$) and the mean plus 1.5 standard deviations ($5.4 = 3.6 + 1.5 \times 1.2$). According to the paragraph preceding (5.1.7), this probability is equal to the probability that a unit normal variable lies between 0.5 and 1.5, namely,

$$\Phi\,(1.5) - \Phi\,(0.5) = 0.933\ 19 - 0.691\ 46 \qquad \text{(table 5.1.1)}$$
$$= 0.241\ 73 .$$

Alternatively, using (5.1.7), the probability is

$$\Phi\left(\frac{5.4 - 3.6}{1.2}\right) - \Phi\left(\frac{4.2 - 3.6}{1.2}\right) = \Phi\,(1.5) - \Phi\,(0.5) = 0.241\ 73 .$$

Example 5.1.2. What is the probability that the normal random variable in example 5.1.1 lies between 1.2 and 5.4?

According to (5.1.7), the probability is

$$\Phi\left(\frac{5.4 - 3.6}{1.2}\right) - \Phi\left(\frac{1.2 - 3.6}{1.2}\right) = \Phi\,(1.5) - \Phi\,(-2.0) .$$

As indicated at the top of table 5.1.1, $\Phi\,(-x) = 1 - \Phi\,(x)$ because of the symmetry of the unit normal probability-density function about the point $x = 0$ (fig. 5.1.2), and the probability becomes

$$\Phi\,(1.5) - [1 - \Phi\,(2.0)] = 0.933\ 19 - (1 - 0.977\ 25)$$
$$= 0.910\ 44 .$$

Example 5.1.3. An insurance company's claim size statistics reveal that, if $X is the size of a claim, the variable $Y = \ln X$ is normally distributed[1] with a mean of 6.012 and variance of 1.792. Calculate the probability that a particular claim is

    (a) greater than $1200;

    (b) between $0 and $200;

    (c) between $200 and $500.

(a) The probability that X is greater than 1200 is the same as the probability that Y is greater than $\ln 1200 = 7.09$, and this is the same as the probability that a unit normal variable Z takes a value greater than $(7.09 - 6.012)/\sqrt{(1.792)}$, namely,

$$1 - \Phi \left(\frac{7.09 - 6.012}{\sqrt{(1.792)}} \right)$$
$$= 1 - \Phi\,(0.805)$$
$$= 0.210\ .$$

Note that $1 - \Phi\,(z)$ is the area under the unit normal probability-density curve to the right of the ordinate at z, since the whole area under the curve is equal to 1.

(b) Since $\ln 0 = -\infty$ and $\ln 200 = 5.298$, the probability that X lies between 0 and 200 is equal to the probability that Y lies between $-\infty$ and 5.298. But Y is normally distributed with mean 6.012 and variance 1.792. According to (5.1.7), therefore, the required probability is

$$\Phi \left(\frac{5.298 - 6.012}{\sqrt{(1.792)}} \right) - \Phi \left(\frac{-\infty - 6.012}{\sqrt{(1.792)}} \right)$$
$$= \Phi\,(-0.533) - \Phi\,(-\infty)$$
$$= 0.297 - 0$$
$$= 0.297\ .$$

Note that, although Y may lie anywhere between $-\infty$ and $+\infty$, the claim size X cannot be negative.

(c) Using the same method as in (b), the probability that a particular claim is between $200 and $500 is

$$= \Phi \left(\frac{\ln 500 - 6.012}{\sqrt{(1.792)}} \right) - \Phi \left(\frac{\ln 200 - 6.012}{\sqrt{(1.792)}} \right)$$
$$= \Phi\,(0.151) - \Phi\,(-0.533)$$
$$= 0.560 - 0.297$$
$$= 0.263\ .$$

[1]   The claim size distribution is log-normal (section 5.3).

Example 5.1.4. A normal random variable U has mean 3.3 and variance 0.64; V is an independent normal random variable with mean 1.6 and variance 0.36. Find the probability that the random variable W is negative, where $W = U - 2V$.

According to the final paragraph of this section, W must be a normal random variable, since it is a linear combination of U and V which are independent normal random variables. Using properties (1) and (2) of means (section 4.1), we see that the mean of W is

$$3.3 - 2 \times 1.6 = 0.1 .$$

Property (2) of variances (section 4.2) indicates that the variance of W will be

$$0.64 + 4 \times 0.36 = 2.08 .$$

From (5.1.7), therefore, the probability that W is less than zero is

$$\Phi \left(\frac{0 - 0.1}{\sqrt{(2.08)}} \right) = \Phi (- 0.07) = 1 - \Phi (0.07) = 0.472\ 10 .$$

Further reading: Feller [9] 174–9**; Hoel [13] 100–5; Hoel [14] 75–9**; Mendenhall & Scheaffer [21] 124–7; Mode [22] 119–46; Mood & Graybill [23] 123–6**; Pollard [26] 90–1; Yamane [30] 113–28.

5.2   The Central Limit Theorem

This powerful theorem, introduced by De Moivre early in the 18th century, says in effect that if S is the sum of n identically distributed independent random variables, each having a mean of μ and standard deviation σ, then the distribution of the standardised variable

$$T = \frac{S - n\mu}{\sigma\sqrt{n}}$$

approaches the unit normal distribution as $n \rightarrow \infty$, *whatever the distribution of each of the n independent random variables may be.*

In other words, even if we do not know the distribution of a particular random variable X, we do know that the distribution of the sum S of a large number n of such variables will approach the normal distribution, and normal tables can then be applied. How large should n be, for reasonably accurate results, using this theorem? This depends on the shape of the distribution of the variable X and of course on what is regarded as 'reasonable'. As a rule of thumb for distributions which are not markedly skew (section 4.6), n should be 25 or larger.

The Central Limit Theorem explains (at least in part) why the normal distribution plays such a central role in statistical theory. For most classes of general insurance, the claim size distribution is markedly skew with a long tail to the right. If an insurer were to experience a large number of claims in respect of a particular class of business, his total payout might, however, be expected to be approximately normal, being the sum of a large number of individual claims. This assumption is reasonable for many purposes. The reader is warned, however, that there may be problems with the extreme tails of the distribution, and distribution tails are important for reinsurance purposes.

Example 5.2.1. A die is tossed n times, and the total score T is noted.

If $n = 1$, T may take the values $1, 2, 3, 4, 5, 6$, each with probability $1/6$. The distribution, which has mean 3.5 and variance 2.916, is plotted at the top of fig. 5.2.1. The normal distribution, with the same mean and variance, is

Fig. 5.2.1. Distribution of the total from n throws of a die for $n = 1, 2$ and 3. The probability-density functions of the normal distributions with the same means and variances are also shown, and the Central Limit Theorem effect is evident.

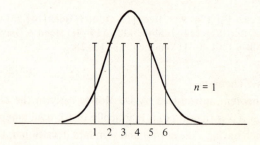

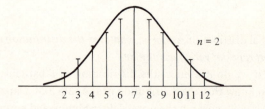

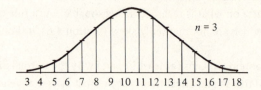

also shown. In the case $n = 2$, T may take the values $2, 3, \ldots, 12$ with probabilities $1/36, 2/36, 3/36, 4/36, 5/36, 6/36, 5/36, \ldots, 1/36$. This distribution, with mean 7 and variance 5.83̇, is depicted in the centre of fig. 5.2.1 together with the normal probability-density function with the same mean and variance. When $n = 3$, T can take the values $3, 4, 5, \ldots, 18$ with probabilities $1/216$, $3/216, 6/216, 10/216, 15/216, 21/216, 25/216, 27/216, 27/216, 25/216, \ldots,$ $1/216$. This distribution has mean 10.5 and variance 8.75, as has the normal probability-density function which is also plotted at the bottom of fig. 5.2.1.

The approach to normality, with increasing n, is very rapid in this case, due to the symmetry of the basic distribution when $n = 1$. Note that the Central Limit Theorem applies whether the underlying distribution is discrete or continuous.

Example 5.2.2. Use the Central Limit Theorem to estimate the probability that, in three tosses of an unbiased die, a total of at least 14 is obtained. Compare the approximate answer with the exact value. What is the probability of obtaining a total of at least 45 with ten tosses of an unbiased die?

Let us redraw the distribution of T, for $n = 3$ in fig. 5.2.1, in the form of a histogram with the area under the histogram between $x - \frac{1}{2}$ and $x + \frac{1}{2}$ representing the probability that T lies between $x - \frac{1}{2}$ and $x + \frac{1}{2}$ (i.e. the probability that $T = x$). The histogram is shown in fig. 5.2.2, together with the normal probability-density function, having the same mean and variance. It is clear that the probability we require is equal to the sum of the spikes in fig. 5.2.1 from 14 onwards, or the area under the histogram from 13.5 onwards. It is also clear that this area is accurately approximated by the area under the normal density curve from

Fig. 5.2.2. The normal (Central Limit) approximation to the distribution of the total T from three tosses of a die. The shaded area under the normal probability-density curve is a close approximation to the area under the histogram from 13.5 onwards. The normal curve is alternately above and below the histogram. It is apparent, therefore, that the area under the normal curve from 13.5 to 14.5 is an accurate approximation to the area under the histogram over the same interval, and so on.

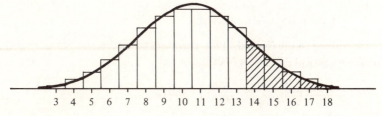

13.5 onwards. The mean and variance of this distribution are 10.5 and 8.75 respectively. The probability we require is, therefore,

$$1 - \Phi \left(\frac{13.5 - 10.5}{\sqrt{(8.75)}} \right) = 0.16 .$$

The exact answer is

$$15/216 + 10/216 + 6/216 + 3/216 + 1/216 = 0.16 .$$

The normal approximation has provided an accurate approximation.

The mean and variance of the result of a single toss of the die are readily shown to be 3.5 and $2.91\dot{6}$ respectively, using (4.1.1) and (4.2.3). Using the additive properties of means and variances of sums of independent random variables (sections 4.1 and 4.2 respectively), we deduce that the total of the outcomes from ten independent tosses of the die has mean 35 and variance $29.1\dot{6}$. Furthermore, from the Central Limit Theorem, the total will be approximately normally distributed. Using the histogram argument demonstrated above, we conclude that an accurate value for the probability is given by

$$1 - \Phi \left(\frac{44.5 - 35}{\sqrt{(29.1\dot{6})}} \right) = 0.0393 .$$

It would be very difficult to determine this probability exactly. We know that the result, using the normal approximation, will be very accurate, however. (It was reasonably good when n was as low as 3.)

This example also demonstrates the importance of the variance of a random variable and the formula for the variance of the sum of independent random variables.

Example 5.2.3. If the mean size of a claim is \$400 and its standard deviation is \$1000, calculate the probability that the sum of 85 such claims, independent of one another, is greater than \$49 000.

Using the additive properties of means and variances of independent random variables, the mean or expected value of the total payout is

$$85 \times 400 = 34\,000,$$

and the variance is

$$85 \times (1000)^2 = 85\,000\,000 .$$

According to the Central Limit Theorem, therefore, the probability that the total payout will exceed \$49 000 is

$$1 - \Phi \left(\frac{49\,000 - 34\,000}{\sqrt{(85\,000\,000)}} \right) = 0.015 .$$

The reader may wonder why there is no adjustment of 1/2 in this example as there was in the previous case. The reason is that, in the present example, the distribution of the total payout may be assumed to be continuous and we are using a continuous distribution (the normal) as an approximation. In the previous case, the distribution of the total score was discrete (on the positive integers) and a continuity correction of 1/2 was necessary to permit the use of a continuous distribution as an approximation (fig. 5.2.2).

> *Further reading:* Feller [9] 182–6**; Hoel [13] 129–32; Hoel [14] 125; Mendenhall & Scheaffer [21] 252–5; Mode [22] 153; Pollard [26] 90; Yamane [30] 123.

5.3   The log-normal distribution

This distribution is often useful as a model for the claim size distribution as it is positively skewed[2], which is a feature of claim size distributions. It has a range from zero to infinity.

A random variable X is said to have the log-normal distribution with parameters μ and σ if $Y = \ln X$ has the normal distribution with mean μ and standard deviation σ. It is clear, therefore, that the random variable X representing claim size in example 5.1.3 has the log-normal distribution with parameters $\mu = 6.012$ and $\sigma = \sqrt{(1.792)}$.

The mean and variance of the log-normal distribution are, respectively,

- mean $= \exp\left(\mu + \tfrac{1}{2}\sigma^2\right);$ (5.3.1)

- variance $= \exp\left(2\mu + \sigma^2\right)\left[\exp\left(\sigma^2\right) - 1\right].$ (5.3.2)

Fig. 5.3.1. The log-normal probability-density function with parameters $\mu = 1.5$ and $\sigma = 0.4$.

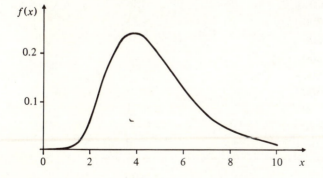

The probability-density function looks rather forbidding:

$$f(x) = \frac{1}{\sigma x \sqrt{(2\pi)}} \exp\left[-\tfrac{1}{2}\left(\frac{\ln x - \mu}{\sigma}\right)^2 \right] \quad (x > 0). \tag{5.3.3}$$

Fortunately, we rarely have to use it. Examples 5.1.3 and 5.3.1 indicate why. The probability-density function of the log-normal distribution with parameters $\mu = 1.5$ and $\sigma = 0.4$ is shown in fig. 5.3.1.

Example 5.3.1. Table 5.3.1 summarises the claim sizes of a sample of 100 claims on an insurance company. Assuming that the log-normal distribution is a suitable model, obtain estimates of its parameters, μ and σ, and estimate the probability that a particular claim exceeds $4000.

The skewness of the distribution is evident when the histogram representing the data is drawn (fig. 5.3.2). Assuming that the number of claims in the right-hand column of table 5.3.1 can be said to refer to claims with sizes equal to the mid-point of the respective claim size interval (which may not be a very accurate assumption with a skew distribution such as this), we obtain the mean claim size of the observed distribution as follows:

$$\text{mean claim size} = \$\left(200 \times \tfrac{2}{100} + 600 \times \tfrac{24}{100} + \ldots + 3400 \times \tfrac{1}{100}\right)$$
$$= \$1216 .$$

Table 5.3.1. *Claim size distribution*

Claim size ($)	Number of claims
0–400	2
400–800	24
800–1200	32
1200–1600	21
1600–2000	10
2000–2400	6
2400–2800	3
2800–3200	1
3200–3600	1
over 3600	0
Total	100

The variance of the observed claim size distribution is calculated as follows using (4.2.3):

$$\text{variance} = \left(200^2 \times \tfrac{2}{100} + 600^2 \times \tfrac{24}{100} + \ldots + 3400^2 \times \tfrac{1}{100} \right) - 1216^2$$
$$= 362\,944 .$$

The mean and variance of the log-normal distribution are given by (5.3.1) and (5.3.2) respectively. To estimate μ and σ^2 we therefore equate (5.3.1) and (5.3.2) to the observed values 1216 and 362 944 respectively. Thus,

$$\exp\left(\mu + \tfrac{1}{2}\sigma^2\right) = 1216 \text{ and } \exp\left(2\mu + \sigma^2\right)\left[\exp\left(\sigma^2\right) - 1\right] = 362\,944 .$$

Squaring the first of these equations and dividing the second equation by this square we obtain

$$\exp\left(\sigma^2\right) - 1 = 0.2455,$$

from which

$$\sigma = 0.469,$$

and so

$$\mu = 6.993.$$

The probability that a particular claim X exceeds \$4000 is equal to the probability that $\ln X$ exceeds 8.294. But $\ln X$ is normally distributed with mean μ and

Fig. 5.3.2. Histogram representing the distribution of claim sizes in a sample of 100 claims on a general insurer. The probability-density function of the log-normal distribution with parameters $\mu = 6.993$ and $\sigma = 0.469$ is also shown.

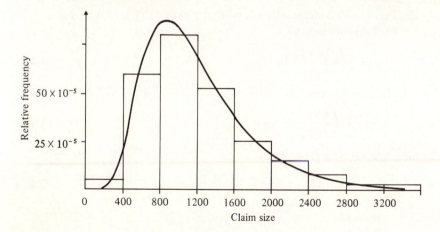

standard deviation σ, and we have estimated μ to be 6.993 and σ to be 0.469. An estimate of the required probability is, therefore,

$$1 - \Phi\left(\frac{8.294 - 6.993}{0.469}\right) = 1 - \Phi(2.77) = 0.002\ 80 \ .$$

In other words, we estimate that about 3 claims in 1000 will exceed \$4000.

A word of warning needs to be given. The procedure we have adopted is essentially one of fitting a curve over the range \$0–\$3600 and then *extrapolating* for all values over \$3600 to estimate the probability of a claim in excess of \$4000. If the log-normal distribution is appropriate (and it does seem reasonable from fig. 5.3.2), then we may have obtained a reasonable estimate of the tail probability. If, on the other hand, the true underlying probability-density function tapers away to zero more slowly than the log-normal, our estimate of the probability will be too low. Reinsurers in particular need to be cautious not to underestimate the tail. We return to this problem again, briefly, in the next section.

Further reading: Benjamin [3] 131–2; Johnson & Kotz [17] 112–36**; Mood & Graybill [23] 131–2; Pollard [26] 97–8*.

*5.4   The Pareto distribution

At the end of example 5.3.1 we gave a warning about the danger of fitting a distribution to claim size data and then using the extrapolated 'tail' to estimate the remote probability of an extremely large claim and the cost of reinsuring such a claim. Clearly, a reinsurer needs to err on the safe side by fitting a 'tail' which does not fade away to zero too quickly, and for this purpose the tail of the Pareto distribution is often more satisfactory than that of the log-normal distribution.

The Pareto distribution, which is positively skewed[3] (fig. 5.4.1), has probability-density function

■ $$f(x) = \frac{\alpha}{\beta}\left(\frac{\beta}{x}\right)^{\alpha+1} \quad (x > \beta),$$ (5.4.1)

and distribution function

■ $$F(x) = 1 - \left(\frac{\beta}{x}\right)^{\alpha} \quad (x > \beta) \ .$$ (5.4.2)

Its mean and variance are given by

■ $$\text{mean} \quad = \frac{\alpha\beta}{\alpha - 1} \ ;$$ (5.4.3)

[3]   section 4.6.

■   variance $= \dfrac{\alpha\beta^2}{\alpha-2} - \left(\dfrac{\alpha\beta}{\alpha-1}\right)^2.$ (5.4.4)

It should be noted that, for the mean to exist, α must be greater than 1 and, for the variance to exist, α must be greater than 2. These restrictions mean that, in practice, the distribution is somewhat more difficult to use than the log-normal.

> **Example 5.4.1.** The log-normal distribution in example 5.3.1 had parameters $\mu = 6.993$ and $\sigma = 0.469$. The tail of its probability-density

function is shown in fig. 5.4.2, together with the tail of the Pareto distribution having the same $f(x)$ values at $x = 2000$ and $x = 3000$ (0.000 184 and 0.000 027

Fig. 5.4.1. The Pareto probability-density function $f(x) = 1.5(2/x)^4$ corresponding to the parameter values $\alpha = 3, \beta = 2$.

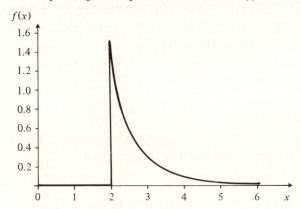

Fig. 5.4.2. The tails of the Pareto and log-normal probability-density functions having common values $f(2000) = 0.000\ 184$ and $f(3000) = 0.000\ 027$.

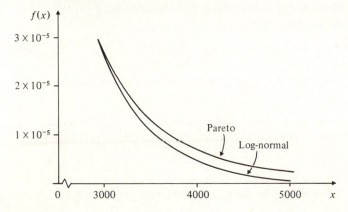

respectively). The Pareto probability-density function tapers away to zero much more slowly than the log-normal, and would therefore be much safer to use for estimating reinsurance premiums in respect of very large claims.

Example 5.4.2. The claim size of an insurance portfolio, measured in $100 units, follows the Pareto distribution illustrated in fig. 5.4.1. Calculate the proportion of claims with size in excess of $500 and the average size of all such claims.

The Pareto distribution in fig. 5.4.1 has parameters $\alpha = 3$ and $\beta = 2$. If X is the size of a claim in $100 units, we require the probability that X is greater than 5, which is

$$1 - F(5) = 1 - \left[1 - \left(\tfrac{2}{5}\right)^3\right] = 0.064 .$$

The probability that a claim lies between $100x$ and $100(x + dx)$ is $f(x)\,dx$, and the probability that the claim is over $500 is 0.064. The conditional probability that the claim lies between $100x$ and $100\,(x + dx)$, $(x > 5)$, given that the claim is over $500, is, therefore, $[f(x)\,dx]/0.064$ (equation 2.3.2)). It follows that the average size of claims which exceed $500 is (in $100 units)

$$\int_5^\infty x\,\frac{f(x)\,dx}{0.064} = \frac{1}{0.064} \int_5^\infty 1.5x \left(\frac{2}{x}\right)^4 dx = \frac{24}{0.064} \int_5^\infty x^{-3}\,dx ,$$

which when evaluated yields 7.5. The average size of claims greater than $500 is, therefore, $750. This average is a conditional mean (section 4.4).

Further reading: Benjamin [3] 132–3.

*5.5   The gamma distribution

The gamma distribution is a continuous distribution which finds application in a number of areas of general insurance (for example, in the study of claim size distributions and in the analysis of heterogeneity of risk (section 5.9)). The probability-density function is

■ $$f(x) = \frac{\beta}{\Gamma(\alpha)}\ e^{-\beta x}\,(\beta x)^{\alpha - 1} \qquad (0 \leqslant x < \infty) , \qquad (5.5.1)$$

where the parameters α and β must be greater than zero and $\Gamma(\alpha)$ is a number[4] which depends on α.

----

[4]   When α is an integer, $\Gamma(\alpha) = (\alpha - 1)!$ For example, $\Gamma(6) = 120$. The gamma function $\Gamma(\alpha)$ is in fact a continuous function passing through the factorial values at integer values of α and obeying the recurrence relation

$\Gamma(\alpha) = (\alpha - 1)\,\Gamma(\alpha - 1).$

$\Gamma(\alpha)$ can be found approximately by interpolating between the factorials or from tables (for example, Chemical Rubber Publishing Company [5] 127).

The mean and variance are, respectively,

-     mean $= \alpha/\beta$;   (5.5.2)

-     variance $= \alpha/\beta^2$.   (5.5.3)

The versatility of the distribution is evident in fig. 5.5.1 which shows the probability-density function for selected combinations of the parameters α and β. When $\alpha = 1$, the density function takes its largest value at $x = 0$, and declines thereafter. For all other values of α, $f(x)$ is zero at $x = 0$, rises to a maximum and then falls away again. The distribution is clearly not symmetrical. It is positively skew[5], but, as α increases, the skewness decreases and the distribution becomes more symmetrical.

The sum of n independent gamma random variables, each with probability-density function (5.5.1), can be shown to have the gamma distribution with parameters $n\alpha$ and β. For large n, the Central Limit Theorem tells us that this distribution will be effectively normal with mean $n\alpha/\beta$ and variance $n\alpha/\beta^2$.

As a corollary, we can deduce that, if X is a gamma random variable with parameters α and β, and α is large, then X will be approximately normal with mean α/β and variance α/β^2, and

- $$\frac{X - (\alpha/\beta)}{\sqrt{(\alpha/\beta^2)}} \qquad\qquad\qquad (5.5.4)$$

will be approximately a unit normal random variable.

Further reading: Freund [10] 127–8, 146–7*; Mendenhall & Scheaffer [21] 128–9; Mood & Graybill [23] 126–31**.

Fig. 5.5.1. Examples of the gamma probability-density function.

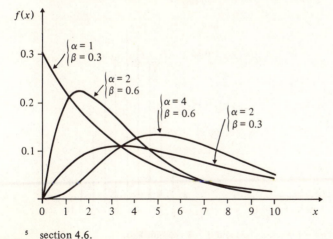

---
[5]   section 4.6.

5.6   The Poisson distribution

The distributions we have discussed so far in this chapter have all been continuous. We now describe a discrete distribution commonly employed for analysing the incidence of claims, a role which it fills very adequately.

The Poisson distribution is a non-negative, integer-valued distribution which plays a prominent role in statistical theory. Traditional examples of its use include the number of alpha particles emitted from a radioactive source in a given time, the number of bacteria visible under the microscope on a fixed area of plate, blood counts, mutations caused by radiation, flying bomb hits on London and deaths of Prussian soldiers from horse kicks. Other examples include defects in materials, and the incidence of insurance claims.

A random variable X taking non-negative integer values is said to have the Poisson distribution[6] with parameter q if

■ $$P(X = x) = e^{-q} \frac{q^x}{x!} \quad (x = 0, 1, 2, \ldots).$$ (5.6.1)

The parameter q must be positive, and the mean and variance of the distribution are given by

■   mean $= q$;   (5.6.2)

■   variance $= q$.   (5.6.3)

The parameter q is both the mean and the variance of the distribution. Poisson distributions with means $q = 0.9$ and $q = 5.0$ are shown in fig. 5.6.1.

Fig. 5.6.1. Poisson distributions with means 0.9 and 5.0 respectively.

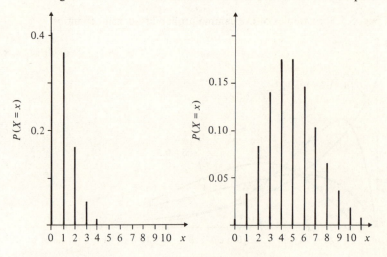

[6]   Note that $q^0 = 1$ (section 1.5) and $0! = 1$ (section 1.3).

An important property of the Poisson distribution is that the sum of n independent Poisson variables is itself a Poisson random variable with mean equal to the sum of the n separate means.

Example 5.6.1. In a particular year, 1000 policies gave rise to 140 claims. Estimate the probability that a particular policyholder makes no claim in nine months.

It is usually reasonably safe to assume that the number of claims on a policy in a given period follows the Poisson distribution. Let us assume, therefore, that the number of claims on an individual policy in a three-month period is a Poisson variable with mean q. Claims in successive intervals of time are assumed to be independent, and we deduce (using the important additive property quoted above) that the total number of claims on a policy in a twelve-month period is Poisson with mean $4q$. For 1000 independent policies, using the same property, we conclude that the total number of claims will be Poisson with mean $4000q$. An estimate of this mean will be provided by the observed number of claims, 140, and we deduce $140/4000 = 0.035$ as an estimate of q.

If the number of claims on a policy in a three-month period is a Poisson random variable with mean 0.035, the number of claims on such a policy in a nine-month period will be Poisson with mean 0.105. According to (5.6.1), therefore, an estimate of the probability of no claims on a given policy during a nine-month period is

$$\frac{(0.105)^0 \, e^{-0.105}}{0!} = e^{-0.105} = 0.90 .$$

In this solution, we have explained all the assumptions and calculations in some detail. A concise solution would be as follows:

Estimated claim frequency per policy per year
$$= \frac{140}{1000}$$
$$= 0.14 .$$

The estimated probability of no claims in 0.75 years is, therefore,

$$\frac{e^{-(0.75 \times 0.14)} (0.75 \times 0.14)^0}{0!} = e^{-0.105} = 0.90 .$$

Example 5.6.2. Using the data of example 5.6.1, estimate the probability that a policyholder has more than two claims in a year.

The estimated mean number of claims a policyholder has in one year is

140/1000 = 0.140. It follows from (5.6.1) that the estimated probabilities of 0, 1 and 2 claims are, respectively,

$$\frac{e^{-0.14}\ (0.14)^0}{0!} = 0.869\ 36\ ;$$

$$\frac{e^{-0.14}\ (0.14)^1}{1!} = 0.121\ 71\ ;$$

and

$$\frac{e^{-0.14}\ (0.14)^2}{2!} = 0.008\ 52\ ;$$

which total 0.999 59. The estimated probability of more than two claims is, therefore, 0.000 41.

Example 5.6.3. Use the data of example 5.6.1 to estimate the probability that, during a given year, two independent policyholders have exactly one claim between them.

Using the important additive property of the Poisson distribution, mentioned above, we conclude that the distribution of the number of claims for the two independent policyholders in a given year is Poisson, with an estimated mean of $0.14 \times 2 = 0.28$. An estimate of the required probability is, therefore,

$$\frac{e^{-0.28}\ (0.28)^1}{1!} = 0.2116\ .$$

Alternatively, an estimate of the probability that the first has a claim and the second does not is

$$\left[\frac{e^{-0.14}\ (0.14)^1}{1!}\right]\left[\frac{e^{-0.14}\ (0.14)^0}{0!}\right] = 0.1058\ .$$

Table 5.6.1. *Observed numbers of policies producing 0, 1, 2 or 3 claims*

Number of claims	Observed number of policies
0	3288
1	642
2	66
3	4
Total	4000

Likewise, an estimate of the probability that the first has no claim and the second has one is

$$\left[\frac{e^{-0.14} \; (0.14)^0}{0!} \right] \; \left[\frac{e^{-0.14} \; (0.14)^1}{1!} \right] = 0.1058 \; .$$

These two events are mutually exclusive. The estimated probability of exactly one claim between the two policyholders is, therefore, the sum of the above two probabilities or 0.2116.

Example 5.6.4. The claim experience of 4000 policies, each exposed to risk for a year, is shown in table 5.6.1. Compare the numbers of policies yielding 0, 1, 2, 3 claims with those that would result assuming the number of claims per policy was a Poisson variable with $q = 0.2$.

If $q = 0.2$, the probability that a policy produces no claim

$$= (0.2)^0 \; e^{-0.2} / 0!$$
$$= 0.819 \; .$$

Similarly, the probabilities of making 1, 2, 3 claims are, respectively,

$$\frac{(0.2)^1 \; e^{-0.2}}{1!} \; , \quad \frac{(0.2)^2 \; e^{-0.2}}{2!} \quad \text{and} \quad \frac{(0.2)^3 \; e^{-0.2}}{3!}$$

or

$$0.164 \; , \qquad 0.016 \qquad \text{and} \; 0.001 \; .$$

We would expect, therefore, that in respect of 4000 policies

$4000 \times 0.819 = 3276$ would produce 0 claims;
$4000 \times 0.164 = 656$ would produce 1 claim each;
$4000 \times 0.016 = 64$ would produce 2 claims each;
$4000 \times 0.001 = 4$ would produce 3 claims each.

These figures are close to the observed numbers in table 5.6.1.

Further reading: Feller [9] 156–64*; Hoel [14] 63–7; Mendenhall & Scheaffer [21] 81–4; Mode [22] 181–4; Mood & Graybill [23] 70–1; Pollard [26] 107–8, 112; Yamane [30] 556–74.

5.7   Normal approximation to the Poisson distribution
The probability of obtaining an outcome between x_1 and x_2 (inclusive) from a Poisson random variable with mean q is obtained by summing (5.6.1) from x_1 to x_2. This sum can be tedious to evaluate, particularly when q is reasonably large and the range from x_1 to x_2 is large.

An important property of the Poisson distribution was noted at the end of section 5.6, namely, that the sum of a number of independent Poisson random variables is also Poisson. Thus, a Poisson random variable with mean 10 may be regarded, for example, as the sum of ten independent Poisson random variables, each with mean 1. Invoking the Central Limit Theorem (section 5.2), we can deduce that, for reasonably large q, the probability that the Poisson random variable X lies between x_1 and x_2, inclusive, is

■ $\qquad P(x_1 \leqslant X \leqslant x_2) \doteqdot \Phi(z_2) - \Phi(z_1),$ (5.7.1)

where

■ $\qquad z_1 = (x_1 - q - \frac{1}{2})/\sqrt{q} \; ;$

■ $\qquad z_2 = (x_2 - q + \frac{1}{2})/\sqrt{q} \; .$ $\qquad$ (5.7.2)

The limits x_1 and x_2 in (5.7.2) have been standardised by subtracting the mean q and dividing by the standard deviation $\sqrt{q}$ (section 5.1). The adjustments of $\pm 1/2$ are continuity corrections to allow the approximation of the discrete Poisson distribution by the continuous normal curve, and the reasoning behind their inclusion should be evident from example 5.2.2 and fig. 5.2.2.

An alternative way of expressing this Central Limit Theorem result is to say that the standardised random variable

■ $\qquad \dfrac{X - q}{\sqrt{q}}$ (5.7.3)

is approximately a unit normal random variable when q is large.

The normal approximation to the Poisson will usually be quite adequate whenever q is greater than about 10. Even for $q = 5$, the shape of the distribution is very similar to the normal (fig. 5.6.1).

Table 5.7.1. *Claims under householders' policies covering fire, theft and public liability*

	Number of policies	Period of observation	Number of claims during period
Fire	1250	1 year	12
Theft	2500	1 year	250
Liability	2000	4 years	35

Example 5.7.1. For one year, 200 insurance policies are observed and in that period 26 claims are made in respect of them. Estimate the probability that in the next year there will be less than 750 claims arising from

the 6000 similar policies in the insurance company's portfolio.

The observed claim frequency is 0.13 per policy per year. We shall base our calculations on this figure. The expected number of claims from 6000 policies, in a year, will therefore be $6000 \times 0.13 = 780$.

The number of claims arising during a year from the 6000 policies will be a Poisson random variable X, with an estimated mean of 780. Using the normal approximation (5.7.1), the estimated probability of 749 or fewer claims is

$$\Phi \left(\frac{749.5 - 780}{\sqrt{(780)}} \right) = \Phi(-1.09) = 0.138 .$$

Example 5.7.2. Using the data of table 5.7.1 and assuming that claim frequencies are unchanging, estimate the probability of less than 250 claims arising from the insurance company's 2178 householders' policies in the ensuing year.

The average numbers of claims per policy per year by type of claim for the data in table 5.7.1 are 0.0096, 0.1000 and 0.0044 respectively. Assuming that these risks are independent, an estimate of the expected number of claims (all types combined) arising from a single policy is $0.0096 + 0.1000 + 0.0044 = 0.1140$.

In respect of 2178 policies, therefore, the estimated expected total number of claims is $2178 \times 0.1140 = 248.3$. Invoking the normal approximation to the Poisson distribution, we conclude that an estimate of the probability that fewer than 250 claims arise in the ensuing year is

$$\Phi \left(\frac{249.5 - 248.3}{\sqrt{(248.3)}} \right) = \Phi(0.08) = 0.53 .$$

Further reading: Pollard [26] 112.

*5.8   The binomial distribution

When a certain coin is tossed, the outcome is a 'head' with probability p and a 'tail' with probability $1 - p$. The probability of obtaining x 'heads' and $n - x$ 'tails' in n independent tosses of the coin is[7]

■ $\quad P(x \text{ 'heads' from } n \text{ tosses}) = \binom{n}{x} p^x (1 - p)^{n - x} .$ (5.8.1)

This probability defines the *binomial distribution,* which has two parameters n and p. Its mean and variance are given by

■ $\quad$ mean $\quad = n p ;$ (5.8.2)

[7] The combinatorial notation $\binom{n}{x}$ is explained in section 1.4.

∎   variance $= n p (1 - p)$.   (5.8.3)

The number of 'heads' in n tosses is the sum of the number of 'heads' at each toss. We would therefore expect the Central Limit Theorem to apply for large n. In fact, for large n, the probability of obtaining a number of 'heads' X between x_1 and x_2 inclusive is

∎ $P (x_1 \leqslant X \leqslant x_2) \doteqdot \Phi (z_2) - \Phi (z_1),$ (5.8.4)

where

∎ $z_1 = (x_1 - np - \frac{1}{2})/\sqrt{[np (1 - p)]}$;   (5.8.5)

∎ $z_2 = (x_2 - np + \frac{1}{2})/\sqrt{[np (1 - p)]}$.   (5.8.6)

The explanation of these formulae is given in fig. 5.8.1.

An alternative way of expressing this Central Limit Theorem result is to say that the standardised random variable

$$\frac{X - np}{\sqrt{[np (1 - p)]}}$$ (5.8.7)

is approximately a unit normal random variable when n is large.

The normal approximation will usually be quite accurate provided both np and $np (1 - p)$ are greater than about 10.

One other important property of the binomial distribution needs to be noted, namely, that for n large and p very small (i.e. $1 - p$ very close to 1), the

Fig. 5.8.1. The normal approximation to the binomial in the case $n = 25, p = 0.5$. The probability that the random variable lies between 9 and 15 inclusive is equal to the sum of the ordinates from 9 to 15 inclusive. This sum is equal to the shaded histogram area, which can be approximated by the area under the normal curve between 8.5 and 15.5. (Reproduced, with permission, from J. H. Pollard, *Handbook of numerical and statistical techniques*, Cambridge University Press.)

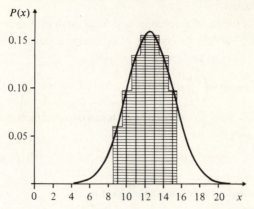

binomial mean and variance become essentially equal and the distribution itself becomes Poisson. This result is demonstrated in example 5.8.3. The example also indicates why the Poisson distribution is so useful for analysing claim frequencies.

Example 5.8.1. When a certain coin is tossed, the outcome is a 'head' with probability p and a 'tail' with probability $1 - p$. Derive from first principles the probability that in five tosses of this coin exactly three 'heads' are obtained.

Consider a particular outcome producing three 'heads':

$$H T H H T$$

The probability of this outcome is

$$p \times (1 - p) \times p \times p \times (1 - p) = p^3 (1 - p)^2,$$

and the same probability will be obtained in respect of any outcome producing exactly three 'heads'.

As there are five positions in the sequence and we need to choose exactly three of these to position 'heads' (the remaining positions being filled by 'tails'), the number of possible outcomes must be the number of ways of choosing exactly three objects out of five, namely,

$$\binom{5}{3} = \frac{5!}{3!\,2!} = 10 .$$

The required probability is, therefore,

$$\binom{5}{3} p^3 (1 - p)^2 \quad \text{or} \quad 10\, p^3 (1 - p)^2 .$$

The general proof of (5.8.1) follows exactly these lines.

Example 5.8.2. An unbiased coin is tossed 1000 times. What is the probability that the number of 'heads' lies between 475 and 525 inclusive?

According to (5.8.1) the probability is

$$\sum_{x=475}^{525} \binom{1000}{x} \left(\tfrac{1}{2}\right)^x \left(\tfrac{1}{2}\right)^{1000-x} = \sum_{x=475}^{525} \binom{1000}{x} \left(\tfrac{1}{2}\right)^{1000} .$$

This sum is very difficult to compute, unless we invoke the Central Limit Theorem. The mean and variance of the number of 'heads' obtained in 1000 tosses of an unbiased coin are, respectively, 500 and 250 so that, according to (5.8.4), the required probability is

$$\Phi\left(\frac{525.5 - 500}{\sqrt{(250)}}\right) - \Phi\left(\frac{474.5 - 500}{\sqrt{(250)}}\right) = \Phi(1.61) - \Phi(-1.61)$$
$$= 0.89 .$$

In other words, it is almost 90% certain that the number of 'heads' will lie in this range.

Example 5.8.3. For an individual, the probability of an accident of a given type in any 24-hour period, leading to an insurance claim, is 0.000 37. The probabilities of claims on successive days are independent, and it is not possible to have more than one accident (leading to a claim) on the same day. Calculate the probabilities that a policyholder makes 0, 1 and 2 claims in a year.

On any day, having an accident can be likened to obtaining a 'head', and not having an accident to obtaining a 'tail'. The probability p is very small (0.000 37). Over a year 365 such 'tosses' are made, and the expected (mean) number of 'heads' (accidents) will be $365 \times 0.000\ 37 = 0.135$. With $n = 365$, large, and $p = 0.000\ 37$, small, the distribution of the number of accidents in a year becomes effectively Poisson with mean $np = 0.135$ (section 5.8 above). In other words,

P (no accident claim) $= e^{-0.135}(0.135)^0/0! = 0.874$;
P (1 accident claim) $= e^{-0.135}(0.135)^1/1! = 0.118$;
P (2 accident claims) $= e^{-0.135}(0.135)^2/2! = 0.008$.

Alternatively, using the binomial formula (5.8.1),

$$P \text{ (no accident claim)} = \binom{365}{0}(0.000\ 37)^0\ (0.999\ 63)^{365} = 0.874 \text{ ;}$$

$$P \text{ (1 accident claim)} = \binom{365}{1}(0.000\ 37)^1\ (0.999\ 63)^{364} = 0.118 \text{ ;}$$

$$P \text{ (2 accident claims)} = \binom{365}{2}(0.000\ 37)^2\ (0.999\ 63)^{363} = 0.007 \text{ .}$$

The Poisson calculation is generally simpler and to be preferred. The example also indicates why the Poisson distribution is so useful as a model of claim incidence.

Further reading: Feller [9] 146–56**; Freund [10] 66–70, 72–5; Hoel [13] 91–114; Hoel [14] 63–6; Mood & Graybill [23] 64–9, 71–2; Pollard [26] 100–3, 108–12; Yamane [30] 499–562.

**5.9   The negative binomial distribution; heterogeneity of risk

A discrete random variable X is said to have the negative binomial distribution with parameters k and p if

$$\blacksquare \qquad P(X = x) = \binom{k + x - 1}{x} p^k (1 - p)^x \qquad (x = 0, 1, 2, \dots). \qquad (5.9.1)$$

The mean and variance are given by

-     mean $= k(1-p)/p$;   (5.9.2)

-     variance $= k(1-p)/p^2$;   (5.9.3)

and examples of the distribution are shown in fig. 5.9.1.

The sum of k independent negative binomial random variables, each with parameters 1 and p, can be shown to be a negative binomial random variable with parameters k and p. For large k, the Central Limit Theorem should, therefore, apply. In fact, for large k,

-     $P(x_1 \leqslant X \leqslant x_2) \doteqdot \Phi(z_2) - \Phi(z_1),$ (5.9.4)

where

-     $z_1 = (x_1 - \text{mean} - \tfrac{1}{2})/\sqrt{(\text{variance})}$;
-     $z_2 = (x_2 - \text{mean} + \tfrac{1}{2})/\sqrt{(\text{variance})}$.   (5.9.5)

An alternative way of expressing this Central Limit Theorem result is to say that, for large k, the standardised random variable

-     $\dfrac{X - \text{mean}}{\sqrt{(\text{variance})}}$ (5.9.6)

is approximately a unit normal random variable.

Fig. 5.9.1. Negative binomial distributions with parameters $k = 1$, $p = 0.3$ and $k = 6$, $p = 0.6$ respectively. The first distribution is also called a geometric distribution. (Reproduced, with permission, from J. H. Pollard, *Handbook of numerical and statistical techniques*, Cambridge University Press.)

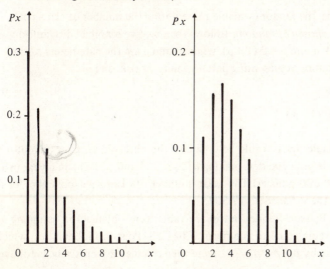

Perhaps the most important application of the negative binomial distribution, as far as general insurance applications are concerned, is in connection with the distribution of claim frequencies when the risks are not homogeneous.

Consider an insurance portfolio in which the distribution of the number of claims a particular policyholder makes in a year is Poisson with mean q (section 5.6). Some policyholders are poor risks (i.e. their q-values are high) while others are good risks (q is small). We saw in section 5.5 that the gamma distribution was continuous and very versatile. Let us, therefore, assume that the q-values of policyholders chosen at random follow the gamma distribution. In other words, for a policyholder chosen at random,

$$P(u < q < u + du) = \frac{\beta}{\Gamma(\alpha)} \; e^{-\beta u} \; (\beta u)^{\alpha - 1} du \; . \tag{5.9.7}$$

For a policyholder *with a q-value in this range,* the probability of x claims is given by the Poisson probability

$$P(X = x \mid u < q < u + du) = \frac{e^{-u} u^x}{x!} \; . \tag{5.9.8}$$

The probability that a policyholder, *chosen at random,* experiences x claims in a year, is obtained by summing (integrating) the product of (5.9.8) and (5.9.7) for all values of u. That is,

$$P(X = x) = \int_0^\infty \left(\frac{e^{-u} u^x}{x!} \right) \frac{\beta}{\Gamma(\alpha)} \; e^{-\beta u} \; (\beta u)^{\alpha - 1} \; du \; , \tag{5.9.9}$$

and it turns out that

$$\blacksquare \qquad P(X = x) = \binom{\alpha + x - 1}{x} \left(\frac{\beta}{1 + \beta} \right)^\alpha \left(\frac{1}{1 + \beta} \right)^x \; . \tag{5.9.10}$$

In other words, the random variable representing the number of claims of a policyholder, *chosen at random,* follows the negative binomial distribution with parameters $k = \alpha$ and $p = \beta/(1 + \beta)$, where α and β are the parameters of the gamma distribution representing heterogeneity of risk, and

$$\blacksquare \qquad \alpha = k \; ; \tag{5.9.11}$$

$$\blacksquare \qquad \beta = p/(1 - p) \; . \tag{5.9.12}$$

Example 5.9.1. Table 5.9.1 shows the observed number of motor vehicle policyholders making 0, 1, 2, 3, 4 and 5 claims in a year in a sample of 100 000 policies. The mean number of claims per policyholder is 0.123 18 and the variance 0.127 507.

The fitted Poisson frequencies in the table were obtained by assuming a theoretical q-value equal to the mean 0.123 18. Poisson probabilities, which we shall denote by $p_0, p_1, p_2, \ldots$, were then calculated recursively as follows:

$p_0 = e^{-0.123\ 18} (0.123\ 18)^0/0! = e^{-0.123\ 18} = 0.884\ 11$;

$p_1 = (p_0 \times 0.123\ 18)/1 = 0.108\ 90$;

$p_2 = (p_1 \times 0.123\ 18)/2 = 0.006\ 71$;

$p_3 = (p_2 \times 0.123\ 18)/3 = 0.000\ 27$;

$p_4 = (p_3 \times 0.123\ 18)/4 = 0.000\ 01$.

The expected numbers of policyholders making 0, 1, 2, 3 and 4 claims were then calculated by multiplying these probabilities by 100 000 (table 5.9.1).

To fit the negative binomial distribution, the theoretical and observed means and variances were equated:

$k(1 - p)/p\ \ = 0.123\ 18$;

$k(1 - p)/p^2 = 0.127\ 507$.

Dividing the first of these two equations by the second, we obtain $p = 0.966\ 065$, whence $k = 3.507$. The fitted negative binomial probabilities $p_0, p_1, p_2, \ldots$, were then calculated recursively as follows:

$p_0 = \binom{2.507}{0}(0.966\ 065)^{3.507}(0.033\ 935)^0 = 0.885\ 97$;

$p_1 = p_0 \times 0.033\ 935 \times (3.507/1) = 0.105\ 44$;

$p_2 = p_1 \times 0.033\ 935 \times (4.507/2) = 0.008\ 06$;

$p_3 = p_2 \times 0.033\ 935 \times (5.507/3) = 0.000\ 50$;

$p_4 = p_3 \times 0.033\ 935 \times (6.507/4) = 0.000\ 03$.

Again, the fitted frequencies in table 5.9.1 were obtained by multiplying these probabilities by 100 000.

Table 5.9.1. *Distribution of number of claims on 100 000 motor vehicle comprehensive policies*

Number of claims	Observed number of policies	Fitted frequencies	
		Poisson	Negative binomial
0	88 585	88 411	88 597
1	10 577	10 890	10 544
2	779	671	806
3	54	27	50
4	4	1	3
5	1	–	–
6	–	–	–
Total	100 000	100 000	100 000

Source: D. Liddy (personal communication).

Example 5.9.2. The negative binomial distribution obviously provides a much better fit than the Poisson to the data in table 5.9.1, and goodness-of-fit tests[8] confirm this. It would appear, therefore, that the risks are heterogeneous. Let us examine this feature of the data.

Applying (5.9.11) and (5.9.12), we obtain $\alpha = 3.507$ and $\beta = 28.47$. According to the formula in footnote 4 of section 5.5, and gamma tables,

$$\Gamma(3.507) = 2.507 \times 1.507 \times \Gamma(1.507)$$
$$= 2.507 \times 1.507 \times 0.886\ 50$$
$$= 3.349\ 24.$$

The probability-density function of the Poisson parameter q is, therefore,

$$f(u) = 8.500\ 44\ e^{-28.47u}\ (28.47u)^{2.507},$$

which is depicted in fig. 5.9.2.

The mode of this gamma distribution is about 0.09 and the mean 0.123 18. By considering the area under the probability-density function to the right of

Fig. 5.9.2. Probability-density function of the claim frequency rate q of a policyholder, chosen at random, based on the data in table 5.9.1. The shaded area is the probability that a policyholder, chosen at random, has a claim frequency rate in excess of 0.24 (twice the average).

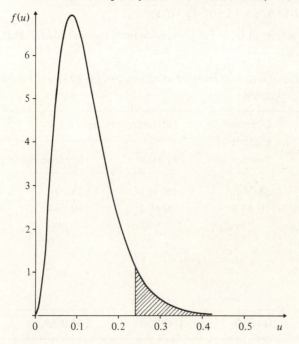

8   See, for example, Pollard [26] 149–51.

$x = 0.24$, we can conclude, for example, that about 6.5% of policyholders have accident frequency rates (q-values) greater than twice the average value of 0.123 18. These are of course the poorer risks.

Further reading: Benjamin [3] 128–9; Johnson & Hey [15] 206–9; Johnson & Kotz [16] 122–42**; Kendall & Stuart [19] 130–1*; Pollard [26] 114–17.

5.10   The importance of theoretical distributions in general insurance

In this chapter we have described a number of theoretical distributions and given examples of their application in general insurance. It is clear that they can be used. Are they essential? The more sceptical reader might observe that many of the calculations we have performed can be carried out with observed claim frequency distributions and observed claim size distributions. Why then need we concern ourselves with these particular theoretical distributions?

When the underlying data are very extensive and have been collected in the most appropriate form for the calculation in hand, it is indeed possible to answer many of the questions which arise in general insurance, using the observed distributions. More often than not, however, the data are far from extensive and may not be in the most convenient form. In such situations, calculations are only possible if certain assumptions are made. In other words, we formulate a model and make use of theoretical distributions. The distributions described in this chapter are very useful for this purpose. Even when the data are extensive, theoretical distributions may still be essential (for example, to estimate the upper tail of a claim size distribution to compute reinsurance premiums).

Other reasons for the importance of these theoretical distributions include:

1. their convenient and well-known properties, which facilitate the analysis of many problems (for example, the Central Limit Theorem; the additive property of independent Poisson random variables);

2. the fact that the distribution is completely summarised by a small number of parameters (one in the case of the Poisson; two in the case of the normal, log-normal, gamma, Pareto and negative binomial) and it is not necessary to operate with a long schedule of observed frequencies;

3. the fact that they allow us to make inferences about the behaviour of insurance portfolios (chapter 6);

4. their convenience for mathematical manipulation allowing the development of useful theoretical results (chapter 11).

For all these reasons, therefore, theoretical distributions are preferable to observed frequency distributions in many situations.

5.11   Exercises

1. Use table 5.1.1 to obtain the values of

    (a) Φ (2.07) ;
    (b) Φ (– 1.65) ;
    and the value of z such that
    (c) the area under the unit normal curve between $– z$ and z is 0.75 ;
    (d) Φ (z) = 0.43 .

2. 1500 plate-glass insurance claims reveal a mean claim size of $120 and a standard deviation of $15. Assuming that the claim size X is normally distributed, calculate the size x of claim such that 800 of the claims might be expected to be less than x and 700 greater. Estimate also the number of claims in the sample with sizes less than $100.

3. If the claim size distribution in question 2 is log-normal rather than normal, estimate the log-normal parameters μ and σ.

4. Solve question 2 assuming a log-normal rather than normal claim size distribution.

5. A Poisson distribution is such that the probability that the random variable takes the value 1 is the same as the probability that it takes the value 2. What is this probability?

6. If the number of claims per policy received by an insurer during a month can be taken as a Poisson variate with mean of 0.01, calculate how many of 80 000 similar policies are expected to give rise to more than two claims each in a year.

7. The claim frequency of a policy insuring against a certain risk A is 0.08 per policy per year and that of another type of policy insuring against another risk B is 0.05 per policy per year. The insurer issues a new type of policy insuring against both of these risks. Calculate approximately the probability of there being more than 140 claims arising in the first policy year out of 1000 of these new policies. State any assumptions necessary.

8. The claim size distribution in respect of a certain risk is log-normal with parameters μ = 5.0, σ = 1.2. What proportion of claims lie between $50 and $5000?

9. For a certain class of risk, the mean claim size is $310 and the standard deviation of the claim size is $420. In one year there are 520 claims arising from this class. Calculate the probability that the sum of these claims exceeds $180 000.

**10. Deduce (5.9.10) from (5.9.9).

6 INFERENCES FROM GENERAL INSURANCE DATA

Summary. In this short chapter we show how the theoretical distributions, described in chapter 5, can be used to make inferences about claim frequencies and claim sizes. We briefly outline the theory behind the testing of statistical hypotheses and give several examples. The basic concepts of point and interval estimation of claim frequency and claim size parameters are also explained. The chapter concludes with a short introduction to multivariate modelling of claim frequency rates.

6.1 Hypothesis testing

We saw in section 2.1 that many of the basic concepts of probability and statistics are readily explained in terms of games of chance. This is certainly true in respect of hypothesis testing, and we start with a coin-tossing example.

A scientist has recently been given a coin and he wishes to test whether it is unbiased. The obvious experiment for him to carry out is to toss the coin a number of times and observe the number of 'head' and 'tail' outcomes. He decides to toss the coin 1000 times. For an unbiased coin, the probability of a 'head' $p = \frac{1}{2}$, and the expected number of 'heads' is 500 (section 5.8). If the number of 'heads' turns out to be 511, the scientist will probably conclude that the coin is unbiased (511 is near 500); if, on the other hand, the number of 'heads' turns out to be 897, he will be rather convinced that the coin is biased, and he will reject any suggestion that it is unbiased.

The hypothesis which is being tested, namely, that $p = \frac{1}{2}$, is referred to as the *null hypothesis* and is usually denoted by H_0.

Both the probability of obtaining exactly 511 'heads' with an unbiased coin and the probability of obtaining exactly 897 'heads' with such a coin are small. Why then do we accept the null hypothesis that the coin is unbiased when we obtain 511 'heads', yet reject it when we obtain 897 'heads'? In the former case we accept the null hypothesis that the coin is unbiased because the probability of obtaining, *with an unbiased coin,* a number of 'heads' differing from the expected number 500 by 11 or more is quite appreciable (about 0.5). The probability of obtaining, *with an unbiased coin,* a number of 'heads' differing from

500 by 397 or more, on the other hand, is extremely remote and we would reject the null hypothesis in this case; we would accept instead the *alternative hypothesis H_1* that $p \neq \frac{1}{2}$.

This type of reasoning underlies all statistical tests. The probability level below which we reject the null hypothesis is known as the *significance level.* The general test procedure may be summarised as follows:

General procedure	*Coin-tossing example*
1. Choose a *level of significance* α.	$\alpha = 0.05$.
2. Formulate the *statistical model.*	The number of 'heads' X has the binomial distribution with parameters $n = 1000$ and p.
3. Specify the *null hypothesis H_0* and the *alternative hypothesis H_1*.	$H_0 : p = \frac{1}{2}$; $H_1 : p \neq \frac{1}{2}$.
4. Select a *test statistic* whose behaviour is known.	$T = (X - np)/\sqrt{[np(1-p)]}$ is approximately a unit normal random variable when n is large (equation (5.8.7)).
5. Find the appropriate *critical region* for testing the null hypothesis. (If the test statistic falls in this region, the null hypothesis will be rejected.) The test statistic has probability α of falling in this region when H_0 is true.	From the normal tables, the critical region is where $|T| > 1.96$.
6. Compute the test statistic on the assumption that the null hypothesis is true.	$T = (511 - 500)/\sqrt{(250)} = 0.696$.
7. Draw conclusions. If the test statistic lies in the critical region, reject the null hypothesis and accept the alternative. Otherwise accept the null hypothesis.	The test statistic is not in the critical region, so we accept the null hypothesis. We have no evidence that the coin is biased.

The fact that the test criterion is not significant does not prove that the null hypothesis is true; it merely tells us that the data do not contradict the null hypothesis. We accept the null hypothesis until evidence is brought forward disproving it. In other contexts this approach might be referred to as *scientific method.*

For a more complete discussion of the theory behind the testing of statistical hypothesis, and a wide range of tests and examples, the reader is referred to Pollard [26] 133–209. We now give some simple general insurance examples.

Example 6.1.1. An insurer bases his premium rates for a certain risk on a claim frequency rate of 0.01 and an average claim size of $980. In 1979, the insurer wrote 1000 such policies and, during the period they were in force, the policies produced 15 claims averaging $989.70. The average claim size does not appear unreasonable. The actual number of claims (15) is 50% higher than the number expected (10) under the premium assumptions. Is the insurer assuming too low a claim frequency rate for calculating the premium, or has he just been unlucky?

Let us assume that the underlying claim frequency rate is in fact 0.01, and see whether the insurer could reasonably have obtained 15 claims purely by chance with such a claim rate. (In other words, we assume as our null hypothesis, H_0, a claim frequency rate of 0.01.) If the underlying claim frequency rate were 0.01, then, with 1000 policies, the number of claims would be a Poisson random variable with mean 10 (section 5.6; example 5.8.3). The probability of 15 or more claims would, therefore, be

$$e^{-10} \frac{10^{15}}{15!} + e^{-10} \frac{10^{16}}{16!} + e^{-10} \frac{10^{17}}{17!} + \ldots$$

$$= 1 - \left(e^{-10} \frac{10^0}{0!} + e^{-10} \frac{10^1}{1!} + \ldots e^{-10} \frac{10^{14}}{14!} \right)$$

$$= 0.083 ,$$

or about 1 chance in 12, which is not so unlikely.

Thus, with an underlying claim frequency rate of 0.01, the insurer with 1000 policies would expect to encounter 15 or more claims about 1 year in 12, which is not so rare. He may or may not feel that he ought to assume a higher claim frequency when calculating his premium rates in the future. Indeed, in a highly competitive market, he may require stronger statistical evidence to put his rates up than to lower them!

Example 6.1.2. The calculation of the individual Poisson probabilities in example 6.1.1 is rather tedious. The Poisson mean (10) is large enough for the Central Limit Theorem to apply, and we may compute the probability of 15 or more claims as

$$1 - \Phi \left(\frac{14.5 - 10}{\sqrt{(10)}} \right) = 1 - \Phi (1.42) = 0.078 .$$

The relevant formulae are (5.7.1) and (5.7.2).

Example 6.1.3. Let us now imagine that the insurer of example 6.1.1 experiences 16 claims in respect of the 1000 policies written the subsequent year 1980. Over the two-year period, he has then experienced 31 claims compared with an expected number (on the premium basis) of 20.

Assuming an underlying claim frequency rate of 0.01 (our null hypothesis) the number of claims in the two-year period is a Poisson random variable with mean 20, and the probability of 31 or more claims is (applying the Central Limit Theorem result of section 5.7)

$$1 - \Phi \left(\frac{30.5 - 20}{\sqrt{(20)}} \right) = 1 - \Phi (2.35) = 0.0094 \ ,$$

or about 1 chance in 106, which is rather a rare event. We would doubt very much whether the underlying claim frequency rate was in fact 0.01, and there would seem to be a very strong case for assuming a higher claim rate in the calculation of future premiums.

Note the simplicity of the calculations when the normal approximation is used. Note also that it would not be possible to answer this type of question working only with means; we have to look at the distribution.

Example 6.1.4. In respect of a certain risk, an insurer has based his premium on an assumed average claim size of $1200. The average claim size in respect of 1243 claims during 1980 under such policies was $1283.70 with an observed standard deviation of $1497.31. Is there any evidence that the insurer is assuming too low an average claim size in his premium calculation?

According to the Central Limit Theorem (section 5.2) and the additive rules for means and variances of sums of independent random variables (sections 4.1, 4.2), we would expect the distribution of the total payout in respect of 1243 independent claims to be approximately normal with mean 1243μ and variance $1243\sigma^2$, where μ and σ^2 are, respectively, the mean and variance of the claim size distribution. Both these parameters are unknown. An adequate estimate of σ^2 for the purpose of this example will, however, be given by $(1497.31)^2$.

Let us assume that the underlying average claim size is in fact the average claim size assumed in the premium basis, namely $1200. Then the total payout in respect of 1243 claims is approximately a normal random variable with mean $1243 \times 1200 = 1\ 491\ 600$ and standard deviation

$$\sqrt{[1243 \times (1497.31)^2]} = 52\ 789 \ .$$

The actual total payout in 1980 was $1283.70 \times 1243 = \$1\ 595\ 639$. Under the null hypothesis that the underlying mean claim size is $1200, the probability of obtaining a total payout of $1 595 639 or more with 1243 claims is

$$1 - \Phi \left(\frac{1\ 595\ 639 - 1\ 491\ 600}{52\ 789} \right) = 1 - \Phi\ (1.97) = 0.024 \ ,$$

or less than 1 in 40. An outcome as extreme as this is thus rather unlikely with an underlying mean claim size of $1200. The results of 1980 suggest very strongly, therefore, that the assumed mean claim size in the premium basis is too low.

Further reading: Freund [10] 237–94**; Hoel [13] 159–64; Hoel [14] 106–12**; Mode [22] 105–11*; Pollard [26] 133–7; Yamane [30] 168–226.

6.2   Point estimation and method of moments

The more important statistical distributions from the general insurance point of view were described in chapter 5, and we noted that each distribution involved one or more parameters which determined its location and spread, and even its shape. Numerous examples were given of the application of these distributions to problems of general insurance.

The parameters of a distribution are seldom known *a priori,* and they need to be estimated from claims data before the distribution can be applied to a particular problem (for example, the estimation of the reinsurance risk premium[1] for excess of loss reinsurance). The function of the observations which we choose, to estimate a parameter, is known as an *estimator,* and the numerical value obtained from it, using a particular set of data is called an *estimate.*

Often, several different functions will suggest themselves as estimators (for example, the sample mean and the sample median can both be used to estimate the mean of a normal population) and we need to decide which to use. The following criteria are used by statisticians:

1. The estimator should be *unbiased,* so that its expectation is equal to the true value of the parameter. Thus, on average, the estimate obtained is equal to the underlying parameter. The estimator should not provide estimates which are on average too high or too low.

2. The estimator should be *consistent.* By this we mean that, for any small quantity ϵ, the probability that the absolute value of the deviation of the estimator from the true parameter value is less than ϵ tends to 1 as n tends to infinity. Thus, for an estimate based on a large number of

---

[1] premium, taking account only of claim frequency and average claim size. No allowance is made for expenses and other loadings.

observations, there is a very small probability that its value will differ seriously from the true value of the parameter.

3. The estimator should be *efficient.* That is, the variance of the estimator should be minimal.

Statisticians have devised a number of different standard methods for producing point[2] estimates of parameters, including the method of moments, least squares, and maximum likelihood. In simple situations, the various methods often produce the same results. When sample sizes are large, they all tend to provide more or less the same answers, even in more complicated cases. In other circumstances, however, markedly different results can emerge, and the three criteria above are often used by statisticians in deciding which estimator to use.

The maximum likelihood method (section 6.3) usually provides estimators which are quite satisfactory as far as the above criteria are concerned. However, the method frequently produces equations which are rather awkward to solve and, for this reason, the simpler method of moments is often preferred, despite the fact that the resulting estimators may be sub-optimal in respect of the above three criteria.

Of the three standard methods, the method of moments is perhaps the most readily understood, and we have already given examples of its use (examples 5.3.1, 5.6.1, and 5.9.1). In the case of a two-parameter distribution, for example, we compute the first two moments of the sample and equate these to the corresponding theoretical moments of the distribution (i.e. we equate the observed and theoretical means and the observed and theoretical variances).

The maximum likelihood method is described in section 6.3. Examples of the use of the method of least squares are given in section 6.5.

> **Example 6.2.1.** Re-read example 5.3.1. The estimation method is an example of the method of moments.

> **Example 6.2.2.** Re-read example 5.6.1. The estimation method is an example of the method of moments.

Further reading: Freund [10] 214–23; Mendenhall & Scheaffer [21] 263–9, 299–301; Pollard [26] 210–12.

*6.3   Maximum likelihood

The method of *maximum likelihood* provides estimators which are usually quite satisfactory. They have the desirable properties of being consistent,

---
[2]   Interval estimators are described in section 6.4.

asymptotically normal and asymptotically efficient for large samples under quite general conditions. They are often biased but the bias is frequently removable by a simple adjustment (Pollard [26] 211–12). Other methods of obtaining estimators are also available (for example, the method of moments outlined above in section 6.2) but the maximum likelihood method is the most frequently used.

The *principle of maximum likelihood* tells us that we should use as our estimate that value which maximises the likelihood[3] of the observed event. The following example demonstrates the technique.

Example 6.3.1. Use the data in table 5.6.1 and the principle of maximum likelihood to estimate the claim frequency rate for the class of risk represented by these data.

Let us denote the unknown claim frequency rate by q. The probability that a specified policy experiences no claim in a year is given by the Poisson probability $e^{-q} q^0/0!$. Similarly, the probabilities of one, two, etc., claims in respect of a specified policy are, respectively, $e^{-q} q^1/1!$, $e^{-q} q^2/2!$, etc.

The 4000 policies in the sample are independent. The probability (likelihood) that 3288 specified policies experience no claims, 642 specified policies experience exactly one claim, 66 specified policies experience two claims, and 4 specified policies experience three claims is

$$L = (e^{-q} q^0/0!)^{3288} (e^{-q} q^1/1!)^{642} (e^{-q} q^2/2!)^{66} (e^{-q} q^3/3!)^4$$

$$= [e^{-4000q} q^{(0 \times 3288 + 1 \times 642 + 2 \times 66 + 3 \times 4)}]/(2^{66} \times 6^4)$$

$$= \left(e^{-4000q} q^{786}\right)/(9.56 \times 10^{22}).$$

According to the principle of maximum likelihood, we choose the value of q which maximises L. This value also maximises

$$\ln L = -4000 q + 786 \ln q - 52.91 .$$

At the maximum, the derivative with respect to q must be zero (section 1.7). That is,

$$\frac{d}{dq} \ln L = -4000 + \frac{786}{q} = 0 ,$$

whence

$$\hat{q} = 786/4000 = 0.196 .$$

---

[3] The distinction between *likelihood* and *probability* is explained in a footnote on page 8 of Kendall & Stuart [20].

(We have followed the usual convention and placed a circumflex over the q to indicate a maximum likelihood estimator.)

The maximum likelihood estimator of the Poisson claim frequency rate is merely the mean number of claims per policy per annum, and we would have obtained the same answer by the method of moments (section 6.2).

> *Further reading:* Freund [10] 223–6; Hoel [14] 58–61**; Mendenhall & Scheaffer [21] 302–5; Mood & Graybill [23] 178–80; Pollard [26] 211–12; Yamane [30] 245–9.

*6.4   Confidence intervals

The methods of sections 6.2 and 6.3 can be used to obtain what are referred to as *point estimates* of a parameter, but we must remember that a point estimator, depending as it does on the sample actually obtained, is a random variable distributed in some way around the true value of the parameter. The true parameter value may be higher or lower than our estimate. It is often useful, therefore, to obtain an interval within which we are reasonably confident the true value will lie, and the generally accepted method is to construct what are known as *confidence limits*.

The following procedure will yield upper and lower 95% confidence limits with the property that, when we say that these limits include the true value of the parameter, 95% of all such statements will be true and 5% will be incorrect.

1. Choose a test statistic involving the unknown parameter and no other unknown parameter.
2. Place the appropriate sample values in the statistic.
3. Obtain an equation for the unknown parameter by equating the statistic to the upper $2\frac{1}{2}\%$ point of the relevant distribution.
4. The solution of the equation gives one limit.
5. Repeat steps (3) and (4) with the lower $2\frac{1}{2}\%$ point of the distribution to obtain the other limit.

Tables and charts are also available from which confidence intervals can be determined for parameters of certain basic distributions (for example, the Poisson and binomial distributions; see Campbell [4] 367, 377).

> **Example 6.4.1.** Obtain a 95% confidence interval for the claim frequency rate for the class of risk represented by the data in table 5.6.1.

Let us again denote the unknown claim frequency rate by q. Then, the number of claims a particular policyholder makes in a year will be distributed as a Poisson random variable with mean q, and the total number of claims N

experienced by 4000 independent policyholders will be a Poisson random variable with mean 4000 q (section 5.6). The Central Limit Theorem (sections 5.2 and 5.7) tells us that N will be approximately normally distributed with mean 4000 q and standard deviation $\sqrt{(4000\ q)}$, so that the standardised random variable

$$(N - 4000\ q)/\sqrt{(4000\ q)} \qquad\qquad (6.4.1)$$

has the unit normal distribution.

To obtain the 95% confidence limits for q, we set N equal to the total number of claims, 786, and equate (6.4.1) to the upper and lower $2\frac{1}{2}$% points of the unit normal distribution: ± 1.96. Thus,

$$(786 - 4000\ q)/\sqrt{(4000q)} = \pm\ 1.96\ .$$

Squaring and re-arranging, we obtain

$$16\ 000\ 000\ q^2 - 6\ 303\ 366\ q + 617\ 796 = 0\ ,$$

whence $q = 0.183$ or 0.211. The 95% confidence interval for q is from 0.183 to 0.211.

Example 6.4.2. A sample of 35 claim sizes is exhibited in table 6.4.1.

Assuming that the distribution of claim size is log-normal, obtain a 95% confidence interval for the log-normal parameter μ.

If the assumption of log-normality is correct, the logarithm (to base e) of the claim size will have the normal distribution with mean μ and variance σ^2. Both these parameters are unknown. Point estimates of them are provided by the mean and variance of the logarithms of the 35 sample claim sizes in table 6.4.1,

Table 6.4.1. *A sample of 35 householders' claims*

Claim sizes ($)				
272.63	21.69	1001.43	157.05	552.92
95.74	183.48	191.44	388.26	125.25
8.06	97.10	59.19	787.43	47.88
35.08	15.44	332.32	71.14	1386.39
744.12	453.61	2811.75	10.54	79.66
148.41	560.80	214.37	265.03	111.85
2002.50	57.54	38.18	327.65	28.37

namely, 5.04 and 2.08 respectively.[4] We require, however, a confidence interval for μ.

The logarithm of the random variable representing claim size has the normal distribution with mean μ and variance σ^2. The sum of the logarithms of 35 independent claim sizes will, therefore, have the normal distribution with mean 35μ and variance $35\sigma^2$ (sections 4.1, 4.2). Dividing the sum by 35, we deduce that the average of 35 logarithms of claim sizes will be normally distributed with mean μ and variance $\sigma^2/35$ (sections 4.1, 4.2). Thus, denoting the average of the 35 logarithms by Y, the standardised random variable.

$$(Y - \mu)/\sqrt{(\sigma^2/35)}$$

has the unit normal distribution.

The parameter σ^2 is unknown. If we substitute the point estimate 2.08 for it, we know that

$$(Y - \mu)/0.244 \qquad\qquad (6.4.2)$$

is approximately a unit normal random variable, and we can use this statistic to obtain a confidence interval for μ.

We substitute the observed mean logarithm 5.04 for Y and equate (6.4.2) to the upper and lower $2\frac{1}{2}\%$ points of the normal distribution (± 1.96) to obtain $\mu = 5.04 \pm 0.48$. In other words, the (approximate) 95% confidence interval for μ is from 4.56 to 5.52. The interval is wide because the sample size is relatively small.

The approximation we made above when we substituted the estimate 2.08 for σ^2 is reasonable provided the sample size is not too small, which, in practice, means that the number of claims should not be less than about 30. A knowledge of Student's t-distribution is required if the sample is less than 30 (Pollard [26] 220).

A confidence interval can also be obtained for the other parameter σ^2. A knowledge of the chi-square distribution is, however, required (Pollard [26] 228).

> *Further reading:* Hoel [14] 234–40**; Mendenhall & Scheaffer [21] 274; Mode [22] 193–8; Mood & Graybill [23] 248–74**; Pollard [26] 212–14; Yamane [30] 259–64.

*6.5   Risk factors; multivariate models; least squares

In general insurance there are many possible sources of heterogeneity with regard to risk of claims; we refer to these as *risk factors*. Examples of risk

---

4   These are the maximum likelihood estimates of μ and σ^2. The estimation method should be contrasted with the method of moments adopted in example 5.3.1.

factors in a motor car insurance portfolio are, age of policyholder, type of motor car, financial encumbrance, etc. In respect of the risk factor, age, policy-holders may be categorised, for example, according to whether they are under 25, 25–70 years of age, or over 70. These categories are often referred to as *levels*. In setting his premium rates, the general insurer must take account of the relevant risk factors and the levels of the policyholders in his experience in respect of these risk factors. If he were not to do so, and the mix of levels were to change, premiums based on the insurer's past experience may well turn out to be inadequate.

The fact that, in respect of most general insurance risks, several risk factors can be identified, means that multivariate methods are often required. We demonstrate the approach with a very simple example.

Table 6.5.1 shows the experience of a small motor insurer in respect of 12 299 policies. The policies and claims have been subdivided according to the age of the policyholder (under 25, or 25 and over) and type of vehicle (family sedan, or high-performance car). If there were no differences in claim frequency rates among the four classes of policyholder, the best estimate of the common underlying rate would be

$$\frac{882 + 248 + 741 + 453}{5827 + 1280 + 3570 + 1622} = 0.188\,96 \,.$$

The fitted number of claims for the four classes, assuming this common under-lying rate, is obtained by multiplying the respective number of policyholders in the four categories by 0.188 96 (table 6.5.2). The deviations (observed minus fitted claims), shown in parenthesis in the table, are large, indicating a poor fit.[5]

Clearly, the claim frequency rate depends upon the class to which a policy

Table 6.5.1. *Claim experience of a motor insurer*

	Number of policies		Number of claims	
Age group	Family sedan	High performance	Family sedan	High performance
25 +	5827	1280	882	248
< 25	3570	1622	741	453

---

[5] A chi-square goodness-of-fit test would produce a highly significant result (Pollard [26] 149–51).

belongs. Let us denote the underlying claim frequency rates f_{ij} of the various classes of policyholder as follows:

f_{11} over 25, family sedan;
f_{12} over 25, high-performance car;
f_{21} under 25, family sedan;
f_{22} under 25, high-performance car;

and assume that the effects of youth and high performance are additive; in other words, assume that

$$f_{11} = A \ ;$$
$$f_{12} = A + B \ ;$$
$$f_{21} = A + C \ ;$$
$$f_{22} = A + B + C \ .$$

The unknown constant A is the underlying claim frequency rate in respect of policyholders aged 25 and over with family sedans. Constant B is the additional claim frequency rate in respect of policyholders having a high-performance vehicle, and C is the additional claim frequency rate for youthful policyholders. The observed and expected numbers of claims would then be as follows:

Observed number	Expected number
882	$5827 \, A$
248	$1280 \, A + 1280 \, B$
741	$3570 \, A + 3570 \, C$
453	$1622 \, A + 1622 \, B + 1622 \, C$

In this model A, B and C are unknown underlying parameters. *Estimates* of these parameters will be denoted by $\hat{A}$, $\hat{B}$ and $\hat{C}$. If the model is in fact valid and is to be of any practical use, it is desirable that the fitted numbers of claims,

Table 6.5.2. *Fitted claims assuming a common underlying claim frequency rate. Deviations (observed minus fitted) are shown in parentheses*

	Fitted number of claims			
Age group	Family sedan		High performance	
25 +	1101	(– 219)	242	(+ 6)
< 25	675	(+ 66)	306	(+ 147)

calculated using $\hat{A}$, $\hat{B}$,and $\hat{C}$, be close to the observed numbers. In other words, we require

$5827\,\hat{A}$	to be close to 882 ;
$1280\,\hat{A} + 1280\,\hat{B}$	to be close to 248 ;
$3570\,\hat{A} + 3570\,\hat{C}$	to be close to 741 ;
$1622\,\hat{A} + 1622\,\hat{B} + 1622\,\hat{C}$	to be close to 453 .

The best fit may be obtained by choosing $\hat{A}$, $\hat{B}$ and $\hat{C}$ to minimise

$$\sum_{\text{all cells}} (\text{observed number} - \text{fitted number})^2, \qquad (6.5.1)$$

the method being known as *'least squares'* (Pollard [26] 255–8).

The reliability of an estimate based on a cell with a small number of observations will not be as great as the reliability of an estimate based on a cell with more claims. It is usual, therefore, to minimise, instead of (6.5.1), the weighted sum of squares

$$\sum_{\text{all cells}} \frac{(\text{observed number} - \text{fitted number})^2}{\text{variance of number of claims}}. \qquad (6.5.2)$$

This *weighted least squares criterion* takes proper account of the relative weight of data in the different cells.

The variance of the number of claims in a particular cell depends upon the underlying claim frequency rate which is unknown. Fortunately, the number of claims in a particular cell will tend to follow the Poisson distribution (section 5.6), for which the mean and variance are equal, and a sufficiently accurate estimate of the variance of the number of claims (for the purpose of (6.5.2)) is given by the observed number of claims. In other words, in our particular example, we choose $\hat{A}$, $\hat{B}$ and $\hat{C}$ to minimise

$$\frac{(882 - 5827\,\hat{A})^2}{882} + \frac{(248 - 1280\,\hat{A} - 1280\,\hat{B})^2}{248}$$

$$+ \frac{(741 - 3570\,\hat{A} - 3570\,\hat{C})^2}{741} + \frac{(453 - 1622\,\hat{A} - 1622\,\hat{B} - 1622\,\hat{C})^2}{453}.$$

At the minimum, the partial derivatives of this criterion, with respect to $\hat{A}$, $\hat{B}$ and $\hat{C}$, must be zero (section 1.8). The effect of differentiating the above criterion, with respect to $\hat{A}$, $\hat{B}$ and $\hat{C}$, and equating the three partial derivatives to zero, is to obtain three simultaneous equations in the three unknowns, which we solve and obtain

$$\hat{A} = 0.149\,503\,3\ ;$$
$$\hat{B} = 0.055\,141\,1;$$
$$\hat{C} = 0.062\,220\,1\ .$$

The fitted claim frequency rates are then as follows:

$\hat{f}_{11} = 0.149\ 503\ 3$;
$\hat{f}_{12} = 0.204\ 644\ 4$;
$\hat{f}_{21} = 0.211\ 723\ 4$;
$\hat{f}_{22} = 0.266\ 864\ 5$;

and we obtain the fitted numbers of claims in table 6.5.3. The fit appears quite reasonable.[6]

The above additive model may be satisfactory in some situations. In others, the appropriateness of the model must be doubted because of the poor fit obtained. The so-called *multiplicative model* is, therefore, sometimes used as an alternative. We assume that

$f_{11} = A$;
$f_{12} = AB$;
$f_{21} = AC$;
$f_{22} = ABC$.

The unknown constant A is again the underlying claim frequency rate in respect of policyholders aged 25 and over with family sedans. Multiplication of A by B produces the claim frequency rate in respect of policyholders over 25 but with high-performance cars. Multiplication by C produces the corresponding claim frequency rates for drivers under 25.

The connection between the claim frequency rates and the parameters A, B and C is multiplicative. The connection between the logarithms is thus linear, and the multiplicative model is, therefore, sometimes referred to as *log-linear*.

Table 6.5.3. *Fitted claims according to the additive model. Deviations* (*observed minus fitted*) *are shown in parentheses*

	Fitted number of claims			
Age group	Family sedan		High performance	
25 +	871	(+ 11)	262	(– 14)
< 25	756	(– 15)	433	(+ 20)

---

[6] It also satisfies the chi-square goodness-of-fit test (Pollard [26] 149–51).

The parameters A, B and C are unknown. Estimates $\hat{A}$, $\hat{B}$ and $\hat{C}$ are obtained by minimising

$$\sum_{\text{all cells}} \frac{[\ln(\text{observed number}) - \ln(\text{fitted number})]^2}{\text{variance of ln of number of claims}} \qquad (6.5.3)$$

by suitable choice of $\hat{A}$, $\hat{B}$ and $\hat{C}$.

The main problem is that of estimating the variance of the logarithm of the number of claims. In the case of a Poisson random variable X with reasonably large expectation q, the random variable $\ln X$ has expectation $\ln q$ (approximately) and variance $1/q$ (approximately).[7] The (Poisson) expected number of claims for each cell is not known, but we can represent it adequately (for weighted least squares weighting purposes) by the observed number of claims in the cell, and minimise

$$\sum_{\text{all cells}} (\text{observed number})\,[\ln(\text{observed number}) - \ln(\text{fitted number})]^2$$

$$(6.5.4)$$

Let us write $\hat{a}$ for $\ln \hat{A}$, $\hat{b}$ for $\ln \hat{B}$ and $\hat{c}$ for $\ln \hat{C}$. Then in our particular case, we have

Observed number	Fitted number	ln (observed number) minus ln (fitted number)
882	$5827\,\hat{A}$	$-(1.888\ 07 + \hat{a})$
248	$1280\,\hat{A}\hat{B}$	$-(1.641\ 19 + \hat{a} + \hat{b})$
741	$3570\,\hat{A}\hat{C}$	$-(1.572\ 32 + \hat{a} + \hat{c})$
453	$1622\,\hat{A}\hat{B}\hat{C}$	$-(1.275\ 52 + \hat{a} + \hat{b} + \hat{c})$

and we minimise

$$882\,(1.888\ 07 + \hat{a})^2 + 248\,(1.641\ 19 + \hat{a} + \hat{b})^2 + 741\,(1.572\ 32 + \hat{a} + \hat{c})^2$$
$$+ (1.275\ 52 + \hat{a} + \hat{b} + \hat{c})^2$$

by suitable choice of $\hat{a}$, $\hat{b}$ and $\hat{c}$. Differentiating partially with respect to $\hat{a}$, $\hat{b}$ and $\hat{c}$, and equating the derivatives to zero (section 1.8), we obtain three simultaneous linear equations in the three unknowns $\hat{a}$, $\hat{b}$ and $\hat{c}$. These equations are then solved to yield $\hat{a} = -1.894\ 55$ ($\hat{A} = 0.150\ 386$), $\hat{b} = 0.276\ 44$ ($\hat{B} = 1.318\ 43$) and $\hat{c} - 0.329\ 96$ ($\hat{C} = 1.390\ 91$).

---

[7] We quote this result without proof.

The resulting fitted numbers of claims are shown in table 6.5.4, and it is clear that the fit is even better than that obtained using the additive model.

The above, artificially simple, example was chosen to demonstrate the numerical techniques of model fitting as simply as possible. The simplicity of the example meant, however, that the main advantages of modelling were not readily apparent.

Let us consider, therefore, a more realistic (and more complicated) motor insurance example where the rating factors are: age (25 + / under 25), sex (male/female), area (metropolitan/other urban/rural), use (private/business), type of vehicle (6 categories) and occupation (5 classes). There are $2 \times 2 \times 3 \times 2 \times 6 \times 5 = 720$ different categories of risk which need to be rated.

Given a large enough experience, it is theoretically possible to estimate the claim frequency rate for each of the 720 categories by dividing the observed number of claims for each category by the exposure (vehicle-years) for that category. The calculations are straightforward. In practice, however, no experience is large enough to produce meaningful claim frequency rates in all cells (exposures in some will be zero or very small). Furthermore, even if exposures were sufficient to produce meaningful claim frequency rates in all cells, the broad effects of age, sex, area, use, type of vehicle, and occupation, would be completely hidden in the huge array of numbers.

Both these problems can be overcome by modelling. The necessary parameters (assuming no interaction between factors) are listed in table 6.5.5. From this table, it is clear, for example, that, under an additive model, the underlying claim frequency rate in respect of a male aged 33, occupation class 2, residing in the country and using a vehicle belonging to category 3, solely for private purposes, would be

$$f = A + D_2 + F_3 + G_2 \ .$$

Table 6.5.4. *Fitted claims according to the multiplicative model. Deviations (observed minus fitted) are shown in parentheses*

Age group	Fitted number of claims			
	Family sedan		High performance	
25 +	876	(+ 6)	254	(− 6)
< 25	747	(− 6)	447	(+ 6)

Under the multiplicative model, the formula would be

$$f = A\,D_2\,F_3\,G_2 .$$

Computer programs are available which will estimate the 15 parameters, from the data, by least squares. These programs are not troubled by zero or near-zero exposures in certain cells. Furthermore, the parameter values obtained indicate immediately the broad effects of the various rating factors and their relative importance. A negative value of $\hat{C}$, for example, would indicate a lower claim frequency rate for females and a positive value of $\hat{E}$ would indicate a higher claim frequency rate for business vehicles. A higher absolute value of $\hat{E}$ than $\hat{C}$ would indicate that 'use' is a more important rating factor than 'sex'.

As well as calculating estimates of the various parameters, least squares computer programs usually provide confidence intervals for these parameters.

One other important point needs to be noted. Instead of having to record separate claim frequency rates for 720 different categories of policyholder, the model approach requires the calculation and recording of only 15 parameter values — a considerable saving. Of course, a model can only be used when an adequate fit is obtained.

Further reading: Benjamin [3] 125–8; Freund [10] 321–5; Hoel [14] 168–77*; Mendenhall & Scheaffer [21] 457–87**; Pollard [26] 255–74, 300–12.

Table 6.5.5. *The 15 parameters necessary to model the claim frequency rate when the rating factors are age (25 + / under 25), sex (male/female), area (metropolitan/other urban/rural), use (private/business), type of vehicle (6 categories), and occupation (5 classes)*

Rating factor	Number of alternatives	Alternatives	Corresponding parameters
age	2	25 + / under 25	$-/B$
sex	2	male/female	$-/C$
area	3	metropolitan/other urban/rural	$-/D_1/D_2$
use	2	private/business	$-/E$
vehicle type	6	categories 0, 1, 2, 3, 4, 5	$-/F_1/F_2/F_3/F_4/F_5$
occupation	5	classes 0, 1, 2, 3, 4	$-/G_1/G_2/G_3/G_4$
base claim frequency level*			A

*For a male policyholder aged 25 +, occupation class 0, residing in the metropolitan area, using a vehicle in category 0 for private purposes.

6.6   Exercises

1. Confirm that the mean claim size for the data in table 6.6.1 is $230.79, and calculate the variance of the claim size. [*Hint*: Assume that all claims within a given size interval are concentrated at the average for the interval.)

2. Use the method of moments to fit a log-normal distribution to the claim size distribution in table 6.6.1. Is your fit satisfactory?

3. Fit both the Poisson and negative binomial distributions to the claim frequency data in table 6.6.2. Which model provides the better fit?

*4. If the probability that a policyholder makes at least one claim in a year is p and an experience involves n policyholders, the distribution of the number of policyholders making at least one claim is binomial with parameters n and p (section 5.8). The number of policyholders making at least one claim is X. Show that the maximum likelihood estimator of p is X/n. Calculate the maximum likelihood estimate of p using the data in table 5.9.1.

*5. If the probability that a policyholder makes at least one claim in a year is p and an experience involves n policyholders, the distribution of the number of policyholders making at least one claim is binomial with mean np and standard deviation $\sqrt{[np(1-p)]}$. When np is large, the Central Limit Theorem (section 5.2) ensures that the distribution of the number of policyholders making at least one claim is approximately normal with mean np and standard deviation $\sqrt{[np(1-p)]}$. Obtain a 95% confidence interval for p using the data in table 5.9.1.

*6. Confirm the estimates of A, B and C for the additive model in section 6.5.

**7. Attempt to fit a Pareto distribution to the data in table 6.6.1 by the method of moments. Comment on any difficulties you encounter.

Table 6.6.1. *Distribution of claim sizes in respect of 1950 householders' contents claims*

Claim size ($)	Average size ($)	Number of claims
0–24	17.14	168
25–49	34.88	474
50–74	60.02	329
75–99	87.73	205
100–199	134.27	367
200–499	282.88	241
500–999	685.29	80
1000–4999	2455.83	84
5000 and over	7170.00	2
All claims	230.79	1950

Source: T.J. Matthews (personal communication).

Inferences from general insurance data 121

Table 6.6.2. *Distribution of number of claims on motor vehicle policies*

Number of claims in year	Observed frequency
0	565 664
1	68 714
2	5 177
3	365
4	24
5	6
6	–

Source: D. Liddy (personal communication).

7 THE RISK PREMIUM

Summary In this chapter we define risk premium and show why the two main components, claim frequency rate and claim size need to be considered separately. Exposure and its measurement are discussed, and examples of the use of the 'eighths method' and census method are given. We also discuss the problem of estimating the claim size distribution and mean claim size, and the calculation of premiums for policies subject to excesses and excess of loss reinsurance.

7.1   Risk premium; claim frequency and claim size

The pure premium or *risk premium* is the premium that would exactly meet the expected cost of the risk covered, ignoring management expenses, commission, contingency loadings, etc. To compute it, we need to estimate the claim frequency rate q and the mean claim size m. The risk premium is then qm.

It is important that the two components: claim frequency rate and claim size be considered separately. Only in exceptional circumstances can the use of 'rate of payment of claims' be considered satisfactory for the assessment of a risk premium. The reasons for this include the following.

1. Some factors affect claim frequency and claim size differently. For example, inflation will affect claim size, but it is unlikely to affect claim frequency; the introduction of a law enforcing the wearing of seatbelts may have only a small effect on the frequency of compulsory third-party motor insurance claims, but it may have a much greater effect on the mean claim size; the introduction of more stringent drink—driving laws may reduce the frequency of claims but have little effect on mean claim size.

2. The effect of introducing an excess, or excess of loss reinsurance, can only be estimated if the claim size distribution is known (section 7.5).

We noted in chapter 5 that the Poisson distribution is usually satisfactory for studying claim frequency, although, in certain special circumstances, the negative binomial may be more appropriate (section 5.9). The reason why the Poisson distribution is usually applicable is suggested by example 5.8.3. Unfortunately, there is no generally applicable distribution for claim size. The log-normal (section 5.3) is sometimes applicable, and certain authors have also employed the gamma (section 5.5) and other distributions for this purpose. Reinsurers sometimes prefer to use the Pareto distribution to estimate the risk premium for excess of loss reinsurance, because of its long tail (section 5.4).

Further reading: Benjamin [3] 114–16.

7.2 Claim frequency rate; exposure

It is often very difficult to choose the most appropriate claim frequency rate for a class of insurance. Consider aviation insurance as an example; should one use claims per aircraft per year, or claims per aircraft–kilometre, or claims per landing, or claims per passenger–kilometre, or claims per tonne of fuel consumed, or what? In each case the numerator of the rate is the number of claims and causes no difficulty. It is the denominator (the *exposure*) which causes the problem. What exposure should we use? Very often the unit of exposure which is used is that which is possible or practical, rather than that which is theoretically more desirable. In motor insurance, for example, the exposure usually adopted is vehicle–year rather than kilometres driven, which might be theoretically more attractive, but is not practicable.

Once the unit of exposure has been chosen, there is still the problem of calculating the exposure. The insurer with adequate records and a sophisticated computer system may be able to compute exposure exactly. Accurate estimates can also be obtained using approximate methods as the following examples indicate.

Example 7.2.1. Table 7.2.1 shows the number of householders' policies issued by a small general insurer in each of the quarters of 1978 and 1979. Relevant details of the 29 policies, which were terminated during 1978 and 1979, are shown in table 7.2.2. Sixteen claims have been reported in respect

Table 7.2.1. *Householders' policies issued or renewed during 1978 and 1979 (by quarter)*

Quarter	Number issued or renewed 1978	1979
1 January–31 March	74	81
1 April–30 June	89	95
1 July–30 September	82	98
1 October–31 December	69	79

Table 7.2.2. *Householders' policies terminated during 1978 and 1979: date of termination, renewal date, and reduction in exposure during 1979 caused by the termination*

Date of termination	Renewal date	Reduction in exposure (days)	Date of termination	Renewal date	Reduction in exposure (days)
4 January 1978	18 June	0	18 January 1979	10 July	173
12 February 1978	1 November	0	13 February 1979	30 October	259
19 February 1978	13 May	0	10 March 1979	5 January	296
17 March 1978	10 August	0	17 March 1979	17 December	275
5 April 1978	31 July	0	21 April 1979	30 November	223
24 April 1978	5 December	0	30 April 1979	17 November	201
1 May 1978	5 January	5	17 May 1979	10 October	146
4 June 1978	15 February	46	6 June 1979	10 December	187
7 July 1978	4 January	4	14 July 1979	15 September	63
29 July 1978	19 October	0	20 August 1979	7 June	133
3 September 1978	21 July	202	5 September 1979	30 April	117
16 September 1978	14 June	165	30 September 1979	5 November	36
1 October 1978	3 April	93	3 October 1979	10 May	89
5 November 1978	9 August	220	18 November 1979	18 July	43
19 November 1978	30 January	30	Total reduction (days)		3006

of policies in force in 1979, and past experience indicates that the company can expect two further incurred but not reported claims. Obtain a point estimate of the claim frequency rate under householders' policies for the company. Obtain also an approximate 95% confidence interval for the claim frequency rate.

Let us ignore, for the moment, the problem of terminations. The 74 policies issued during the first quarter of 1978 will have been issued 'on average' in mid-February or one-eighth of the way through 1978. They will be in force for seven-eighths of 1978 and one-eighth of 1979. We assume that each of the 74 policies issued in the first quarter of 1978 contributes one-eighth of a year exposure to the risk of a claim during 1979. Similarly, the contribution of each policy to the exposure during 1979 will be

$\frac{3}{8}$ year for policies written in the second quarter 1978;

$\frac{5}{8}$ year for policies written in the third quarter 1978;

$\frac{7}{8}$ year for policies written in the fourth quarter 1978;

$\frac{7}{8}$ year for policies written in the first quarter 1979;

$\frac{5}{8}$ year for policies written in the second quarter 1979;

$\frac{3}{8}$ year for policies written in the third quarter 1979;

$\frac{1}{8}$ year for policies written in the fourth quarter 1979.

The above argument (the 'eighths rule') assumes that all policies remain in force for a full year. This is not the case, and the 1979 exposure, calculated by the 'eighths rule', needs to be reduced to take account of terminations during 1978 and 1979. The calculation of the reduction is set out in table 7.2.2, and we deduce that the total number of years of exposure during 1979 is

$$74 \times \frac{1}{8} + 89 \times \frac{3}{8} + 82 \times \frac{5}{8} + 69 \times \frac{7}{8} + 81 \times \frac{7}{8} + 95 \times \frac{5}{8} + 98 \times \frac{3}{8}$$

$$+ 79 \times \frac{1}{8} - \frac{3006}{365}$$

or 322.9 years.

Our point estimate of the claim frequency rate is, therefore, $18/322.9 = 0.056$.

To obtain a 95% confidence interval for the claim frequency rate q, we note first that the number of claims X will be a Poisson random variable with mean $322.9q$ (section 5.6). Provided q is not too small, the standardised random variable

$$(X - 322.9q) / \sqrt{(322.9q)} \tag{7.2.1}$$

will be approximately unit normal (section 5.7). Approximate 95% confidence limits for q can therefore be obtained by setting X equal to 18 and equating

(7.2.1) to the upper and lower $2\frac{1}{2}\%$ points of the unit normal distribution (section 6.4). We need to solve

$$\frac{18 - 322.9q}{\sqrt{(322.9q)}} = \pm 1.96.$$

Squaring this equation and re-arranging the terms, we obtain

$$104\,264.41q^2 - 12\,864.852q + 324 = 0,$$

with roots $q = 0.035$ and $q = 0.088$. The approximate 95% confidence interval is from 0.035 to 0.088, which is rather wide because of the small size of the experience.

The same approach can be used when the policies issued are grouped by month of issue rather than quarter. The *'twenty-fourths rule'* is then employed.

Example 7.2.2. The number of policies in force in a motor vehicle damage-only portfolio, on the first day of each quarter of 1979 and the first quarter of 1980, is shown in table 7.2.3 according to no-claim discount level. The number of claims in respect of incidents during 1979 total 1125 (including IBNR[1]): 364 from policyholders paying full premium, 299 from those on a 20% discount, and 462 from those on a 40% discount. Estimate the claim frequency rates for the three categories of policyholder.

Let us imagine that the number of full premium policies in force at time t years after 1 January 1979 is $P(t)$. We shall only be interested in (and our data only provide) values of $P(t)$ for t in the range $0 \leqslant t \leqslant 1$.

During the short interval of time δt immediately following time t, the change in the number of policyholders on full premium will be negligible. Each of the $P(t)$ full-premium policyholders currently on the books will contribute δt years

Table 7.2.3. *Motor vehicle damage-only policies. Number of policies in force at the beginning of each quarter during 1979, by no claim discount category*

Date	Number of policies in force		
	Full premium	20% discount	40% discount
1 January 1979	2560	2142	3967
1 April 1979	2627	2247	4120
1 July 1979	2689	2289	4175
1 October 1979	2835	2446	4384
1 January 1980	2977	2597	4488

[1] incurred but not reported claims.

of exposure during that small time interval so that the total number of years' exposure during the interval of time δt following time t will be $P(t)\,\delta t$. The total exposure during 1979 will, therefore, be approximately

Sum $P(t)\,\delta t$.
$t = 0$ to 1
in steps
of δt

The calculation becomes more and more accurate the smaller δt becomes, and exact when δt becomes infinitesimally small. As we saw in section 3.3, mathematicians then write dt instead of δt, and the exposure becomes

$$\int_0^1 P(t)\,dt, \tag{7.2.2}$$

i.e. the area under the $P(t)$ curve between $t = 0$ and $t = 1$.

To be able to evaluate this area, we need to know the value of $P(t)$ for every single instant between $t = 0$ and $t = 1$. However, we only know that $P(0) = 2560$, $P(0.25) = 2627$, $P(0.50) = 2689$, $P(0.75) = 2835$ and $P(1.00) = 2977$. An approximate estimate of the area under the $P(t)$ curve can be obtained by assuming that $P(t)$ changes in a linear fashion between the known values (fig. 7.2.1). The area under the curve between $t = 0$ and $t = 0.25$ is then

$$\tfrac{1}{2}\,[P(0) + P(0.25)] \times 0.25.$$

Similarly for the other sections of the curve, and we deduce that the total exposure for full-premium policyholders during 1979 is, approximately,

$$\tfrac{1}{2}\,(2560 + 2627) \times 0.25 + \tfrac{1}{2}\,(2627 + 2689) \times 0.25$$

$$+ \tfrac{1}{2}\,(2689 + 2835) \times 0.25 + \tfrac{1}{2}\,(2835 + 2977) \times 0.25,$$

Fig. 7.2.1. Values of $P(t)$ for $t = 0, 0.25, 0.50, 0.75$ and 1.00. The values at intermediate points are unknown and have been estimated by joining the known points by straight lines.

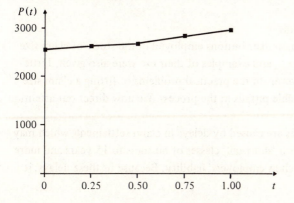

or 2729.9. The point estimate of the claim frequency rate for full-premium policyholders is, therefore,

$$364/2729.9 = 0.133.$$

The claim frequency rates for those in the 20% and 40% discount categories are obtained similarly (0.128 and 0.109 respectively). Confidence intervals can also be obtained using the method of example 7.2.1.

The method used in this example for estimating exposure is usually referred to as a *census method*. It is simpler to apply than the 'eighths' or 'twenty-fourths' methods because it automatically allows for policies terminated during the period of the investigation. Variations of the 'census method' are available, as the following example shows.

Example 7.2.3. Estimate the claim frequency rates for policyholders on full premium, 20% discount and 40% discount, using the data of example 7.2.2, but assuming that only the censuses on 1 April 1979 and 1 January 1980 are available.

In the case of the full-premium policyholders, the exposure is still given exactly by (7.2.2). The difficulty is that we only know $P(0.25) = 2627$ and $P(1.00) = 2977$. If we assume that $P(t)$ is approximately linear over the whole year and passes through these two points, the height of the $P(t)$ curve at $t = 0.5$ (the average height of the curve over the year) is $[2P(0.25) + P(1.0)]/3 = 2743.7$, and the estimated claim frequency rate is

$$364/2743.7 = 0.133.$$

Similarly, the claim frequency rates for policyholders on 20% and 40% discounts are estimated to be 0.126 and 0.109 respectively.

The reader should note that the assumption that $P(t)$ is linear over the whole year is much more likely to introduce error than the assumption that it varies linearly between quarterly censuses.

Further reading: Benjamin [3] 114–21.

7.3   Claim size; pitfalls

The more common distributions employed in the study of claim size were described in chapter 5, and examples of their use were also given. Little attention was given, however, to the practical problems of fitting a claim size distribution and the possible pitfalls in the process. We now direct our attention to these aspects.

Most of the difficulties are caused by delays in claim settlement, which may vary from a year or so with 'short-tail' classes of business to 15 years and more with 'long-tail' classes such as employers' liability. Because of these delays, it may be necessary to wait many years to estimate the mean claim size and claim size distribution in respect of claims arising from losses in a particular period, and by then the information is completely out of date.

It is tempting, therefore, to consider instead the sizes of claims actually settled in a given recent period, irrespective of their year of origin. This approach is suspect and can be positively dangerous, particularly when the rate of inflation is changing rapidly, or the rate at which new business is written changes suddenly, or the rate at which claims are settled varies.

The following examples demonstrate problems which may arise. Methods for getting around the difficulty of delay in claim settlement are described in section 7.4.

Example 7.3.1. A general insurer commenced operations in 1975 and, each year up to 1979, wrote 10 000 identical policies on 1 January. Then on 1 January 1979, the number of these yearly contracts increased 50% to 15 000. Inflation over the entire period was negligible, and the claim frequency rate remained constant at 0.1. In the year of origin 50% of claims were settled, and 50% the following year, the average settlements in those development years being $100 and $500 respectively. Calculate the average size of claims settled in each of the years 1976, 1977, 1978 and the most recently available year 1979.

The calculations are set out in table 7.3.1. Because of the sudden increase in business in 1979, settlements that year included a higher proportion of early-settled claims than previous years. Claims settled early are smaller than those settled later and, as a result, the average settled claim by year of settlement (which had remained constant at $300 from 1976 to 1978) dropped to $260 in 1979 (bottom line of table 7.3.1). The average claim settled by year of origin, on the other hand, remained constant at $300 (final column of table 7.3.1).

Example 7.3.2. The insurer described in example 7.3.1 charged a premium in 1975 and 1976 of $30. The premium charged in subsequent years was based on the observed constant claim rate of 0.1 and the average claim settled the previous year. On 1 January 1980, the insurer wrote 20 000 of these policies. He ceased to write business on 31 December 1980.

Ignoring the problem of loadings in the premium for commission and other expenses, contingencies, profit, etc., calculate

(a) the premium charged in each of the years 1977 to 1980;
(b) the total premium income of the company over the entire period of its operation;
(c) the total claim outgo of the company over the entire period of its operation.

Table 7.3.1. *Calculation of average settled claim by year of settlement and by year of origin (example 7.3.1)*

Year of origin	Year of settlement												Totals		Average claim size ($)
	1975		1976		1977		1978		1979		1980				
	No.	Amount ($)	No.	Amount ($)	No.	Amount ($)	No.	Amount ($)	No.	Amount ($)	No.	Amount ($)	No.	Amount ($)	
1975	500	50 000	500	250 000									1000	300 000	300
1976			500	50 000	500	250 000							1000	300 000	300
1977					500	50 000	500	250 000					1000	300 000	300
1978							500	50 000	500	250 000			1000	300 000	300
1979									750	75 000	750	375 000	1500	450 000	300
Total	500	50 000	1000	300 000	1000	300 000	1000	300 000	1250	325 000	750	375 000	5500	1 650 000	–
Average claim size ($)				300		300		300		260		–		–	

The average sizes of claims settled in the years 1976 to 1979 are shown on the bottom line of table 7.3.1. As the company based its premium in a given year on a claim rate of 0.1 and the average claim settled the previous year, the premiums charged in the various years would be those shown in column (2) of table 7.3.2.

The number of policies written each year is shown in column (3) of table 7.3.2, and the premium income (column (4)) is obtained by multiplying the entries in columns (2) and (3). The claim outgo figures in column (5) are taken from the penultimate line of table 7.3.1, updated to include claims in respect of year of origin 1980.

Over the entire period of operation, the insurer made an (underwriting) loss of $80 000. The loss was due solely to the invalid manner in which the premium was calculated, and was relatively small because the premium charged was inadequate in only one of the six years. It is clear, however, that an insurer with continually increasing business would be very unwise to compute his premium in this manner.

Example 7.3.3. All claims in respect of policies issued by the insurer in example 7.3.1 were settled by the end of the year following the year of issue. The appropriate premium to be charged in respect of policies written in 1980, for example, can therefore, be based on the claims experience of those written in 1978; similarly for other years. In other words, we can base the

Table 7.3.2. *Premium income and claim outgo for the insurer of example 7.3.2*

Calendar year (1)	Premium charged (2)	Number of policies (3)	Premium income (4)	Claim outgo (5)
	($)		($'000)	($'000)
1975	30	10 000	300	50
1976	30	10 000	300	300
1977	30	10 000	300	300
1978	30	10 000	300	300
1979	30	15 000	450	325
1980	26	20 000	520	475
1981	(27)	–	–	500
Total	–	75 000	2170	2250

premium on the observed constant claim frequency rate 0.1 and the most recent average claim size available in the final column of table 7.3.1, updated for 1980 year of origin.

If the insurer of examples 7.3.1 and 7.3.2 had computed his premiums in this manner, they would have been adequate. This is demonstrated in table 7.3.3.

Example 7.3.4. A general insurer commenced operation on 1 January 1975. That year, 10 000 identical policies were written (all on 1 January). The number of policies written by the insurer in subsequent years (all on 1 January) has grown at a compound rate of 30% per annum. The claim frequency rate in 1975 was 0.1, but this has grown at a compound rate of 10% per annum subsequently. Over the period, the claim settlement pattern has remained stable with 50% of claims (by number) being settled in the calendar year in which the policy was written and 50% in the subsequent year. The claim payments made in 1975 and 1976, in respect of policies issued in 1975, totalled $50 000 and $275 000 respectively, and claim sizes have grown with inflation at the rate of 10% per annum. Calculate the average size of claims settled in each of the years 1976, 1977, 1978 and 1979. Calculate also the average size of claims settled in respect of policies written in each of the years 1975, 1976, 1977, 1978 and 1979.

Table 7.3.3. *Premium income and claim outgo for the insurer of example 7.3.2, had he calculated his premiums in the manner of example 7.3.3*

Calendar year (1)	Premium charged (2)	Number of policies (3)	Premium income (4)	Claim outgo (5)
	($)		($'000)	($'000)
1975	30	10 000	300	50
1976	30	10 000	300	300
1977	30	10 000	300	300
1978	30	10 000	300	300
1979	30	15 000	450	325
1980	30	20 000	600	475
1981	(30)	–	–	500
Total	–	75 000	2250	2250

The results are shown in table 7.3.4. The calculations are quite straightforward. For example,

$$715 = 0.5 \times 10\,000 \times 1.3 \times 0.1 \times 1.1;$$
$$432\,575 = 275\,000 \times 1.3 \times 1.1 \times 1.1;$$
$$1022 = 715 \times 1.3 \times 1.1;$$
$$680\,440 = 432\,575 \times 1.3 \times 1.1 \times 1.1;$$
$$306\,115 = 194\,606 \times 1.3 \times 1.1 \times 1.1.$$

*Example 7.3.5. The insurer described in example 7.3.4 charged a premium in 1975 of \$33 and in 1976 of \$39. The premium charged in subsequent years was based on the average claim settled the previous calendar year, the observed claim frequency rate the previous year adjusted upwards by 10% (all claims are notified immediately), and inflation in claim size of 10%. The insurer ceased to write business at the end of 1979.

Ignoring the problem of loadings in the premium for commission and other expenses, contingencies, profit, etc., calculate

(a) the premium charged in each of the years 1977 to 1979;
(b) the total premium income of the company over the entire period of its operation; and
(c) the total claim outgo of the company over the entire period of its operation.

All claims were settled within two years of the date the policy was written and it would appear that the average time to settlement was no greater than 1.5 years (possibly less). Let us assume 1.5 years.

All policies written in 1977 were written on 1 January. Claims arising from these policies would be settled about 1.5 years later on average, i.e. about 30 June 1978. If we assume that claims settled in 1976 were settled on average at the middle of the year, the average claim size of claims settled in 1976 would need to be adjusted upwards at 10% per annum for two years.

The observed claim frequency rate for 1976 was $1430/13\,000 = 0.11$, so that the estimated rate for 1977 was $0.11 \times 1.10 = 0.121$. We deduce that the premium charged in 1977 was

$$0.121 \times 291 \times (1.10)^2 = \$43 \ .$$

Premiums for 1978 and 1979 are obtained similarly (table 7.3.5).

Over the entire period of operation of the company, claim outgo exceeded premium income by \$440 000 (table 7.3.6) indicating that the premiums charged were inadequate.

Table 7.3.4. *Calculation of average settled claim by year of settlement and by year of origin (example 7.3.4)*

Year of origin	Year of settlement												Totals		Average claim size ($)
	1975		1976		1977		1978		1979		1980				
	No.	Amount ($)	No.	Amount ($)	No.	Amount ($)	No.	Amount ($)	No.	Amount ($)	No.	Amount ($)	No.	Amount ($)	
1975	500	50 000	500	275 000									1000	325 000	325
1976			715	78 650	715	432 575							1430	511 225	358
1977					1022	123 716	1022	680 440					2044	804 156	393
1978							1462	194 606	1462	1 070 333			2924	1 264 939	433
1979									2091	306 115	2091	1 683 633	4182	1 989 748	476
Total	500	50 000	1215	353 650	1737	556 291	2484	875 046	3553	1 376 448	2091	1 683 633			
Average claim size ($)			291		320		352		387						—

Example 7.3.6. All claims in respect of policies issued by the insurer in example 7.3.5 were settled by the end of the year following the year of issue of the policy. The appropriate premium to be charged in respect of policies to be written in 1977 can, therefore, be based on the claim experience of those written in 1975; similarly for other years.

The average claim size in respect of policies written in 1975 was $325. Assuming no change in the settlement pattern for policies issued in 1977, the

Table 7.3.5. *Premiums charged by the insurer of example 7.3.5*

Calendar year	Base year	Average claim size in base year	Claim frequency rate	Inflation adjustment	Premium (3) × (4) × (5)
(1)	(2)	(3)	(4)	(5)	(6)
		($)			($)
1975	–	–	–	–	33*
1976	–	–	–	–	39*
1977	1976	291	0.121	1.21	43
1978	1977	320	0.133	1.21	51
1979	1978	352	0.146	1.21	62
1980	1979	387	0.161	1.21	75

* Given as data.

Table 7.3.6. *Premium income and claim outgo for the insurer of example 7.3.5*

Calendar year	Premium charged	Number of policies	Premium income	Claim outgo
(1)	(2)	(3)	(4)	(5)
	($)		($'000)	($'000)
1975	33	10 000	330	50
1976	39	13 000	507	354
1977	43	16 900	727	556
1978	51	21 970	1120	875
1979	62	28 561	1771	1376
1980	(75)	–	–	1684
Total	–	–	4455	4895

figure of $325 needs to be adjusted upwards for exactly two years inflation at 10% per annum.

The observed claim frequency rate for 1976 is known to be 0.11, so that the estimated rate for 1977 is $0.11 \times 1.10 = 0.121$ and the appropriate premium is

$$325 \times (1.10)^2 \times 0.121 = \$48 .$$

Table 7.3.7. *Premiums based on average settled claim by year of origin*

Calendar year (1)	Base year of origin (2)	Average claim size by year of origin (3)	Claim frequency rate (4)	Inflation adjustment (5)	Premium (3) × (4) × (5) (6)
		($)			($)
1975	–	–	–	–	33*
1976	–	–	–	–	39*
1977	1975	325	0.121	1.21	48
1978	1976	358	0.133	1.21	58
1979	1977	393	0.146	1.21	69
1980	1978	433	0.161	1.21	84

* Given as data.

Table 7.3.8. *Premium income and claim outgo for the insurer of example 7.3.5 had he based his premium on average settled claim by year of origin*

Calendar year (1)	Premium[a] (2)	Number of policies (3)	Premium income (4)	Claim outgo[b] (5)
	($)		($'000)	($'000)
1975	33	10 000	330	50
1976	39	13 000	507	354
1977	48	16 900	811	556
1978	58	21 970	1274	875
1979	69	28 561	1971	1376
1980	(84)	–	–	1684
Total	–	–	4893	4895

[a] table 7.3.7;
[b] table 7.3.4 (penultimate line).

If the insurer had calculated his premiums in this manner, the values would be those shown in table 7.3.7, and they would have been adequate. This is demonstrated in table 7.3.8.

Further reading: Benjamin [3] 121–2.

7.4   Claim settlement pattern

We saw, in section 7.3, that to use claims settled in a particular period to estimate the cost of claims in respect of policies in force during a given period is wrong, and can be very dangerous. Is there any alternative other than waiting, perhaps many years, until all the claims in respect of a particular base year have been settled, and then making use of this out-of-date information?

For most classes of business, the majority of claims are settled within a few years, and only a relatively small number of claims (which may be quite large) may be outstanding after, say, three years. It is possible for the insurer to construct a table like 7.4.1 representing the settlement pattern of claims in respect of policies in force many years earlier, and then apply this settlement pattern table to claims settled so far, in respect of a much more recent cohort of policies, to obtain a reasonably up-to-date estimate of average claim size. Obviously, the claim settlement pattern table needs to be continually monitored to ascertain whether it is still appropriate. Example 7.4.1 demonstrates the technique.

If, in respect of an earlier period, all claims are settled and the claim size distribution is known, and if the shape of the distribution has not changed (apart from scaling, due to inflation), then the above approach can be used to estimate the mean claim size from more recent data, and the claim size distribution can then be used to assess, for example, the effects of excesses and excess of loss reinsurance.

Apart from causing a long period to elapse before a claim amount distribution can be completed, delays in settlement mean that the sample is usually heterogeneous. In the employers' liability class of insurance, for example, court verdicts, legislation, community attitudes and money values all change with time, sometimes drastically. Claims in respect of a particular year of cover, but settled at different times, may produce quite a heterogeneous sample.

Example 7.4.1. The numbers of policies in force at the beginning of each quarter during 1979 for a particular class of business of a general insurer are shown in table 7.4.2. Claims settled by the end of 1980 in respect of incidents which occurred during 1979 number 98 and cost $48 906. An additional 10 claims have been notified, but not yet settled. Obtain

Table 7.4.1. *Claim settlement pattern for a long-tail class of business. Payments have been adjusted for inflation and expressed in constant dollars*

Duration since occurrence of incident leading to claim (quarters) (1)	Average settled claim (up to end of quarter) as a percentage of ultimate average settled claim[a] (2)	Percentage of claims settled (up to end of quarter) by	
		number (3)	amount[b] (4)
1	26	7	2
2	34	20	7
3	41	35	14
4	47	60	28
5	53	76	40
6	58	85	49
7	66	90	59
8	72	95	68
12	80	97.6	78
16	86	99.1	85
20	92	99.4	91
24	95	99.7	95
∞	100	100	100

Notes: (a) column (2) × column (3) ÷ 100 = column (4);
  (b) *excludes* payments on claims not treated as settled. The actual amount paid will usually be greater, sometimes much greater.

Table 7.4.2. *Inforce of a general insurer during 1979*

Date	Number of policies in force
1 January 1979	6213
1 April 1979	6435
1 July 1979	6522
1 October 1979	6899
1 January 1980	7138

(a) an estimate of the claim frequency rate for this class of business;

(b) an estimate of the mean claim size (in July 1979 dollars) of claims arising out of incidents during 1979;

(c) the risk premium which ought to be charged throughout 1981, assuming inflation at 15% per annum after 1 January 1980 and ignoring investment earnings; and

(d) the gross premium, assuming a loading for profit, commission, expenses and contingencies equal to 30% of the gross premium.

A record of the index of inflation appropriate to this class of business is shown in table 7.4.3. You may assume that the average time to payment of benefit following an incident is two years, and that the relevant claim settlement pattern is that shown in table 7.4.1.

(a) The exposure during 1979 can be obtained from table 7.4.2 using the census method of example 7.2.2. The mean number of policies in force is

$$\frac{1}{4}\left[\left(\frac{6213+6435}{2}\right)+\left(\frac{6435+6522}{2}\right)+\left(\frac{6522+6899}{2}\right)\right.$$
$$\left.+\left(\frac{6899+7138}{2}\right)\right]$$

or 6633.

On average, claims in respect of 1979 will have arisen out of incidents at the middle of the year. At the end of 1980, therefore, six quarters will have elapsed. According to column (3) of table 7.4.1, an estimate of the total number of claims arising from incidents in 1979 is provided

Table 7.4.3. *Inflation index*

Date	index
1 January 1972	100
1 January 1973	105
1 January 1974	115
1 January 1975	145
1 January 1976	157
1 January 1977	169
1 January 1978	183
1 January 1979	201
1 January 1980	227

by 98/0.85 = 115. So far, 98 + 10 = 108 claims have been notified. It may be that there are some incurred but not reported claims. Even if this is not so, an observed number of claims of 108 is not statistically different from an expected number of 115 (exercise 6). An estimate of the claim frequency rate is provided by 115/6633 = 0.0173.

(b) The average claim settled by the end of 1980 was 48 906 ÷ 98 = $499. This figure includes an element of inflation. Assuming an inflation rate of about 10% (table 7.4.3) for about one year (a guess at the mean time to the payment of benefit of claims settled within 18 months), the average claim settled by the end of 1980 was (in July 1979 dollars)

$$499 \div 1.10 = \$454.$$

We now make use of the entry in column (2) of table 7.4.1 to estimate the ultimate average settled claim size (in July 1979 dollars):

$$454 \div 0.58 = \$783.$$

(c) Policies written in 1981 will be written on average on 30 June 1981 and incur claims on average on 31 December 1981. From the question, we know that claim payments will be made on average two years later on 31 December 1983. Inflation during 1979 was approximately 10% per annum (table 7.4.3), and we are to assume thereafter 15% per annum. If the claim frequency rate does not change, the risk premium for 1981 should be

$$0.0173 \times 783 \times (1.10)^{\frac{1}{2}} (1.15)^4 = \$24.85.$$

(d) The various loadings consume 30% of the gross premium. As a result, 70% of the gross premium should be equal to the risk premium. It follows that the gross premium is

$$24.85/0.70 = \$35.50.$$

Example 7.4.2. Table 7.4.4 lists the payments made by an insurer in respect of claims arising out of incidents which occurred in the two-month period December 1971–January 1972. For each payment, the quarter in which the payment was made is shown in parentheses. An index of inflation relevant to this class of business was given in table 7.4.3. Obtain a claim settlement pattern akin to table 7.4.1, assuming that there are no further claims to be settled.

We first need to express all the payments in constant dollars, as on (say) 1 January 1972. On average, the incidents in the two-month period will have occurred at 1 January 1972. The $500 payment in respect of claim 19 was made in the 15th quarter or about $3\frac{5}{8}$ years after 1 January 1972. In terms of 1 January 1972 dollars, therefore, this payment was

$$500 \div \left[1.45 \times \left(\frac{157}{145} \right)^{\frac{5}{8}} \right] = 328.$$

This figure is shown in table 7.4.5. The other payments are adjusted similarly.

Column (3) in the claim settlement pattern table 7.4.6 can be derived directly from the data table 7.4.4 (2 out of the 21 claims or, 10%, were settled, for example, in the first quarter). The figures in column (4) are obtained by dividing

Table 7.4.4. *Claim payments arising in respect of incidents in the two-month period December 1971–January 1972. Claims have been ordered according to date of settlement*

Claim number	Payment (quarter)[a] ($)			
1	100 (1)			
2	100 (1)			
3	100 (1)	100 (2)		
4	100 (1)	200 (2)		
5	100 (1)	300 (3)		
6	100 (1)	100 (3)		
7	100 (1)	100 (2)	200 (3)	
8	400 (3)			
9	500 (3)	200 (4)		
10	100 (1)	600 (5)		
11	200 (3)	600 (5)		
12	200 (1)	100 (5)	500 (6)	
13	300 (3)	200 (4)	400 (6)	
14	100 (2)	100 (3)	700 (7)	
15	100 (3)	700 (6)	200 (8)	
16	800 (7)	300 (10)		
17	300 (6)	800 (12)		
18	1500 (14)			
19	1400 (12)	500 (15)		
20	200 (3)	500 (7)	2000 (19)	
21	100 (1)	800 (7)	300 (9)	1000 (22)

Note: (a) quarter 1 is the first three months following the date of the incident causing the loss.

the relevant cumulative totals (asterisked) in table 7.4.5 by the total in that table (15 143).

Column (2) in table 7.4.6 can be obtained either by dividing column (4) by column (3) or by dividing the average settled claim up to and including the relevant quarter by the ultimate average settled claim. In the case of quarter 16, for example,

$$77/90 = 0.85 = 85\%,$$

or

$$\left(\frac{11\ 636}{19}\right) \div \left(\frac{15\ 143}{21}\right) = 85\%.$$

Table 7.4.5. *Claim payments arising in respect of incidents in the two-month period December 1971–January 1972, expressed in 1 January 1972 dollars*

Claim number	Payments (quarter) ($)			Total	Cumulative total
1	99 (1)			99	99
2	99 (1)			99	198*
3	99 (1)	98 (2)		197	395
4	99 (1)	196 (2)		295	690*
5	99 (1)	291 (3)		390	1080
6	99 (1)	97 (3)		196	1276
7	99 (1)	98 (2)	194 (3)	391	1667
8	388 (3)			388	2055*
9	491 (3)	192 (4)		683	2738*
10	99 (1)	565 (5)		664	3402
11	194 (3)	565 (5)		759	4161*
12	199 (1)	94 (5)	460 (6)	753	4914
13	291 (3)	192 (4)	368 (6)	851	5765*
14	98 (2)	97 (3)	630 (7)	825	6590*
15	97 (3)	644 (6)	176 (8)	917	7507*
16	720 (7)	239 (10)		959	8466
17	276 (6)	568 (12)		844	9310*
18	1004 (14)			1004	10 314
19	994 (12)	328 (15)		1322	11 636*
20	194 (3)	450 (7)	1217 (19)	1861	13 497*
21	99 (1)	720 (7)	253 (9) 574 (22)	1646	15 143*
Total				15 143	–

Example 7.4.3. In respect of the 21 claims enumerated in table 7.4.4, calculate

(a) the mean time between incident and payment of claim benefit;
(b) the mean time between incident and settlement of claim.

(a) In calculating the mean time to payment of benefit, the intervals between incidents and payments are weighted by the sizes of the payments. To avoid inflating the mean time, it is necessary to express the claim payments in constant dollars (table 7.4.5). The payments by quarter can then be summarised as a table 7.4.7. Assuming that payments during a quarter are made on average at the mid-point of that quarter, the mean time (in quarters) between incident and payment of benefit is

$$(0.5 \times 1090 + 1.5 \times 490 + \ldots + 21.5 \times 574)/15\,143 = 7.72,$$

or slightly less than two years.

Table 7.4.6. *Claim settlement pattern (example 7.4.1). Payments have been adjusted for inflation and expressed in constant dollars*

Duration since occurrence of incident leading to claim (quarters) (1)	Average settled claim (up to end of quarter) as a percentage of ultimate average settled claim[a] (2)	Percentage of claims settled (up to end of quarter) by	
		number (3)	amount[b] (4)
1	14	10	1
2	24	19	5
3	36	38	14
4	42	43	18
5	52	52	27
6	61	62	38
7	65	67	44
8	69	71	50
12	76	81	61
16	85	90	77
20	94	95	89
24	100	100	100

Notes: (a) column (2) × column (3) ÷ 100 = column (4);
(b) *excludes* payments on claims not treated as settled.

(b) The entries in columns (2) and (3) of table 7.4.8 are obtained by differencing the entries in columns (3) and (4) respectively of table 7.4.6. The mean time (in quarters) between incident and settlement is then

$$(0.5 \times 10 + 1.5 \times 9 + \ldots + 22.5 \times 5)/100 = 6.82,$$

or about 20 months.

The above calculation gives equal weight to all claims. From the financial point of view of the insurer, the larger claims are of greater consequence, particularly as they tend to take longer to settle and as a result are more affected by inflation. The mean time (in quarters) between incident and settlement, weighted by claim size is

$$(0.5 \times 1 + 1.5 \times 4 + \ldots + 22.5 \times 11)/100 = 10.45$$

or about $2\frac{1}{2}$ years.

Example 7.4.4. The data in table 7.4.4 were collected to monitor the claim settlement pattern of an insurer. Are these data consistent with the settlement pattern in table 7.4.1?

Table 7.4.7. *Payments* (*in constant dollars*) *made each quarter in respect of the 21 claims in table 7.4.4*

Quarter	Payments made during quarter ($)
1	1090
2	490
3	2334
4	384
5	1224
6	1748
7	2520
8	176
9	253
10	239
12	1562
14	1004
15	328
19	1217
22	574
Total	15 143

According to table 7.4.1, 25% of claims should be settled in the fifth and sixth quarters combined (85 – 60 = 25). Of 21 claims, therefore, we should expect 5.2 to be settled during this period. This figure appears in the third column of table 7.4.9. The other expected numbers of claims settled are calculated similarly and are also listed.

The observed numbers of claims settled in the various periods and shown in the second column of table 7.4.9 were derived from the data in table 7.4.4. Although the sample size is small, it would appear from the figures that settlement is much slower than predicted by table 7.4.1. The same conclusion is reached when the costs of settled claims are examined (final two columns of table 7.4.9).

Statistical methods can be used to test whether the observed differences are significant or not. The chi-square test of goodness-of-fit (Pollard [26] 149–51), for example, indicates that the differences between the observed and expected numbers of claims settled are very highly significant.

Further reading: Benjamin [3] 122–4.

*7.5   Excesses and excess of loss reinsurances

The distribution function and probability-density function of the loss amount X for a certain risk are $F(x)$ and $f(x)$ respectively. Let us imagine that

Table 7.4.8. *Percentage of claims settled each quarter, by number and by amount (constant dollars)*

Quarter	Percentage settled in quarter by	
	number	amount
(1)	(2)	(3)
1	10	1
2	9	4
3	19	9
4	5	4
5	9	9
6	10	11
7	5	6
8	4	6
9–12	10	11
13–16	9	16
17–20	5	12
21–24	5	11
Total	100	100

the insurer introduces an *excess* of $A; if a loss is less than this amount, the insured meets it himself; if, on the other hand, the loss is greater, the insured meets the first $A himself and the excess is met by the insurer.

The probability that the loss will be less than $A is $F(A)$, in which case the insurer pays nothing. The probability that X lies between x and $x + \delta x$ is approximately $f(x)\,\delta x$, and if x is greater than A, the insurer must pay $x - A$. We deduce that the mean amount payable by the insurer, in respect of all losses *including those which involve no claim payment*, is

$$\int_A^\infty (x - A)\, f(x)\, dx, \tag{7.5.1}$$

which may be written

■ $$\int_A^\infty x\, f(x)\, dx - A\,[1 - F(A)], \tag{7.5.2}$$

since the integral of $Af(x)$ from A to ∞ is $A\,[1 - F(A)]$.

No claim payment is made by the insurer in a fraction $F(A)$ of all losses. The average non-zero claim payment (*excluding* losses below $A, for which no payment is made) is obtained by dividing (7.5.2) by $1 - F(A)$:

■ $$\left(\int_A^\infty x\, f(x)\, dx\right) \Big/ \left(1 - F(A)\right) - A. \tag{7.5.3}$$

The same type of argument can be used to derive the mean amount payable by the direct insurer when there is no excess, but an *excess of loss treaty* exists under which the excess of any claim over $B is met by the reinsurer. The formula turns out to be

■ $$\int_0^B x\, f(x)\, dx + B\,[1 - F(B)]. \tag{7.5.4}$$

Table 7.4.9. *Comparison of the observed claim settlement pattern in table 7.4.2 with the pattern expected according to table 7.4.1*

Period (quarters)	Claims settled during period		Costs of claims settled during period	
	Observed number	Expected number	Observed cost ($)	Expected cost ($)
1–2	4	4.2	690	1060
3–4	5	8.4	2048	3180
5–6	4	5.2	3027	3180
7–8	2	2.1	1742	2877
9–16	4	0.9	4129	2574
17+	2	0.2	3507	2271
Totals	21	21.0	15 143	15 142

General reasoning tells us that the mean amount paid by the reinsurer on a claim (*including* claims which involve no reinsurances) is given by (7.5.1) or (7.5.2) with B replacing A. The sum of (7.5.4), and (7.5.2) with B written instead of A is the mean claim size (4.1.3).

Only claims in excess of $\$B$ involve the reinsurer, and the probability that a particular claim involves the reinsurer is $1 - F(B)$. The mean amount payable by the reinsurer on any claim involving him is given, therefore, by (7.5.3) with B written instead of A.

Readers less familiar with the integral calculus and interested primarily in principles are again advised to interpret each integral as an area under a curve and forget about formal integration. Those familiar with the integral calculus, however, should actually perform the integrations implied by the examples below.

In the case of a log-normal claim size distribution with parameters μ and σ^2 (section 5.3), the mean amount met by the insured himself on any claim when there is an excess of $\$A$ is

$$\blacksquare \qquad \exp\left(\mu + \tfrac{1}{2}\sigma^2\right) \Phi\left(\frac{\ln A - \mu - \sigma^2}{\sigma}\right) + A\left[1 - \Phi\left(\frac{\ln A - \mu}{\sigma}\right)\right]. \qquad (7.5.5)$$

The derivation of this formula from (7.5.2), using (5.3.3), is set as exercise 10. The mean amount payable by the insurer is obtained by subtracting (7.5.5) from (5.3.1). The mean amounts payable by direct insurer and reinsurer, when there is an excess of loss treaty for claims over $\$B$, are obtained using the same formulae but replacing A by B.

Example 7.5.1. An insurance company has made reinsurance arrangements so that, should a claim exceed $\$3000$, the excess is paid by the reinsurer. Claim statistics reveal that the distribution function of the random variable X, being the size of a claim, is $F(x)$ where

$$F(x) = 1 - e^{-0.001x} \qquad (x \geqslant 0).$$

Calculate the mean net sum paid on a claim by the insurer after allowing for this reinsurance.

We know from example 4.1.1 that the probability-density function of the claim size is

$$f(x) = \frac{d}{dx} F(x) = 0.001\, e^{-0.001x} \qquad (x \geqslant 0),$$

and $f(x) = 0$ for $x < 0$.

According to (7.5.4), therefore, the mean net sum paid on a claim by the direct insurer is

$$\int_0^{3000} 0.001x\, e^{-0.001x}\, dx + 3000\, e^{-3.0}.$$

The integral in this formula may be obtained by estimating the area under the $g(x)$ curve in fig. 4.1.3 between $x = 0$ and $x = 3000$ (i.e. by counting the small squares on the graph paper in this region). The area is about 800, and the mean net sum payable by the direct insurer is, therefore,

$$800 + 3000\,e^{-3.0} = \$949.$$

Formal integration produces an exact answer of $\$950.21$.

Example 7.5.2. An insurer underwriting risks with the claim size distribution $F(x) = 1 - e^{-0.001x}$ proposes the introduction of a $\$500$ excess. What percentage reduction in the risk premium is theoretically possible?

The claim size probability-density function $f(x)$ is known from examples 4.1.1 and 7.5.1. According to (7.5.2), therefore, the mean amount payable by the insurer in respect of all losses, after an excess of $\$500$ is introduced is

$$\int_{500}^{\infty} 0.001x\,e^{-0.001x}\,dx \; - \; 500\,e^{-0.5}.$$

The integral in this formula can be obtained by estimating the area under the $g(x)$ curve in fig. 4.1.3 between $x = 500$ and $x = \infty$. The area is about 918. The mean amount payable by the insurer after the introduction of the excess is, therefore, $\$615$ (formal integration gives an exact answer of $\$606.53$).

Loss frequency is not (theoretically) affected by the introduction of the excess. The average claim payment per loss, on the other hand, is reduced by about 38% from $\$1000$ (example 4.1.1) to $\$615$. The risk premium could be reduced by this same percentage.

The reader should note that, by general reasoning, the reduction in this case must be less than 50%.

Example 7.5.3. A company's claim size distribution this year is seen to be approximately log-normal with mean claim size of $\$200$ and standard deviation of $\$120$. It is expected that, next year, all claims will be inflated by 10% and the company's retention under an excess of loss treaty (currently $\$1000$) will be increased by the same percentage. A policy excess of $\$100$ will also be introduced. Estimate

(a) the proportion of incidents in which the loss is borne entirely by the insured;

(b) the proportion of incidents which will involve the reinsurer;

(c) the average loss met by the insured himself;

(d) the average amount paid by the direct insurer in respect of all losses;

(e) the average amount paid by the reinsurer in respect of all losses; and

(f) the average amount paid by the reinsurer in respect of claims in which he is involved.

The effect of 10% inflation will be to change the mean and standard deviation of the claim size distribution to $220 and $132 respectively, next year. The company's retention will become $1100. Denote the loss size by X. Then, as demonstrated in example 5.3.1, we equate the log-normal mean and variance to 220 and 132 respectively, to estimate the parameters μ and σ^2:

$$\exp\left(\mu + \tfrac{1}{2}\sigma^2\right) = 220; \quad \exp\left(2\mu + \sigma^2\right)\left[\exp\left(\sigma^2\right) - 1\right] = (132)^2.$$

Dividing the second equation by the square of the first, we obtain

$$\exp\left(\sigma^2\right) - 1 = (132/220)^2,$$

whence $\sigma = 0.5545$
and $\mu = 5.240$.

(a) We require $P(X < 100)$ and this is the same as $P(\ln X < 4.605)$. Since $\ln X$ has the normal distribution with mean 5.240 and standard deviation 0.5545, the required probability is

$$\Phi\left(\frac{4.605 - 5.240}{0.5545}\right) = \Phi\left(-1.145\right) = 0.126$$

(about 1 incident in 8).
(b) We require $P(X > 1100)$ which is the same as $P(\ln X > 7.003)$, namely,

$$1 - \Phi\left(\frac{7.003 - 5.240}{0.5545}\right) = 0.000\,74$$

(about 1 incident in 1350).
(c) The average loss met by the insured himself (either wholly or in part) is given by (7.5.5) with $A = 100$, namely,

$$\exp\left(5.394\right)\Phi\left(\frac{\ln(100) - 5.547}{0.5545}\right) + 100\left[1 - \Phi\left(\frac{\ln(100) - 5.240}{0.5545}\right)\right],$$

or $97.10.
(d) The same formula with $B = 1100$, instead of A, is used to compute the average amount met by the insured and direct insurer combined in respect of all losses, namely

$$\exp\left(5.394\right)\Phi\left(\frac{\ln(1100) - 5.547}{0.5545}\right)$$

$$+ 1000\left[1 - \Phi\left(\frac{\ln(1100) - 5.240}{0.5545}\right)\right],$$

or $219.88. The average net amount paid by the direct insurer is, therefore, $(219.88 - 97.10) = $122.78.

(e) The average amount paid by the reinsurer in respect of all losses is $220 − $219.88 = $0.12.

(f) The average amount paid by the reinsurer in respect of claims which involve him is $0.12/0.000 74 = $160.[2]

Further reading: Benjamin [3] 206–18.

7.6   Exercises

1. According to the data in table 7.2.2 a householders' policy written on 3 April 1978 was terminated on 1 October 1978. As a result, the exposure according to the 'eighths' method was reduced by 93 days. The 'eighths' method, however, treats all policies written in the quarter following 1 April as having been written on 15 May (the mid-point of the quarter). It could be argued, therefore, that to be consistent with the 'eighths' method, the renewal date for the policy should be taken as 15 May and a reduction of 135 days made. Re-work example 7.2.1 following this approach in respect of all terminations.

2. Estimate the claim frequency rate for policyholders paying full premium, using the data of example 7.2.2, but assuming that only the censuses on 1 January 1979 and 1 January 1980 are available.

3. Update table 7.3.1 to include policies written in 1980 and confirm the figures in table 7.3.2.

4. Obtain 95% confidence limits for the claim frequency rate of policyholders paying full premium using the data of example 7.2.2.

5. Confirm the claim frequency rates quoted in example 7.2.2 in respect of policyholders enjoying 20% and 40% discounts respectively.

6. What is the probability of obtaining 108 or fewer claims when the expected number of claims is 115?

*7. The claim size distribution for a certain risk is log-normal with mean $980 and standard deviation $1560. The claim rate is 0.05. An excess of loss reinsurance treaty has been entered into, under which the reinsurer meets the excess of any claim over and above $2000. Calculate the reinsurance risk premium in respect of 1500 such policies.

*8. What is the general reasoning referred to in the final paragraph of the solution to example 7.5.2?
(*Hint*: Make use of the mean loss size of $1000).

**9. A normal distribution with mean μ and variance σ^2 is truncated at $x = a$ and all values of the random variable less than a are discarded. Show that the mean of the truncated distribution is

$\mu + \sigma\phi(\alpha)/(1 - \Phi(\alpha))$ where $\alpha = (a-\mu)/\sigma$.

(*Hint*: Note that $\dfrac{d}{dw} \dfrac{1}{\sqrt{(2\pi)}} \exp(-\tfrac{1}{2}w^2) = - \dfrac{w}{\sqrt{(2\pi)}} \exp(-\tfrac{1}{2}w^2)$.)

**10. Derive (7.5.5) from (7.5.2) using (5.3.3).

[2] With only two significant figures in both numerator and denominator it would be false accuracy to quote the answer to more than two significant figures.

8   EXPERIENCE RATING

Summary. In this chapter we explain the need for experience rating and introduce some elementary credibility theory which finds application in this area. We also show how Bayes' methods can be used to update estimates of a claim frequency rate in the light of experience, and examine briefly a particular form of experience rating: no claim discount (NCD).

8.1   Introduction

In section 5.9 we saw that, for most classes of general insurance, many possible sources of heterogeneity of risk exist. A premium rate based on the observed claim rate for a heterogeneous portfolio might prove quite inadequate if, as is likely, the mix of risks were to change. To reduce this danger, policies are usually grouped according to the different levels of the various risk factors involved. Claim frequency rates and premiums for the different groups are then calculated. This approach to the problem is called *group rating*. Multivariate methods can also be used to estimate the effects of the various levels of each risk factor on the claim frequency rate and premium.

Even when policies are grouped according to the different levels of various relevant risk factors, the residual heterogeneity within the groups is often still considerable. Many policies will have underlying claim frequency rates near the mean rate for the group. Some, however, will have considerably higher underlying rates, and some considerably lower, and it is desirable that we distinguish between these. We may attempt further subdivision of the groups using additional risk factors or additional intermediate levels of existing factors. This approach, however, soon produces diminishing returns, and may be impossible or at least impracticable. The solution frequently adopted is to use some form of *experience rating* whereby the premium rate for an individual (or small group of risks) depends on the claims experience of this same individual risk (or small group of risks).

Experience rating methods can be either *retrospective* or *prospective*. When, for example, a part refund of premium is made in respect of a risk (or group of risks), upon expiry of the risk and following a favourable experience, the experience rating method is retrospective. Under the no claim discount (NCD) system common in motor insurance, the premium the *following* year depends on the motorist's own experience. The NCD approach is, therefore, prospective.

If we could determine the underlying claim frequency rate for each individual policy in a large group, and were to draw the relative frequency curve of the rates, a unimodal distribution[1] like that shown in fig. 8.1.2 would probably emerge. The two-parameter gamma distribution is very versatile (section 5.5) and it is often used, therefore, to represent the distribution of the underlying claim frequency rates.

Example 8.1.1. Table 8.1.1 shows the experience of a motor insurer in respect of damage-only policies during 1979. Policies are subdivided according to two risk factors: age of policyholder (under 25 years; 25 or over) and type of vehicle (family sedan; high performance).

Table 8.1.1. *Experience of a motor insurer in respect of damage-only policies during 1979. Policies are subdivided according to two risk factors: age (under 25; 25 or over) and vehicle type (family sedan; high performance).*

Age group		25+	25+	< 25	< 25	Whole portfolio
Vehicle type		Family sedan	High performance	Family sedan	High performance	
Exposure		5826	1281	3570	1622	12 299
Number of policies experiencing n claims	$n = 0$	5019	1068	2907	1232	10 226
	$n = 1$	738	182	592	334	1846
	$n = 2$	65	27	66	50	208
	$n = 3$	4	4	5	6	19
	$n = 4$	0	0	0	0	0
Number of claims		880	248	739	452	2319
Average cost of a claim		$1020	$1486	$1097	$1413	$1171

[1] The distribution has a single peak or mode (section 4.1). A bimodal distribution would suggest that an important risk factor had been overlooked.

The risk premium, taking no account of the separate risk factors and based on these 1979 figures, would be

$$(2319/12\ 299) \times 1171 = \$221.$$

If the insurer were to charge the same premium for all policyholders based on this figure, the mature family-sedan drivers would be penalised and the young high-performance vehicle drivers subsidised. Market forces would soon ensure that the mature family-sedan drivers bought their insurance elsewhere and the young high-performance vehicle drivers were attracted to this cheap insurer. The insurer would then have to increase his premium. He should, in fact, base his premiums on separate risk premiums for the four categories. These are respectively

$$(880/5826) \times 1020 = \$154;$$
$$(248/1281) \times 1486 = \$288;$$
$$(739/3570) \times 1097 = \$227;$$
$$(452/1622) \times 1413 = \$394.$$

By subdividing the policies into these four categories, the insurer has separated the data into sub-groups which should be substantially more

Table 8.1.2. *Parameters for the claim frequency distributions and claim frequency rate distributions in respect of the data in table 8.1.1. Policies are subdivided according to two risk factors: age (under 25; 25 or over) and vehicle type (family sedan; or high performance).*

Age group		25+	25+	< 25	< 25
Vehicle type		Family sedan	High performance	Family sedan	High performance
Mean number of claims		0.151 047	0.193 599	0.207 003	0.278 668
Variance of number of claims		0.154 665	0.217 008	0.209 531	0.284 859
Negative binomial	p	0.976 607	0.892 126	0.987 935	0.978 266
parameters	k	6.305 843	1.601 078	16.950 214	12.543 190
Gamma	α	6.306	1.601	16.950	12.543
parameters	β	41.749	8.270	81.884	45.012

homogeneous than the portfolio as a whole. Let us examine whether this is the case using the negative binomial/gamma distribution method of example 5.9.2.

We begin by calculating the mean and variance of the number of claims of policyholders in each risk group using the claim frequency distributions shown in table 8.1.1. The results are given in table 8.1.2. We substitute these moments into (5.9.2) and (5.9.3) to obtain the estimates of the negative binomial parameters p and k shown in table 8.1.2 (cf example 5.9.2). The resulting negative binomial distributions should then be compared with the observed claim frequency distributions in table 8.1.1 (exercise 1).

Having confirmed that the negative binomial distributions provide adequate

Fig. 8.1.1. Gamma distributions representing heterogeneity of risk *within* each of the four risk categories: (a) over 25/family sedan, (b) over 25/high performance, (c) under 25/family sedan and (d) under 25/high performance. The means and standard deviations are, respectively: (a) 0.151, 0.60; (b) 0.194, 0.153; (c) 0.207, 0.050; and (d) 0.279, 0.079.

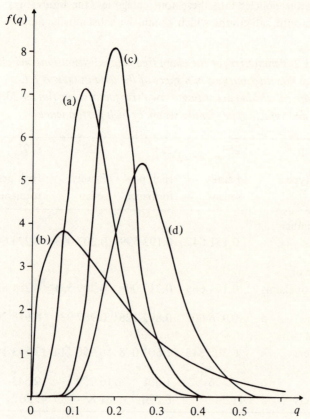

representations of the underlying claim frequency distributions, we calculate the gamma parameters shown at the bottom of table 8.1.2 using (5.9.11) and (5.9.12), and plot the distributions (fig. 8.1.1).

The gamma distribution, describing heterogeneity of risk for a particular group, will be tall and thin with a small standard deviation for a very homogeneous group, and short and broad with a large standard deviation for a heterogeneous group. It appears from fig. 8.1.1 that the risk groups (a) over 25/family sedan and (c) under 25/family sedan are both reasonably homogeneous, but that the other two groups are still quite heterogeneous, particularly (b) over 25/high performance. The introduction of another risk factor (for example, use of vehicle: business or private) might possibly reduce the remaining heterogeneity significantly.

The heterogeneity in the group (b), over 25/high performance, is in fact greater than the heterogeneity in the aggregate portfolio. This can be seen by comparing the heterogeneity distribution for the whole portfolio in fig. 8.1.2 with curve (b) in fig. 8.1.1, or by comparing standard deviations (table 8.1.3).

Fig. 8.1.2. The distribution of underlying claim frequency rates for the aggregate portfolio in example 8.1.1. (The height of this curve at any point is obtained by considering the heights of the curves in fig. 8.1.1, multiplying these by 5826, 1281, 3570 and 1622 respectively, adding and then dividing by 12 299 (table 8.1.1). The resulting curve is *not* of the gamma type, even though it looks like one and one could be drawn very close to it.)

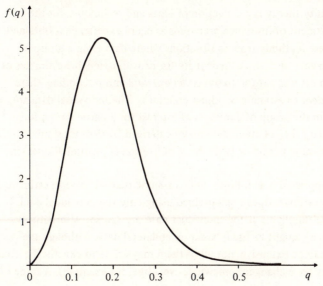

Table 8.1.3. *Mean and standard deviation of the distribution of underlying claim frequency rates: four risk groups separately, and whole portfolio*

Risk group	Distribution of claim frequency rate	
	Mean	Standard deviation
(a) 25+/family sedan	0.151	0.060
(b) 25+/high performance	0.194	0.153
(c) < 25/family sedan	0.207	0.050
(d) < 25/high performance	0.279	0.079
Whole portfolio	0.189	0.087

The heterogeneous sub-group is, however, only a small proportion of the whole portfolio (10%).

The reader should note that this approach to the examination of residual heterogeneity within classes can only be used when the data are extensive and the negative binomial parameters can be accurately estimated.

Further reading: Benjamin [3] 177–9; Johnson & Hey [15] 216–20.

8.2   Credibility theory

Credibility theory is a collection of ideas and techniques for the systematic adjustment of insurance premiums as claim experience is obtained. The need for these methods arose in situations where data from a group of contracts were scanty and hence inadequate for providing reliable estimates of the risk premium. It was natural to use *collateral data* and to combine these with *individual data* to estimate or adjust premiums. The individual data are data derived from the group of contracts of interest for a particular period (usually a year) and the collateral data may be derived from other similar contracts for the same period or from the same contracts (or similar ones) in earlier periods.

The general approach is as follows. Let us assume that we need to estimate a parameter α. An estimate $\hat{\alpha}_I$ can be obtained using only the individual data. It will, however, be unreliable if the individual data are sparse. Alternatively, another estimate $\hat{\alpha}_C$ might be used, based on collateral data. Although the collateral data may be extensive, not all of them may relate to exactly the same risk (the risk may have changed somewhat, over time, for example). A trade-off is needed between the estimate $\hat{\alpha}_C$, based on these extensive data, and the estimate $\hat{\alpha}_I$, based on the sparse individual data.[2]

The credibility theorist assigns a credibility factor Z to the individual data. The credibility factor Z is a number between 0 and 1, which is usually determined by both the individual and collateral experiences. It is close to 1 when the individual data are extensive and close to zero when they are sparse. A credibility estimate of the parameter of interest α is then given by

■ $(1 - Z)\, \hat{\alpha}_C + Z\, \hat{\alpha}_I.$ (8.2.1)

In assigning a value to Z, account is taken of

> 1. the volume of the individual data relative to the volume of the collateral data; and
> 2. differences between the individual and collateral data.
> *Further reading*: Beard *et al*. [2] 69−75.

8.3   Full credibility

Let N be the random variable representing the number of claims in respect of an insurance portfolio during a given period (a year, say). We shall denote the expected value (or mean) of N by n. It is usually appropriate to assume that N has the Poisson distribution, in which case (section 5.6),

$$E(N) = \text{Var}(N) = n. \tag{8.3.1}$$

The size of the ith claim will be a random variable X_i. We shall assume that N and $X_1, X_2, \ldots X_N$ are independent and that the claim sizes are identically distributed with expectations and variances given by

$$E(X_i) = m; \tag{8.3.2}$$

$$\text{Var}(X_i) = \sigma^2. \tag{8.3.3}$$

The conditional formulae (4.4.3) and (4.5.2) can then be used to show that the random variable,

$$C = X_1 + X_2 + \ldots + X_N, \tag{8.3.4}$$

representing the total cost of claims during the period, has expectation

$$E(C) = c = nm \tag{8.3.5}$$

and variance

$$\text{Var}(C) = n(\sigma^2 + m^2). \tag{8.3.6}$$

---

[2] Sometimes a trade-off between $\hat{\alpha}_I$ and the estimate $\hat{\alpha}_T$ based on the total data (individual and collateral) is used. Formula (8.2.1) is then replaced by

$(1 - Z)\, \hat{\alpha}_T + Z\hat{\alpha}_I.$

The proof is given in section 11.4, where α_2 is written instead of $\sigma^2 + m^2$ (α_2 is the second moment about the origin of the claim size distribution (section 4.2).

The insurer is interested in estimating the total risk premium $c = nm$ for the portfolio. At the outset, only an approximation $\hat{c}_C$ is available, based on subjective estimates of risk and claim amounts or on statistics from a similar portfolio. At the end of the year, however, the total claim cost C is known. According to section 8.2, therefore, a revised estimate of the appropriate risk premium for the following year will be given by

■ $$\hat{c}_Z = (1 - Z)\,\hat{c}_C + ZC,$$ (8.3.7)

where Z is the credibility factor.

The question naturally arises: how large should the experience be in order that the insurer can safely ignore the collateral estimate $\hat{c}_C$ and base his estimate wholly on the individual estimate C? In other words, when is an experience large enough to assign *full credibility* ($Z = 1$) to it?

The insurer might be willing to assign full credibility to the estimate C, based solely on the individual data, provided the estimate is within, say, 10% of the true value with a high probability, say, 95%. That is, when

$$P(0.9\,c < C < 1.1\,c) = 0.95,$$ (8.3.8)

or

$$P\left(\frac{-0.1c}{\sqrt{\text{Var}\,(C)}} < \frac{C - c}{\sqrt{\text{Var}\,(C)}} < \frac{0.1\,c}{\sqrt{\text{Var}\,(C)}}\right) = 0.95.$$ (8.3.9)

According to the Central Limit Theorem (section 5.2), if the experience is reasonably large $(C - c)/\sqrt{(\text{Var}\,C)}$ will be approximately distributed as a unit normal random variable. Referring to table 5.1.1, therefore, we see that

$$\frac{0.1\,c}{\sqrt{\text{Var}\,(C)}} = 1.96.$$ (8.3.10)

Substituting nm for c, (8.3.6) for Var (C), and re-arranging, we obtain

$$n = 384\,[1 + (\sigma/m)^2].$$ (8.3.11)

The coefficient 384 in this formula is the direct result of the choice of the range ± 10% of the true value and the probability level 0.95. Both these parameters were chosen arbitrarily. In the more general situation, when full credibility is defined in terms of a range of ± $100k\%$ of the true value and probability $100P\%$, the formula for the minimum number of expected claims for full credibility becomes

■ $$n_F = n_0\,[1 + (\sigma/m)^2],$$ (8.3.12)

where

$$n_0 = y^2/k^2,$$ (8.3.13)

and y is the point on the unit normal distribution such that the area between $-y$ and y is equal to P. The ratio σ/m of the standard deviation to the mean of the claim size distribution is sometimes referred to as the *coefficient of variation* of the distribution.

Values of n_0 for various combinations of k and P are shown in table 8.3.1. The entry 1082, corresponding to $k = 0.05$ and $P = 0.9$, is an often-quoted figure for full credibility.

The confidence interval approach to estimation was described in section 6.4. It should be apparent to the reader that, in determining the expected number of claims for full credibility, all we are really doing is determining the sample size required in order to produce a $100P\%$ confidence interval of a given width.

> **Example 8.3.1.** A sample of 100 claims on a general insurer in respect of a certain class of business is given in table 5.3.1. The claim frequency rate is about 0.015. Calculate the minimum size of the portfolio if full credibility ($k = 0.05, P = 0.9$) is to be assigned to the experience.

From example 5.3.1, we know that the mean m of the claim size distribution is 1216 and the variance σ^2 is 362 944. The ratio σ/m is, therefore, 0.50. Substituting this figure and the n_0 value corresponding to $k = 0.05, P = 0.9$ from table 8.3.1, into (8.3.12), we deduce that the minimum expected number of claims n_F for full credibility is 1353. We are told that the claim frequency rate is about 0.015. The minimum portfolio size for full credibility is, therefore, about 90 000 policies.

> *Further reading*: Benjamin [3] 162–5.

Table 8.3.1. *The credibility parameter n_0 corresponding to various combinations of the range parameter k and probability level P*

P \ k	0.3	0.2	0.1	0.05	0.01
			Value of n_0		
0.9	30	68	271	1082	27 060
0.95	43	96	384	1537	38 416
0.99	74	166	663	2654	66 358
0.999	120	271	1083	4331	108 274

8.4   Partial credibility

In many practical situations, the experience is too small to assign full credibility to it for rating purposes. Only partial credibility ($Z < 1$) is possible, and we need to determine Z for substitution in the credibility estimation formula (8.3.7).

In this formula, $\hat{c}_C$ is a fixed value based on collateral data prior to the experience; C is a random variable depending on the experience. If we invoke a principle of limited fluctuation whereby the credibility estimate $\hat{c}_Z$ must be in a range no wider than the full credibility range $2kc$ with probability P, then we must have ZC in the range $Zc \pm kc$ with probability P. In other words,

$$P\left[(Zc - kc) < ZC < (Zc + kc)\right] = P; \tag{8.4.1}$$

i.e.

$$P\left[\frac{-kc}{Z\sqrt{(\text{Var } C)}} < \frac{C-c}{\sqrt{(\text{Var } C)}} < \frac{kc}{Z\sqrt{(\text{Var } C)}}\right] = P. \tag{8.4.2}$$

Provided the experience is not too small, we can use the unit normal approximation for $(C - c)/\sqrt{(\text{Var } C)}$ and write

$$\frac{kc}{Z\sqrt{(\text{Var } C)}} = y, \tag{8.4.3}$$

where y is again the point on the unit normal distribution such that the area between $-y$ and y is P. Substituting nm for c, $\sqrt{n_0}$ for y/k and the formula (8.3.12) for n_F into (8.4.3) and re-arranging, we obtain the partial credibility formula

■ $$Z = \sqrt{(n/n_F)}. \tag{8.4.4}$$

Example 8.4.1. The insurer in example 8.3.1 has 19 307 policies in its portfolio. The total risk premium charged was \$366 833. Claims during the year totalled \$340 575. Obtain a credibility estimate of the risk premium the insurer should charge the following year in respect of each contract.

According to example 8.3.1 the minimum expected number of claims for full credibility is about 1353. The expected number of claims n with a portfolio of 19 307 and a claim frequency rate of about 0.015 is 290. According to (8.4.4), therefore, the partial credibility factor Z is 0.46.

The credibility estimate of the total risk premium which should be charged in respect of 19 307 policies is given by (8.3.7) with $\hat{c}_C = 366\,833$, $Z = 0.46$ and $C = 340\,575$. We obtain $\hat{c}_Z = 354\,754$. The credibility estimate of the risk premium the insurer should charge the following year in respect of each contract is, therefore,

354 754/19 307 = \$18.37,

compared with the current \$19.00.

Further reading: Beard *et al*. [2] 69–75.

*8.5 Bayes' Theorem

This important theorem is the basis of one of the fundamental approaches to statistical inference, and it finds application in the area of updating premiums and claim frequency rates in the light of experience (section 8.6). We introduce the theorem with a simple urn example.

Consider an urn containing 57 black balls and 96 red balls. Some of the balls also have a white dot on them. Indeed, 37 of the black balls do and so do 13 of of the red balls. The situation is summarised in table 8.5.1. A ball is chosen at random from the urn and it turns out to be black. What is the probability that it also has a dot?

Without too much thought, we can see that the answer is

$$37/(37 + 20),$$

which may be written

$$\frac{\frac{50}{153} \times \frac{37}{50}}{\frac{50}{153} \times \frac{37}{50} + \frac{103}{153} \times \frac{20}{103}}$$

or

$$\frac{P\,(\text{Dot})\,P\,(\text{Black}|\text{Dot})}{P\,(\text{Dot})\,P\,(\text{Black}|\text{Dot}) + P\,(\text{No dot})\,P\,(\text{Black}|\text{No dot})}$$

The latter formula is an example of Bayes' Theorem

- $$P\,(X = x_0\,|Y = y) = \frac{P\,(X = x_0)\,P\,(Y = y|X = x_0)}{\sum_x P\,(X = x)\,P\,(Y = y|X = x)}\,, \qquad (8.5.1)$$

which is readily derived using the conditional probability formula (2.3.2) (exercise 4). When the random variable X is continuous, the sum in the denominator of (8.5.1) becomes an integral.

Table 8.5.1. *Urn demonstration of Bayes' Theorem*

		Colour of ball		
		Black	Red	Total
Other	Dot	37	13	50
characteristic	No dot	20	83	103
	Total	57	96	153

It was clearly simpler to solve the above urn problem from first principles than to invoke Bayes' Theorem. The theorem, however, can be very useful with more complicated problems.

Example 8.5.1. Of the claims on a motor insurer from urban policyholders, 90% are in respect of urban incidents and 10% are in respect of non-urban incidents. The corresponding figures for non-urban policyholders are: urban 15%; non-urban 85%. It is known that 80% of the insurer's policyholders are urban dwellers.

A claim is received in respect of a non-urban incident. What is the probability that the policyholder is an urban dweller?

Let us denote the dwelling location of the policyholder by D and the incident location by L. The dwelling location D can be either urban (u) or rural (r), and the same is true of L. We are given

$P(L = u|D = u) = 0.9$;
$P(L = r|D = u) = 0.1$;
$P(L = u|D = r) = 0.15$;
$P(L = r|D = r) = 0.85$;
$P(D = u) = 0.8$;
$P(D = r) = 0.2$;

and we are required to find $P(D = u|L = r)$.

According to Bayes' formula (8.5.1),

$$P(D = u|L = r) = \frac{P(D = u)\,P(L = r|D = u)}{P(D = u)\,P(L = r|D = u) + P(D = r)\,P(L = r|D = r)}$$

$$= \frac{0.8 \times 0.1}{0.8 \times 0.1 + 0.2 \times 0.85}$$

$$= 0.32.$$

The probability that a claim in respect of a non-urban incident is from an urban policyholder is almost one in three.

Further reading: Mendenhall & Scheaffer [21] 54–5.

**8.6   A Bayesian approach to the updating of claim frequency rates

The claim frequency rate for a class of insurance business may lie anywhere between 0 and ∞. An insurer with a large experience may have a quite an accurate estimate of the rate. Nevertheless, it is an estimate and needs to be updated as further data come to hand. A new insurer in the market will have little or no data of his own upon which to base the estimate of his claim frequency rate. The estimate will be rather uncertain (based perhaps on industry statistics and certain subjective judgements), and it is imperative that it be updated as soon as the insurer obtains reliable data of his own. In either case, Bayesian methods may be employed in the updating.

The gamma distribution (section 5.5) is very convenient for representing uncertainty in the current estimate of a claim frequency rate. The distribution is over the whole positive range from 0 to ∞, and the mean α/β can be set equal to the current best estimate. Uncertainty is represented by the variance α/β^2 of the gamma distribution. A reliable estimate will have a small variance (large β) while a less reliable estimate will have a larger variance (smaller β). Both these situations are depicted in fig. 8.6.1.

Let us denote the unknown underlying claim frequency rate by Q. Our uncertainty about its actual value may be expressed by using the gamma distribution and making the statement[3]

$$P(Q = q) = \frac{\beta}{\Gamma(\alpha)} \, e^{-\beta q} \, (\beta q)^{\alpha - 1} \, dq. \qquad (8.6.1)$$

With an underlying claim frequency rate of q, and N policies, the distribution of the number of claims Y will be Poisson with mean Nq, and we can write

$$P(Y = y | Q = q) = \frac{e^{-Nq} \, (Nq)^y}{y!}. \qquad (8.6.2)$$

Fig. 8.6.1. Two Bayesian prior distributions for the claim frequency rate q. Both have the same mean 0.125. The variance of distribution (b) is only one third of the variance of (a), indicating considerably less uncertainty.

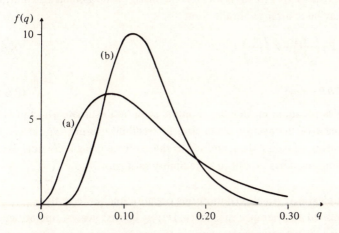

[3] Strictly speaking, the left-hand side of (8.6.1) should be written $P(q < Q \leqslant q + dq)$. We shall, however, adopt the more concise form.

A year now goes by and y claims are sustained by the N policies in force. We need to update our best estimate of the unknown underlying claim frequency rate Q and our measure of uncertainty surrounding it. In other words, we need to update our prior distribution of Q, given by (8.6.1), and obtain $P(Q = q|Y = y)$.

Bayes' Theorem is very useful for this purpose. According to (8.5.1) we can write[4]

$$P(Q = q|Y = y) = \frac{P(Q = q) P(Y = y|Q = q)}{\int_{q=0}^{\infty} P(Q = q) P(Y = y|Q = q)}.$$ (8.6.3)

Substituting (8.6.1) and (8.6.2) for the probabilities in the right-hand side of this equation, and simplifying, we obtain

■ $$P(Q = q|Y = y) = \frac{B}{\Gamma(A)} e^{-Bq} (Bq)^{A-1} dq,$$ (8.6.4)

where

■ $$A = \alpha + y;$$ (8.6.5)

■ $$B = \beta + N.$$ (8.6.6)

The effect of the additional information is to increase the α-parameter by y and the β-parameter by N. The best estimate of the underlying claim frequency rate Q changes from α/β to $(\alpha + y)/(\beta + N)$. The distribution remains gamma, and the process (which is very simple) can be repeated as soon as further data come to hand.

It is worth noting that the updated best estimate of the underlying claim frequency rate Q is $(\alpha + y)/(\beta + N)$, which is the mean of the gamma distribution (8.6.4), and may be re-arranged in the form

$$(1 - Z)\left(\frac{\alpha}{\beta}\right) + Z\left(\frac{y}{N}\right),$$ (8.6.7)

where

$$Z = P/(P + m\alpha),$$ (8.6.8)

P is the total risk premium income based on the prior best estimate α/β, and m is the prior estimate of the average claim size. In credibility terms, α/β is the estimate of Q using collateral data, and y/N is the estimate using individual data. The Bayesian approach has produced a credibility estimator.

Example 8.6.1. A national motoring organisation has recently established an insurance subsidiary. During its first year of operation, the insurer based his premium scale on the published industry claim frequency

---

[4] See footnote 3 on page 163.

rate two years earlier, namely, 0.148. The management was aware of the uncertainty involved in using this figure, but felt it highly probable that the underlying rate for their operation would lie within about 25% of it. The average number of policies in force during the first year of operation was 2427, and 320 claims were incurred. Obtain an updated estimate of the underlying claim frequency rate for the insurer.

Let us equate the management's subjective judgement that it is highly probable that the true underlying rate will lie within about 25% of the assumed rate of 0.148 with two standard deviations. In other words, one standard deviation is, approximately,

$$\frac{1}{2} \times 0.25 \times 0.148 = 0.0185.$$

An assumed gamma prior distribution for the unknown underlying claim frequency rate Q will, therefore, have

$$\text{mean} = \alpha/\beta = 0.148,$$

and

$$\text{variance} = \alpha/\beta^2 = (0.0185)^2.$$

Dividing the mean by the variance, we deduce that $\beta = 432.5$ and, by back substitution in the mean, that $\alpha = 64.0$.

The updated gamma parameters are calculated as follows using (8.6.5) and (8.6.6):

$$A = 64.0 + 320 = 384.0;$$
$$B = 432.5 + 2427 = 2859.5.$$

Fig. 8.6.2. Bayesian prior distributions of the claim frequency rate q: (a) before the first year's experience; (b) after the first year's experience; and (c) after the first and second years' experiences.

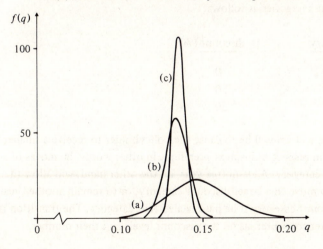

The updated estimate of the underlying claim frequency rate is $A/B = 0.134$. The gamma distributions prior to, and after the year's experience, are shown in fig. 8.6.2 (curves (a) and (b) respectively).

Example 8.6.2. During the second year of operation of the insurer in example 8.6.1, the average number of policies in force was 6982 and 951 claims were incurred. Obtain an updated estimate of the insurer's underlying claim frequency rate as at the end of the second year's operation.

The gamma parameters are updated as follows using (8.6.5) and (8.6.6):

$$A = 384.0 + 951 = 1335.0;$$
$$B = 2859.5 + 6982 = 9841.5.$$

The updated estimate of the claim frequency rate is, therefore, $A/B = 0.136$.

The updated gamma distribution is included in fig. 8.6.2 as curve (c). Note the increasing certainty about the underlying claim frequency rate as further data are accumulated.

Further reading: Benjamin [3] 165–6; De Vylder [7] 19–27*.

8.7   No claim discount (NCD)

We have already alluded to the fact that a person effecting a motor car policy for the first time is initially group rated according to such risk factors as age, type of car, financial encumbrance, etc. (section 8.1). The new policyholder starts by paying, in his first year, the full premium appropriate to his group. Thereafter, the premium he pays depends on his own experience.

If, during that first year, he makes no claim on the insurer, his next premium will be reduced by a discount, which may be, say, 30%. A further claim-free year might result in an even greater discount, an extra 20%, say. We shall number the various discount categories as follows:

category	discount (%)
0	0
1	30
2	50

The effect of a claim will be to cause the policyholder to receive a smaller (or zero) discount in respect of his next premium. In other words, he moves to a lower discount category. A claim-free year, on the other hand, will allow the policyholder to move to a larger discount category, or to remain another year in the largest discount category if he has reached that category. The transition rules vary from insurer to insurer, as do the discount levels and their number.

The *bonus-malus system*, popular on the Continent of Europe, is really a variation of the NCD system whereby a policyholder with a poor claim record may receive a negative discount (i.e. pay more than the "full" premium).

The concept of no claim discount appears to have been developed in the early days of motor insurance with the idea of encouraging good risks to renew with the same company. The discount in the early days was small. Nowadays, the maximum discount may be as much as 60%.

Arguments put forward in support of an NCD system include the following.

1. An NCD system helps reduce heterogeneity within rating categories.
2. It also discourages small claims and so reduces claim costs and management expenses.
3. It may enable an insurer to charge premiums which more closely reflect individual risks.
4. It may encourage safer driving.

We shall see that the NCD system does not reduce heterogeneity very much, so that the insurer is not really able to charge premiums closely reflecting individual risks. It does discourage small claims, but there is little evidence that it encourages safer driving. The system is, however, firmly established in the motor insurance markets of many countries and it is not really possible for an insurer to follow a different approach if he wishes to obtain and maintain a share of the market. NCD has only been used to a limited extent in respect of other classes of business.

Example 8.7.1. An NCD system involves three levels of discount: 0%, 30% and 50%. In the event of a claim-free year, the policyholder moves to the immediately higher discount level. A claim causes the policyholder to move back to the zero discount category. If the full premium is $100, how large should a loss be before it is worthwhile for a policyholder to make a claim?

Let us imagine first that the policyholder has a one-year time horizon. He will compare the size of the loss with the increase in premium the following year if a claim is made, and only make a claim if the latter is smaller than the former. A policyholder in category 0 (no discount) will make a claim if the loss exceeds $30. For discount categories 1 (30%) and 2 (50%), the minimum losses to make claiming worthwhile are both $50. These figures are shown in row (3) of table 8.7.1.

The minimum worthwhile claim amounts for motorists with two- and three-year time horizons are shown in rows (7) and (11) of table 8.7.1. The figures all assume that no further losses occur before the time horizon is reached.

Note that, in respect of an NCD system with $n + 1$ categories $0, 1, 2, \ldots,$

n, time horizons up to n years need to be considered. In practice, most of the effect on premium payments of claiming is felt in the first few years. Furthermore, a policyholder is unlikely to have a time horizon beyond two years. If he did, allowance ought to be made for compound interest and the likelihood of further losses. These points need to be borne in mind in the simulation example 9.11.1.

Example 8.7.2. How would your answer to example 8.7.1 be altered if the step-back rule were one category per claim instead of automatically moving back to the full-premium category?

The calculations are set out in table 8.7.2 for the various possible time horizons. As we might expect, only policyholders in category 2 at the time of the loss are affected.

*Example 8.7.3. In this example we shall assume that the claim frequency rate of a policyholder is unaffected by the NCD category he is in. From examples 8.7.1 and 8.7.2, we know that this is not strictly true, but

Table 8.7.1. *The cost of making a claim in terms of discounts foregone (example 8.7.1)*

NCD category at time of loss (year 0)		0	1	2
		($)	($)	($)
Year 1				
Premium if claim in year 0	(1)	100	100	100
Premium if no claim in year 0	(2)	70	50	50
Difference: (1) – (2)	(3)	30	50	50
Year 2				
Premium if claim in year 0	(4)	70	70	70
Premium if no claim in year 0	(5)	50	50	50
Difference: (4) – (5)	(6)	20	20	20
Cumulative difference: (3) + (6)	(7)	50	70	70
Year 3				
Premium if claim in year 0	(8)	50	50	50
Premium if no claim in year 0	(9)	50	50	50
Difference: (8) – (9)	(10)	0	0	0
Cumulative difference: (7) + (10)	(11)	50	70	70

to make allowance for it we would need to know the distribution of loss size, and the mathematical analysis then becomes more complicated (example 8.7.6). The problem can also be handled by simulation (example 9.11.1).

We shall assume that irrespective of his NCD category, the policyholder has a claim frequency rate of q, so that the probabilities p_0, p_1 and p_{2+} of 0, 1 and more than 1 claim during the year are given by the Poisson distribution as follows:

$$p_0 = e^{-q};$$ (8.7.1)

$$p_1 = qe^{-q};$$ (8.7.2)

$$p_{2+} = 1 - p_0 - p_1.$$ (8.7.3)

The step-back rule is that given in example 8.7.2. The transition matrix of the process is a two-way table showing the probability of moving from category i ($i = 0, 1, 2$) to category j ($j = 0, 1, 2$):

$$\begin{array}{c} \\ i=0 \\ i=1 \\ i=2 \end{array} \begin{array}{ccc} j=0 & j=1 & j=2 \\ \left[\begin{array}{ccc} 1-p_0 & p_0 & 0 \\ 1-p_0 & 0 & p_0 \\ 1-p_0-p_1 & p_1 & p_0 \end{array}\right] \end{array}$$

Table 8.7.2. *The cost of making a claim in terms of discounts foregone (example 8.7.2).*

NCD category at time of loss (year 0)		0 ($)	1 ($)	2 ($)
Year 1				
Premium if claim in year 0	(1)	100	100	70
Premium if no claim in year 0	(2)	70	50	50
Difference: (1) – (2)	(3)	30	50	20
Year 2				
Premium if claim in year 0	(4)	70	70	50
Premium if no claim in year 0	(5)	50	50	50
Difference: (4) – (5)	(6)	20	20	0
Cumulative difference: (3) + (6)	(7)	50	70	20
Year 3				
Premium if claim in year 0	(8)	50	50	50
Premium if no claim in year 0	(9)	50	50	50
Difference: (8) – (9)	(10)	0	0	0
Cumulative difference: (7) + (10)	(11)	50	70	20

Let us assume that there are initially 10 000 policyholders all in category 0. Furthermore, they remain with the insurer from one year to the next. Matrix theory tells us that, after several years, the number of policyholders in the various categories will become stable (Pollard [25] 37–50). If x_i denotes the stable number of policies in category i, the following relationships must hold:

$$x_0 + x_1 + x_2 = 10\ 000; \tag{8.7.4}$$

$$x_0 = (x_0 + x_1)(1 - p_0) + x_2(1 - p_0 - p_1); \tag{8.7.5}$$

$$x_1 = x_0 p_0 + x_2 p_1; \tag{8.7.6}$$

$$x_2 = (x_1 + x_2) p_0. \tag{8.7.7}$$

Equation (8.7.4) states that the total number of policyholders in the risk group is 10 000. Equations (8.7.5)–(8.7.7) then describe the movement of policyholders between categories in successive years, assuming a stable position has been reached. For example, equation (8.7.5) says that the number of policyholders in category 0 is equal to a proportion $(1 - p_0)$ of policyholders in categories 0 and 1 the previous year (who experienced at least one claim), plus a proportion $(1 - p_0 - p_1)$ of those in category 2 (who experienced at least two claims).

From (8.7.7)

$$x_1 = x_2(1 - p_0)/p_0, \tag{8.7.8}$$

and from (8.7.6)

$$x_0 = (x_1 - x_2 p_1)/p_0. \tag{8.7.9}$$

Substituting (8.7.8) into (8.7.9) we have

$$x_0 = x_2(1 - p_0 - p_0 p_1)/p_0^2. \tag{8.7.10}$$

When (8.7.10) and (8.7.8) are substituted into (8.7.4), we obtain

$$x_2(1 - p_0 - p_0 p_1)/p_0^2 + x_2(1 - p_0)/p_0 + x_2 = 10\ 000, \tag{8.7.11}$$

whence

$$x_2 = 10\ 000\ p_0^2/(1 - p_0 p_1). \tag{8.7.12}$$

We deduce from (8.7.8) and (8.7.10) that

$$x_1 = 10\ 000\ p_0(1 - p_0)/(1 - p_0 p_1); \tag{8.7.13}$$

$$x_0 = 10\ 000\ (1 - p_0 - p_0 p_1)/(1 - p_0 p_1). \tag{8.7.14}$$

Numerical values of x_0, x_1 and x_2 are shown in table 8.7.3 for two separate values of the claim frequency rate q:

    (a) $q = 0.1$;
    (b) $q = 0.2$.

In both cases, category 2 contains the vast majority of policyholders.

Example 8.7.4. A motor insurer operates an NCD system with three categories of discount: 0% (category 0), 30% (category 1) and 50% (category 2). The full premium is $200. In the event of a claim-free year, a policyholder moves forward to the immediately higher discount category, or remains in the highest category if he has already reached it. The step-back rule in respect of claims is one category per claim.

The insurer has 20 000 policyholders on his books. Of these, 10 000 are good risks with claim frequency rate $q = 0.1$, and 10 000 are poor risks with $q = 0.2$. According to the calculations in example 8.7.3, we would expect to find, after a few years, 145 of the good risk policyholders in category 0, 938 in category 1 and 8917 in category 2. The total premium income from the good risks would be

$$145 \times 200 + 938 \times 200 \times 0.70 + 8917 \times 200 \times 0.50 = \$1\ 052\ 020.$$

At the same time, we would expect 545 of the poor risks to be in category 0, 1714 to be in category 1, and 7741 to be in category 2 (table 8.7.3). The total premium income from this group would be

$$545 \times 200 + 1714 \times 200 \times 0.70 + 7741 \times 200 \times 0.50 = \$1\ 123\ 060.$$

The average poor risk will pay, therefore, only 7% more for his insurance than the average good risk. His claim frequency rate, however, is twice that of the good risk, and he should really be paying twice the premium of the good risk (assuming the same average claim size for both low- and high-risk policyholders).

Table 8.7.3. *Stable numbers in NCD categories 0, 1 and 2 corresponding to $q = 0.1$ and $q = 0.2$ (example 8.7.3)*

Claim frequency rate q		0.1	0.2
e^{-q}		0.904 84	0.818 73
$p_0 = e^{-q}$		0.904 84	0.818 73
$p_1 = q\,e^{-q}$		0.090 48	0.163 75
$p_{2+} = 1 - p_0 - p_1$		0.004 68	0.017 52
Stable number in NCD categories 0, 1 and 2	x_0	145	545
	x_1	938	1714
	x_2	8917	7741

We shall see in example 8.7.5 that this inequity is also present in the years preceding stability. We conclude, therefore, that this NCD system does little to reduce heterogeneity of risk. The same can be said of all such systems.

*Example 8.7.5. All 20 000 policyholders of the motor insurer described in example 8.7.4 commence in category 0 at time $t = 0$. Calculate the expected number of the low-risk ($q = 0.1$) and high-risk ($q = 0.2$) policyholders in the various NCD categories during the first five years of the portfolio, the premium receipts each year for the low- and high-risk categories and the ratios of these receipts.

Equations (8.7.4) to (8.7.7) describe the behaviour of this system once stability has been reached. Prior to stability the numbers in the various categories will change from year to year. Let us, therefore, denote the number in category i during the year of interest by X_i and the number in that category the previous year by x_i. The equations connecting the X_i and x_i are then simple modifications of (8.7.5), (8.7.6) and (8.7.7), namely,

$$X_0 = (x_0 + x_1)(1 - p_0) + x_2(1 - p_0 - p_1); \qquad (8.7.15)$$

$$X_1 = x_0 p_0 + x_2 p_1; \qquad (8.7.16)$$

$$X_2 = (x_1 + x_2) p_0. \qquad (8.7.17)$$

The explanation is given under (8.7.7).

Initially, for the low-risk group, $x_0 = 10\,000$, $x_1 = 0$ and $x_2 = 0$. Substituting these values, and $p_0 = 0.904\,84$, $p_1 = 0.090\,48$ (from table 8.7.3) into (8.7.15), (8.7.16) and (8.7.17), we obtain the expected numbers in the various categories at time 1, namely, $X_0 = 952$, $X_1 = 9048$ and $X_2 = 0$. We then repeat the process with $x_0 = 952$, $x_1 = 9048$ and $x_2 = 0$ to obtain the expected numbers at time 2: $X_0 = 952$, $X_1 = 861$ and $X_2 = 8187$; and so on. Similarly for the high-risk group. Premium receipts are calculated in exactly the same manner as in example 8.7.4.

The results are summarised in table 8.7.4. It is clear from column (10) that the NCD system is not very successful in separating the two levels of risk. Ideally, the ratio should be 2.0 (assuming the same average claim size for both low- and high-risk policyholders).

**Example 8.7.6. An insurer operates an NCD system with discounts 0%, 30% and 50%. In the event of at least one claim during the year, the policyholder moves back one position (i.e. from 50% discount to 30% discount, or from 30% discount to 0% discount), or remains in the 0% discount position. In the event of a claim-free year, on the other hand, the policyholder moves to the next larger discount level (i.e. from 0% to 30% discount, or from 30% to 50% discount) or remains in the largest discount category (50%).

Table 8.7.4. *Motor insurance portfolio with 10 000 policyholders at low risk (q = 0.1) and 10 000 policyholders at high risk (q = 0.2): Numbers of low-risk and high-risk policyholders in the various NCD categories, premium receipts and ratio of high-risk to low-risk premium receipts during the early years of the portfolio.*

Year t	Low-risk group Number in category			Total premiums	High-risk group Number in category			Total premiums	Ratio of premiums (9)/(5)
	0	1	2		0	1	2		
(1)	(2)	(3)	(4)	(5)	(6)	(7)	(8)	(9)	(10)
				$'000				$'000	
0	10 000	0	0	2000	10 000	0	0	2000	1.00
1	952	9048	0	1457	1813	8187	0	1509	1.04
2	952	861	8187	1130	1813	1484	6703	1241	1.10
3	211	1602	8187	1085	715	2582	6703	1175	1.08
4	211	932	8857	1058	715	1683	7602	1139	1.08
5	150	993	8857	1055	568	1830	7602	1130	1.07
8	145	938	8917	1052	545	1714	7741	1123	1.07

(a) The full office premium for these insurance contracts is $300 per annum. Calculate the size of claim below which it is not worthwhile claiming, assuming that the policyholder has a two-year time horizon.
(b) The loss size distribution for this portfolio is known to be lognormal with parameters $\mu = 6.012$ and $\sigma^2 = 1.792$. Calculate the probability that, in respect of a given loss, a policyholder with a two-year time horizon will choose to claim under the policy.
(c) On the assumption that all policyholders have the same loss incidence rate of 0.1 and the same two-year time horizon, obtain the underlying transition matrix for the policyholders of the company, and estimate the proportions of policyholders in the various NCD categories in a stationary non-growth situation.

(a) Using the method of examples 8.7.1 and 8.7.2, we find that the loss below which it is not worthwhile claiming is $150 for a policyholder on full premium, $210 for a policyholder in the 30% discount category, and $60 for a policyholder in the 50% discount category.
(b) A policyholder paying the full premium will claim if the loss is above $150. The probability that the loss is above $150 is equal to the probability that the logarithm of the loss is above 5.011. But the logarithm of the loss has the normal distribution with mean 6.012 and variance 1.792 (section 5.3). For a policyholder paying full premium, therefore, the probability that he will claim for a particular loss is

$$1 - \Phi\left((5.011 - 6.012)/\sqrt{(1.792)} \right) = 0.773.$$

The probabilities in respect of policyholders in the other two discount classes are 0.691 and 0.923 respectively.
(c) A policyholder paying full premium has a loss frequency rate of 0.1, but he will only claim in respect of a fraction, 0.773, of claims. His claim frequency rate is, therefore, 0.0773. For such a policyholder, the probabilities of no claims during the year and at least one claim are, according to the Poisson distribution with mean 0.0773,

$$p_0 = e^{-0.0773} = 0.9256,$$

and

$$p_{1+} = 1 - 0.9256 = 0.0744$$

respectively. For a policyholder in the 30% discount category the corresponding probabilities are 0.9332 and 0.0668; and for a policyholder in the 50% discount category, 0.9118 and 0.0882.

The required transition matrix is therefore,

$$\begin{pmatrix} 0.0744 & 0.9256 & 0 \\ 0.0668 & 0 & 0.9332 \\ 0 & 0.0882 & 0.9118 \end{pmatrix}.$$

Let us denote the proportions of policyholders in NCD categories 0%, 30% and 50% in the stationary state by x_0, x_1 and x_2. Then, the following equations must be true:

$$\begin{cases} x_0 + x_1 + x_2 = 1; \\ x_0 = 0.0744\,x_0 + 0.0668\,x_1; \\ x_1 = 0.9256\,x_0 + 0.0882\,x_2; \\ x_2 = 0.9332\,x_1 + 0.9118\,x_2. \end{cases}$$

Solving these simultaneous equations, we obtain the required proportions:

$$x_0 = 0.0062;$$
$$x_1 = 0.0858;$$
$$x_2 = 0.9080.$$

Further reading: Benjamin [3] 181–205; Johnson & Hey [15] 199–232.

8.8   Exercises

1. The four pairs of negative binomial parameters in table 8.1.2 were derived using the data in table 8.1.1. Examine the goodness-of-fit of the negative binomial distributions.

2. Deduce (8.4.4) from (8.4.3).

3. The insurer in example 8.3.1 has 5000 policies in his portfolio. The total risk premium received during the year was $95 000, and claims totalled $88 200. Obtain a credibility estimate of the risk premium the insurer should charge the following year in respect of each contract. Ignore inflation and investment income.

*4. (a) Use the conditional probability formula

$P[(Y = y) \cap (X = x)] = P(Y = y|X = x)\,P(X = x)$

to prove that

$P(Y = y) = \sum_x P(Y = y|X = x)\,P(X = x).$

(b) Deduce Bayes' formula (8.5.1) using the above formulae as well as

$P(X = x|Y = y) = P[(Y = y) \cap (X = x)]/P(Y = y).$

(*Note*: All these formulae are derived from (2.3.2).)

*5. Use the data of example 8.5.1 to find the probability that a claim in respect of an incident which occurred in an urban area is from an urban policyholder.

**6. Confirm (8.6.4).

**7. Confirm (8.6.8).

*8. An NCD system involves three levels of discount: 0%, 30% and 50%. In the event of a claim-free year, the policyholder moves to the immediately higher discount level. A claim causes the policyholder to move back to the zero discount category.

(a) Write down the equations connecting the numbers of policyholders in the various categories once stability has been achieved. Assume a total of 10 000 policyholders and no exits.

(b) Solve these equations and obtain numerical values for the numbers in the various categories when the underlying claim frequency rate is

(i) $q = 0.1$;
(ii) $q = 0.2$.

(c) Is this NCD system any better at distinguishing high from low risks than the system studied in example 8.7.4?

(d) Assuming that all 10 000 policyholders are in category 0 at time $t = 0$, estimate the expected numbers in the various categories at times $t = 1, 2, 3, 4$ and 5.

**9. How would your answer to part (c) of example 8.7.6 be altered if policyholders took no account of loss of NCD benefits?

9 SIMULATION

Summary. Simulation can be a useful technique for solving quite difficult problems in general insurance. In this chapter we introduce some of the basic ideas and give a few elementary examples. We conclude with a more complicated NCD simulation example.

9.1 Random numbers and simulation

Problems often arise in statistical analysis which call for the use of random numbers. Survey samplers use such numbers to select random individuals from a population in order to estimate the parameters of the population. Experimental agriculturalists often find it necessary to assign different treatments (for example, fertilisers) to different blocks in a random manner in order to avoid biasing comparisons between treatments. Such an assignment relies on random numbers.

The theoretician may use random numbers to study the distribution of a complicated random variable which is defined in terms of other random variables with known distributions. Random observations on the variables with known distributions are generated using random numbers, and these random observations are then used to calculate random observations on the complicated random variable. From the simulated values, the theoretician can make inferences about the unknown distribution (shape, mean, variance, skewness, etc.).

Various tables of random numbers have been published. For example:

Fisher, R.A. and Yates, F. (1963). *Statistical Tables for Use in Biological, Agricultural and Medical Research* (sixth edition). Oliver and Boyd.

Rand Corporation. (1955). *A Million Random Digits and 100 000 Normal Deviates.* The Free Press, Glencoe, Illinois.

These tables are made up of equally-likely decimal digits arranged in groups, and the groups usually contain five digits, although some tables use smaller groupings. Table 9.1.1 (from a more extensive table prepared by the Bureau of Transport Economics and Statistics of the Interstate Commerce Commission, Washington D.C.) uses groups of five. Individual digits, or pairs of digits or

Table 9.1.1. *A table of random numbers*

Line/Col.	(1)	(2)	(3)	(4)	(5)	(6)	(7)	(8)	(9)	(10)	(11)	(12)	(13)	(14)
1	10 480	15 011	01 536	02 011	81 647	91 646	69 179	14 194	62 590	36 207	20 969	99 570	91 291	90 700
2	22 368	46 573	25 595	85 393	30 995	89 198	27 982	53 402	93 965	34 095	52 666	19 174	39 615	99 505
3	24 130	48 360	22 527	97 265	76 393	64 809	15 179	24 830	49 340	32 081	30 680	19 655	63 348	58 629
4	42 167	93 093	06 243	61 680	07 856	16 376	39 440	53 537	71 341	57 004	00 849	74 917	97 758	16 379
5	37 570	39 975	81 837	16 656	06 121	91 782	60 468	81 305	49 684	60 672	14 110	06 927	01 263	54 613
6	77 921	06 907	11 008	42 751	27 756	53 498	18 602	70 659	90 655	15 053	21 916	81 825	44 394	42 880
7	99 562	72 905	56 420	69 994	98 872	31 016	71 194	18 738	44 013	48 840	63 213	21 069	10 634	12 952
8	96 301	91 977	05 463	07 972	18 876	20 922	94 595	56 869	69 014	60 045	18 425	84 903	42 508	32 307
9	89 579	14 342	63 661	10 281	17 453	18 103	57 740	84 378	25 331	12 566	58 678	44 947	05 585	56 941
10	85 475	36 857	53 342	53 988	53 060	59 533	38 867	62 300	08 158	17 983	16 439	11 458	18 593	64 952
11	28 918	69 578	88 231	33 276	70 997	79 936	56 865	05 859	90 106	31 595	01 547	85 590	91 610	78 188
12	63 553	40 961	48 235	03 427	49 626	69 445	18 663	72 695	52 180	20 847	12 234	90 511	33 703	90 322
13	09 429	93 969	52 636	92 737	88 974	33 488	36 320	17 617	30 015	08 272	84 115	27 156	30 613	74 952
14	10 365	61 129	87 529	85 689	48 237	52 267	67 689	93 394	01 511	26 358	85 104	20 285	29 975	89 868
15	07 119	97 336	71 048	08 178	77 233	13 916	47 564	81 056	97 735	85 977	29 372	74 461	28 551	90 707
16	51 085	12 765	51 821	51 259	77 452	16 308	60 756	92 144	49 442	53 900	70 960	63 990	75 601	40 719
17	02 368	21 382	52 404	60 268	89 368	19 885	55 322	44 819	01 188	65 255	64 835	44 919	05 944	55 157
18	01 011	54 092	33 362	94 904	31 273	04 146	18 594	29 852	71 585	85 030	51 132	01 915	92 747	64 951
19	52 162	53 916	46 369	58 586	23 216	14 513	83 149	98 736	23 495	64 350	94 738	17 752	35 156	35 749
20	07 056	97 628	33 787	09 998	42 698	06 691	76 988	13 602	51 851	46 104	88 916	19 509	25 625	58 104
21	48 663	91 245	85 828	14 346	09 172	30 168	90 229	04 734	59 193	22 178	30 421	61 666	99 904	32 812
22	54 164	58 492	22 421	74 103	47 070	25 306	76 468	26 384	58 151	06 646	21 524	15 227	96 909	44 592
23	32 639	32 363	05 597	24 200	13 363	38 005	94 342	28 728	35 806	06 912	17 012	64 161	18 296	22 851
24	29 334	27 001	87 637	87 308	58 731	00 256	45 834	15 398	46 557	41 135	10 367	07 684	36 188	18 510
25	02 488	33 062	28 834	07 351	19 731	92 420	60 952	61 280	50 001	67 658	32 586	86 679	50 720	94 953
26	81 525	72 295	04 839	96 423	24 878	82 651	66 566	14 778	76 797	14 780	13 300	87 074	79 666	95 725
27	29 676	20 591	68 086	26 432	46 901	20 849	89 768	81 536	86 645	12 659	92 259	57 102	80 428	25 280
28	00 742	57 392	39 064	66 432	84 673	40 027	32 832	61 362	98 947	96 067	64 760	64 584	96 096	98 253
29	05 366	04 213	25 669	26 422	44 407	44 048	37 937	63 904	45 766	66 134	75 470	66 520	34 693	90 449
30	91 921	26 418	64 117	94 305	26 766	25 940	39 972	22 209	71 500	64 568	91 402	42 416	07 844	69 618

31	00 582	04 711	87 917	77 341	42 206	35 126	74 087	99 547	81 817	42 607	43 808	76 655	62 028	76 630
32	00 725	69 884	62 797	56 170	86 324	88 072	76 222	36 086	84 637	93 161	76 038	65 855	77 919	88 006
33	69 011	65 795	95 876	55 293	18 988	27 354	26 575	08 625	40 801	59 920	29 841	80 150	12 777	48 501
34	25 976	57 948	29 888	88 604	67 917	48 708	18 912	82 271	65 424	69 774	33 611	54 262	85 963	03 547
35	09 763	83 473	73 577	12 908	30 883	18 317	28 290	35 797	05 998	41 688	34 952	37 888	38 917	88 050
36	91 567	42 595	27 958	30 134	04 024	86 385	29 880	99 730	55 536	84 855	29 080	09 250	79 656	73 211
37	17 955	56 349	90 999	49 127	20 044	59 931	06 115	20 542	18 059	02 008	73 708	83 517	36 103	42 791
38	46 503	18 584	18 845	49 618	02 304	51 038	20 655	58 727	28 168	15 475	56 942	53 389	20 562	87 338
39	92 157	89 634	94 824	78 171	84 610	82 834	09 922	25 417	44 137	48 413	25 555	21 246	35 509	20 468
40	14 577	62 765	35 605	81 263	39 667	47 358	56 873	56 307	61 607	49 518	89 656	20 103	77 490	18 062
41	98 427	07 523	33 362	64 270	01 638	92 477	66 969	98 420	04 880	45 585	46 565	04 102	46 880	45 709
42	34 914	63 976	88 720	82 765	34 476	17 032	87 589	40 636	32 427	70 002	70 663	88 863	77 775	69 348
43	70 060	28 277	39 475	46 473	23 219	53 416	94 970	25 832	69 975	94 884	19 661	72 828	00 102	66 794
44	53 976	54 914	06 990	67 245	68 350	82 948	11 398	42 878	80 287	88 267	47 363	46 634	06 541	97 809
45	76 072	29 515	40 980	07 391	58 745	25 774	22 987	80 059	39 911	96 189	41 151	14 222	60 697	59 583
46	90 725	52 210	83 974	29 992	65 831	38 857	50 490	83 765	55 657	14 361	31 720	57 375	56 228	41 546
47	64 364	67 412	33 339	31 926	14 883	24 413	59 744	92 351	97 473	89 286	35 931	04 110	23 726	51 900
48	08 962	00 358	31 662	25 388	61 642	34 072	81 249	35 648	56 891	69 352	48 373	45 578	78 547	81 788
49	95 012	68 379	93 526	70 765	10 592	04 542	76 463	54 328	02 349	17 247	28 865	14 777	62 730	92 277
50	15 664	10 493	20 492	38 391	91 132	21 999	59 516	81 652	27 195	48 223	46 751	22 923	32 261	85 653
51	16 408	81 899	04 153	53 381	79 401	21 438	83 035	92 350	36 693	31 238	59 649	91 754	72 772	02 338
52	18 629	81 953	05 520	91 962	04 739	13 092	97 662	24 822	94 730	06 496	35 090	04 822	86 774	98 289
53	73 115	35 101	47 498	87 637	99 016	71 060	88 824	71 013	18 735	20 286	23 153	72 924	35 165	43 040
54	57 491	16 703	23 167	49 323	45 021	33 132	12 544	41 035	80 780	45 393	44 812	12 515	98 931	91 202
55	30 405	83 946	23 792	14 422	15 059	45 799	22 716	19 792	09 983	74 353	68 668	30 429	70 735	25 499
56	16 631	35 006	85 900	98 275	32 388	52 390	16 815	69 298	82 732	38 480	73 817	32 523	41 961	44 437
57	96 773	20 206	42 559	78 985	05 300	22 164	24 369	54 224	35 083	19 687	11 052	91 491	60 383	19 746
58	38 935	64 202	14 349	82 674	66 523	44 133	00 697	35 552	35 970	19 124	63 318	29 686	03 387	59 846
59	31 624	76 384	17 403	53 363	44 167	64 486	64 758	75 366	76 554	31 601	12 614	63 072	60 332	92 325
60	78 919	19 474	23 632	27 889	47 914	02 584	37 680	20 801	72 152	39 339	34 806	08 930	85 001	87 820

This table was prepared by the Bureau of Transport and Statistics of the Interstate Commerce Commission, Washington D.C. and is used herein with their permission.

groups of digits can be used for sampling purposes. To choose 30 men at random from a population of 926, for example, we may number all the men in the population from 1 to 926 and then choose 30 three-digit numbers from a table of random numbers. If a three-digit number we have chosen falls outside the range 1–926, we discard it and select three more digits.

A random fraction between 0 and 1 can be obtained by choosing a group of digits (for example, five or ten digits) and imagining a decimal point in front of the group. We usually regard the distribution of such random fractions as continuous although it is clear that the fractions can only take on values that are multiples of 10^{-n}, where n is the number of digits used in each fraction.

Tables of random numbers must be used carefully, and in such a way that the randomness of the digits used is preserved from one occasion to the next. One method is to start at the beginning of the table and keep a record of how much of the table has been used. Next time the table is used, start with the first unused number, and so work through the table gradually. We shall adopt this approach.

Alternatively, open the table and, without looking, place a finger on a block of numbers. Use this block of numbers in a *predetermined* manner to choose the page, row, column and direction in which the required random numbers are to be read.

> **Example 9.1.1.** In a game of chance, an unbiased coin is tossed twice and the number of 'heads' noted. The coin is tossed two further times and the number of 'tails' in the latter two throws is noted. The maximum of the number of 'heads' in the first two throws and the number of 'tails' in the second two throws is some number X, which is the dollar amount the player pays to the bank. Use the method of simulation to study the distribution of the amount paid to the bank.

Each of the digits in a table of random numbers is equally likely. If a single digit is chosen at random there is a 50% chance that the digit will be less than or equal to 4 (0, 1, 2, 3, 4) and a 50% chance that it will be greater than 4 (5, 6, 7, 8, 9). It is possible to simulate the game by selecting digits from a table of random numbers. If a digit is less than or equal to 4, we can record a 'head'; otherwise a 'tail'.

The random digits for the simulation summarised in table 9.1.2 were taken from the first column of table 9.1.1, and a line has been placed under the line 24 random number so that we know where to continue from in the random number table when next we need a random number.

From our simulation, we conclude that the chance of a payment of $0 is

Table 9.1.2. *Simulation of a game of chance*

Simulation number	First random digit	Second random digit	Number of 'heads'	Third random digit	Fourth random digit	Number of 'tails'	Payment ($)
1	1	0	2	4	8	1	2
2	0	2	2	2	3	0	2
3	6	8	0	2	4	0	0
4	1	3	2	0	4	0	2
5	2	1	2	6	7	2	2
6	3	7	1	5	7	2	2
7	0	7	1	7	9	2	2
8	2	1	2	9	9	2	2
9	5	6	0	2	9	1	1
10	6	3	1	0	1	0	1
11	8	9	0	5	7	2	2
12	9	8	0	5	4	1	1
13	7	5	0	2	8	1	1
14	9	1	1	8	6	2	2
15	3	5	1	5	3	1	1
16	0	9	1	4	2	0	1
17	9	1	1	0	3	0	1
18	6	5	0	0	7	1	1
19	1	1	2	9	5	2	2
20	1	0	2	8	5	2	2
21	0	2	2	3	6	1	2
22	8	0	1	1	0	0	1
23	1	1	2	5	2	1	2
24	1	6	1	2	0	0	1
25	7	0	1	5	6	2	2
26	4	8	1	6	6	2	2
27	3	5	1	4	1	0	1
28	6	4	1	3	2	0	1
29	6	3	1	9	2	1	1
30	9	3	1	3	4	0	1
Total							44

very small and chances of payments of $1 or $2 are almost equal. Estimates of these probabilities are:

$$P (\$0 \text{ payment}) \doteqdot 1/30 = 0.03 \;;$$
$$P (\$1 \text{ payment}) \doteqdot 14/30 = 0.47 \;;$$
$$P (\$2 \text{ payment}) \doteqdot 15/30 = 0.50 \;;$$
$$\text{Average payment} \doteqdot 44/30 = \$1.47 \;.$$

More precise estimates of these probabilities and the mean payment can be obtained by increasing the number of simulations.

Further reading: Pollard [26] 236–7.

*9.2   How many simulations?

The answer to this question depends upon what we are trying to estimate and how accurately we wish to estimate it.

Let us imagine that we wish to estimate the expected payment in the game of chance described in example 9.1.1 to within 1% of its true value with a high probability (95%, say). The data in table 9.1.2 may be regarded as results from a pilot study. We shall denote the mean and variance of the payment resulting from a single simulation by μ and σ^2 respectively. According to the additive rules for means and variances of sums of independent random variables (sections 4.1 and 4.2), the total payment T, in respect of n independent simulations, will have mean $n\mu$ and variance $n\sigma^2$. Furthermore, by the Central Limit Theorem (section 5.2),

$$\frac{(T - n\mu)}{\sqrt{(n\sigma^2)}}$$

will be approximately normally distributed with zero mean and unit variance for large n.

The simulation estimate of the mean μ is provided by T/n. We require

$$P \left(0.99\mu < \frac{T}{n} < 1.01\mu\right) = 0.95 \;.$$

That is,

$$P (0.99\mu n < T < 1.01\mu n) = 0.95 \;,$$

or

$$P \left(\frac{-0.01n\mu}{\sqrt{(n\sigma^2)}} < \frac{T - n\mu}{\sqrt{(n\sigma^2)}} < \frac{0.01n\mu}{\sqrt{(n\sigma^2)}}\right) = 0.95 \;.$$

The 95% points of the unit normal distribution are ± 1.96, so that

$$\frac{0.01n\mu}{\sqrt{(n\sigma^2)}} = 1.96 .$$

whence

$$n = \left(\frac{1.96\sigma}{0.01\mu}\right)^2 .$$

The expectation μ and the standard deviation σ are of course unknown. We do know from the pilot study, however, that the mean payment was about 1.47; the sample standard deviation of the payment is readily calculated to be 0.56. The approximate number of simulations required is, therefore,

$$n \doteq \left(\frac{1.96 \times 0.56}{0.01 \times 1.47}\right)^2 = 5500 \text{ (say) .}$$

Alternatively, we might wish to estimate the proportion p of \$2 payments to within 1% of its true value with probability 0.95. Let us denote the number of occasions on which a \$2 payment is made in n trials by the random variable X. The outcome at a particular trial is either a \$2 payment with probability p or not \$2 with probability $1 - p$. The trials are independent, so that X is a binomial random variable with parameters n and p (section 5.8). According to (5.8.2) and (5.8.3), therefore, the expected value of X is np and the variance $np(1 - p)$. Furthermore, for large n,

$$\frac{X - np}{\sqrt{[np(1 - p)]}}$$

will be approximately normally distributed with zero expectation and unit variance (formula (5.8.7)).

We require

$$P(0.99p < \frac{X}{n} < 1.01p) = 0.95 .$$

That is,

$$P\left(\frac{-0.01\,np}{\sqrt{[np(1-p)]}} < \frac{X - np}{\sqrt{[np(1-p)]}} < \frac{0.01\,np}{\sqrt{[np(1-p)]}}\right) = 0.95 .$$

The 95% points of the unit normal distribution are ± 1.96, so that

$$\frac{0.01\,np}{\sqrt{[np(1-p)]}} = 1.96 ,$$

whence

$$n \doteq \left(\frac{1.96}{0.01}\right)^2 \frac{(1-p)}{p} .$$

The probability p is of course unknown. We do know from the pilot study, however, that 15 of the 30 trials resulted in a $2 payment. The approximate number of simulations required is, therefore,

$$n = \left(\frac{1.96}{0.01}\right)^2 \frac{1/2}{1/2} = 38\,500 \text{ (say)} .$$

In each of these cases, the number of simulations required is very large. This is because we required the true value to lie in a narrow range with a high probability. Manual simulation would be very tedious. Fortunately, fast computer methods are available.

9.3   Computer generation of random numbers

Random numbers are also generated by computers and programmable calculators. These numbers are usually fractions distributed uniformly over the unit interval $(0, 1)$. Again, we normally regard the distribution as continuous, although it is clear that on a digital computer only multiples of some small number such as 2^{-31} are possible. The numbers are perhaps better referred to as *pseudo-random,* because they are generated by a completely specified rule. Once the first number has been chosen, the whole sequence is determined. The mathematical procedure for generating the sequence is so devised that no reasonable statistical test will detect lack of randomness. The great advantage of a specified rule is that the sequence can always be reproduced for checking purposes. The 'mid-square' method was the first procedure devised for generating pseudo-random numbers: the middle digits of the square of a random number are used to form the next random number. This method, however, was soon shown to be unsatisfactory. All modern computers have random number packages and *linear congruential generators* are now most commonly used. These generators operate with integers and produce random observations on the unit interval by division.

*9.4   Linear congruential generators

All modern computers and many programmable calculators have random number packages, and it is not necessary for the user to know how these numbers are actually generated. The linear congruential method, however, is simple and quite interesting, and we therefore describe it briefly in this asterisked section. Only on *rare* occasions will the user find it necessary to write his own generator.

When a first-order linear congruential generator is used, the random integer W_{n-1} at time $n-1$ is multiplied by a constant integer k_1, and the product is divided by another constant integer p. The remainder is an integer W_n, and this is used as the random integer at time n. The following equation represents the process:

■ $W_n = k_1 W_{n-1} \pmod{p}$.   (9.4.1)

The random integer W_n is divided by p to produce a random observation on the unit interval. An initial 'seed' needs to be supplied by the user. The constants p and k_1 need to be chosen carefully. J. G. Skellam, in some unpublished notes, recommends the constants $p = 999\,563$ and $k_1 = 470\,001$. The full cycle length of $p - 1$ is attained.

Second- and third-order linear congruential generators are defined by the equations

■ $W_n = k_1 W_{n-1} + k_2 W_{n-2} \pmod{p}$;   (9.4.2)

■ $W_n = k_1 W_{n-1} + k_2 W_{n-2} + k_3 W_{n-3} \pmod{p}$.   (9.4.3)

In each case, the random integer W_n is divided by p to produce a random observation on the unit interval. The constants p, k_1, k_2 and k_3 in table 9.4.1 are recommended by Skellam.

Table 9.4.1. *Integer constants recommended by J. G. Skellam for use in linear congruential generators. In each case the full cycle of p^{s-1} is attained (s is the order of the generator)*

Order of generator (s)	Recommended constants			
	p	k_1	k_2	k_3
1	999 563	470 001	—	—
2	998 917	366 528	508 531	—
2	999 563	254 754	529 562	—
3	997 783	360 137	519 815	616 087
3	997 783	286 588	434 446	388 251

Example 9.4.1. Use Skellam's first-order linear congruential generator to generate five random numbers on the unit interval (i.e. five random fractions in the range 0 to 1). Use as your seed $W_0 = 671\,800$.

W_1 is calculated as follows:

$$470\,001 \times 671\,800 = 315\,746\,671\,800 ;$$

$$315\,746\,671\,800 \div 999\,563 = 315\,884 + 713\,108/999\,563 ;$$

W_1 = 713 108 and *the first random fraction is*

713 108/999 563 = 0.713 419 76 .

The process is now repeated:

470 001 × 713 108	= 335 161 473 108 ;
335 161 473 108 ÷ 999 563	= 335 308 + 2704/999 563 ;

W_2 = 2704 and *the second random fraction is*

2704/999 563   = 0.002 705 18 .

470 001 × 2704	= 1 270 882 704 ;
1 270 882 704 ÷ 999 563	= 1271 + 438 131/999 563 ;

W_3 = 438 131 and *the third random fraction is*

438 131/999 563   = 0.438 322 55 .

470 001 × 438 131	= 205 922 008 131 ;
205 922 008 131 ÷ 999 563	= 206 012 + 35 375/999 563 ;

W_4 = 35 375 and *the fourth random fraction is*

35 375/999 563   = 0.035 390 47

470 001 × 35 375	= 16 626 285 375 ;
16 626 285 375 ÷ 999 563	= 16 633 + 553 996/999 563 ;

W_5 = 553 996 and *the fifth random fraction is*

553 996/999 563   = 0.554 238 20

The computer will follow the same sequence of operations. The reader should note that all integers in the calculation *must* be recorded exactly. Rounding is not permissible.

Further reading: Croucher [6] 167–72; Pollard [26] 236–9.

9.5   Random observations on the normal distribution

The normal distribution occupies a central position in statistical theory, and random observations from the unit normal distribution are often required. These can be generated using a table of random numbers and a table of the normal integral i.e. the area under the unit normal curve to the left of x, and denoted by $\Phi(x)$ in table 5.1.1. A random fraction U between 0 and 1 is read from the table of random numbers, and the normal table is used inversely to find X such that $\Phi(X) = U$. Then X is a random observation from the unit normal distribution.

The same method can be used on a computer or programmable calculator, but it is usually inconvenient to store a table of the normal integral and it is not practical to compute the inverse of the normal integral each time it is required. Other methods are usually employed.

One method relies on the central limit theorem (section 5.2). We generate N random fractions on the unit interval and add these together. The sum is a random variable with mean $N/2$ and variance $N/12$. We then subtract $N/2$ from the total and divide by $\sqrt{(N/12)}$. The resulting random variable has zero mean and unit variance, and it is approximately normal for reasonably large N. When speed of calculation is important and the problem does not depend critically on the extreme tails of the normal distribution, there is some advantage in choosing N equal to 12.

An elegant method has been devised by Box & Müller, which is convenient for computer work. Two independent random fractions on the unit interval U_1 and U_2 are obtained. We then calculate[1]

$$
\left.
\begin{aligned}
X_1 &= (- 2 \ln U_1)^{\frac{1}{2}} \cos (2\pi U_2) \; ; \\[6pt]
X_2 &= (- 2 \ln U_1)^{\frac{1}{2}} \sin (2\pi U_2) \, .
\end{aligned}
\right\}
\tag{9.5.1}
$$

Then X_1 and X_2 are independent random observations from the unit normal distribution. The Box–Müller method may not be as fast as the above Central Limit procedure.

To generate a random observation from the normal distribution with mean μ and variance σ^2, obtain a random observation from the unit normal distribution. Multiply this observation by σ and add μ.

Table 9.5.1. *Fifty observations on the unit normal distribution genera-ted by the Central Limit Theorem method*

- 0.49	0.32	- 0.62	- 1.75	1.31
0.23	- 1.65	- 0.19	0.31	0.11
- 1.37	- 0.37	- 0.83	- 0.37	1.92
0.83	- 0.84	1.14	1.70	0.83
- 0.13	- 1.04	1.87	- 0.26	- 2.68
1.01	1.28	- 1.29	- 0.75	- 0.41
- 0.98	0.23	- 0.65	- 1.21	0.60
0.66	- 0.51	0.74	- 0.85	1.30
- 0.45	- 0.43	- 0.67	- 0.41	- 1.47
- 0.32	- 1.06	1.41	- 0.10	- 0.56

[1] logarithms to base e, and angles measured in radians $(180° = \pi)$.

Example 9.5.1. A random observation from the normal distribution with mean 10 and variance 4 is required. We consult our table of random numbers and obtain the random fraction 0.024 88. Interpolating in the normal integral table we find that $\Phi(-1.962) = 0.024\ 88$. Our random observation from the normal distribution with mean 10 and variance 4 is, therefore, $10 + 2 \times (-1.962) = 6.076$.

Example 9.5.2. (Central Limit Theorem.) Each random number generated by the linear congruential generator method is an observation on the uniform distribution over the unit interval $(0, 1)$. The Central Limit Theorem (section 5.2) tells us that when we add together a large number of such uniform random variables, the sum has the normal distribution. In fact, one of the methods outlined above for generating normal random variables uses this fact.

Each of the numbers in table 9.5.1 was obtained by adding together twelve random uniform variables and subtracting six from the total. The uniform random variables were generated on a programmable calculator using Skellam's first-order linear congruential generator (table 9.4.1) and the seed $W_0 = 346\ 295$.

The sample mean and variance of the 50 observations in table 9.5.1 are -0.14 and 1.0157 respectively, both of which are close to the unit normal values of 0 and 1. The values in table 9.5.1 have been grouped and plotted as a histogram in fig. 9.5.1, and the comparison with the unit normal curve (also shown) is good.

Fig. 9.5.1. Comparison of observations generated by the Central Limit Theorem method and the unit normal distribution.

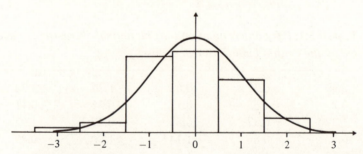

Further reading: Croucher [6] 172–80; Hammersley & Handscomb [12] 39–40; Pollard [26] 239–40.

9.6   Random observations on the log-normal distribution

In an earlier chapter, we saw that a random variable X has the (two-parameter) log-normal distribution if $\ln X$ is normally distributed. The parameters of the log-normal distribution are the mean μ and variance σ^2 of the related normal distribution.

From this definition it is clear that to generate a random observation on the log-normal distribution, all one has to do is to generate a random observation on the corresponding normal distribution and exponentiate the result (section 1.9).

Example 9.6.1. Generate five random observations on the log-normal distribution with parameters $\mu = 5.0$, $\sigma^2 = 4.0$.

The next unused random fraction in table 9.1.1 is 0.81525, and our calculation of five random observations on the log-normal distribution may be set out as follows:

Random fraction (1)	Random unit normal variable (2)	Random normal variable (3)	Random log-normal variable (4)
.815 25	0.90	6.80	897.8
.296 76	− 0.53	3.94	51.4
.007 42	− 2.44	0.12	1.1
.053 66	− 1.61	1.78	5.9
.919 21	1.40	7.80	2440.6

Column (2) is obtained from column (1) using the normal tables 5.1.1 inversely. Column (3) is equal to column (2) multiplied by $\sqrt{4.0}$ plus a constant 5.0, while column (4) is the exponential of column (3).

Further reading: Pollard [26] 240.

9.7 Random observations on the Poisson distribution

The Poisson distribution is often useful in the general insurance context, and we need to be able to generate Poisson random variables for simulation purposes.

Let us imagine that we require a random observation on the Poisson distribution with mean 1.0. According to table 9.7.1, a fraction 0.367 88 of random observations on the Poisson distribution with mean 1.0 should be 0, a fraction 0.735 76 should be less than or equal to 1.0, a fraction 0.919 70 should be less than or equal to 2.0, and so on. A random observation on the Poisson distribution with mean 1.0 can therefore be obtained using a table of ordinary (uniform) random numbers (or a computer random number generator) as follows:

1. Denote the random Poisson variable by Y.
2. Obtain a random fraction U.
3. If $U \leqslant 0.367\ 88$, $Y = 0$;
   if $0.367\ 88 < U \leqslant 0.735\ 76$, $Y = 1$;
   if $0.735\ 76 < U \leqslant 0.919\ 70$, $Y = 2$;

and so on.

The above method is basically very simple, but it does require the calculation and tabulation of the relevant Poisson distribution. A method[2] is available which avoids this task, and is possibly even simpler to apply. Let us imagine that we require a random observation on the Poisson distribution with mean q. All we have to do is to keep generating random fractions until their product is less than e^{-q}. Assume $N + 1$ fractions are required. Then N is a random observation on the Poisson distribution with mean q.

Both the above methods are straightforward, but they can be tedious to apply when the Poisson mean q is large. In this situation, however, the Central Limit Theorem (section 5.7) allows us to reduce the amount of arithmetic by employing the normal distribution.

The approximation makes use of the fact that, for large q, the Poisson distri-

Table 9.7.1. *Poisson distribution with mean 1.0*

j	Probability of j claims $P(j)$	Cumulative distribution $P(j$ or fewer claims$)$
0	.367 88	.367 88
1	.367 88	.735 76
2	.183 94	.919 70
3	.061 31	.981 01
4	.015 33	.996 34
5	.003 07	.999 41
6	.000 51	.999 92
7	.000 07	.999 99
.	.	.
.	.	.
.	.	.

[2]   The method makes use of a mathematical relationship between the Poisson distribution and the gamma distribution. See, for example, Parzen [24] 135–6.

bution with mean q has a shape very similar to the normal distribution with mean q and standard deviation $\sqrt{q}$. The procedure is as follows:

1. Obtain a random fraction U.
2. Calculate the corresponding random unit normal deviate Z (section 9.5 above).
3. Calculate $q + Z\sqrt{q}$.
4. Round this value to the nearest non-negative integer and use it as the random Poisson observation Y.

This normal approach will be reasonably adequate even when q is as small as 10.

Example 9.7.1. Generate five random observations on the Poisson distribution with mean 1.0.

Let us use the first method outlined in the text. The next unused fraction in our table of random numbers is 0.005 82. This value is less than 0.367 88. So our first random observation on the Poisson distribution with mean 1.0 is 0. We repeat the process. The results may be summarised as follows:

Random fraction	Random Poisson observation
.005 82	0
.007 25	0
.690 11	1
.259 76	0
.097 63	0

Example 9.7.2. Generate five random observations on the Poisson distribution with mean 11.0.

Let us adopt the Central Limit Theorem approach. The calculation may be set out as follows:

Random fraction U	Unit normal random variable Z	$11 + Z\sqrt{(11)}$	Poisson random variable Y
0.915 67	1.38	15.58	16
0.179 55	− 0.92	7.95	8
0.465 03	− 0.09	10.70	11
0.921 57	1.41	15.68	16
0.145 77	− 1.06	7.48	7

Further reading: Croucher [6] 180–5; Pollard [26] 243–4.

*9.8   Random observations on the negative binomial distribution

Two of the methods we have outlined in connection with the Poisson distribution are also applicable to the negative binomial distribution.

Let us imagine, for example, that we require a random observation on the negative binomial distribution in table 9.8.1. According to that table, a fraction 0.0467 of observations should be 0, a fraction 0.1120 should be 1, a fraction 0.1568 should be 2, a fraction 0.1672 should be 3 and so on. A random observation on the negative binomial distribution in table 9.8.1 can, therefore, be obtained using a table of random numbers (or a computer random number generator) as follows:

1. Denote the random negative binomial variable by Y.
2. Obtain a random fraction U.

Table 9.8.1. *Negative binomial distribution with parameters $k = 6$ and $p = 0.6$.*

j	P (j claims)	P (j or fewer claims)
0	.0467	.0467
1	.1120	.1587
2	.1568	.3155
3	.1672	.4827
4	.1505	.6332
5	.1204	.7536
6	.0883	.8419
7	.0605	.9024
8	.0394	.9418
9	.0245	.9663
10	.0147	.9810
11	.0085	.9895
12	.0048	.9943
13	.0027	.9970
14	.0015	.9985
15	.0008	.9993
16	.0004	.9997
17	.0002	.9999
.	.	.
.	.	.
.	.	.

3. If $U \leqslant 0.0467$, $Y = 0$;
    if $0.0467 < U \leqslant 0.1587$, $Y = 1$;
    if $0.1587 < U \leqslant 0.3155$, $Y = 2$;

and so on.

Because of the need to form a cumulative distribution table for the negative binomial distribution under consideration, this procedure can be very tedious when the mean and variance are large. Fortunately, when the parameter k is large, we can invoke the Central Limit Theorem (section 5.9) and use a normal approximation. The procedure is as follows (for large k):

1. Obtain a random fraction U.
2. Calculate the corresponding unit normal deviate Z (section 9.5).
3. Calculate $(k(1-p)/p) + Z\sqrt{[k(1-p)/p^2]}$.
4. Round this value to the nearest non-negative integer and use it as the random negative binomial observation Y.

Example 9.8.1. Generate five random observations on the negative binomial distribution in table 9.8.1.

The next unused random fraction in our table of random numbers is 0.984 27. This value lies between 0.9810 and 0.9895. So our first random observation on the negative binomial distribution is 11. We then repeat the process. The results may be summarised as follows:

Random fraction	Random negative binomial value
0.984 27	11
0.349 14	3
0.700 60	5
0.539 76	4
0.760 72	6

9.9   A simulation example

Example 9.9.1. In a certain population, the average male driver has 1 accident every 10 years and the average female driver 1 accident every 20 years. These results (based on statistics compiled by the insurance subsidiary of the national automobile association) were published in the daily newspapers and led to numerous marital arguments.

The debate has even led one irate head of household to enter into an agreement with his wife to pay her, at the end of 10 years $1000 for every accident he himself experiences during the next 10 years over and above the greater of the number of accidents his wife and elder daughter experience during the same 10-year period.

If the man, his wife and daughter are average drivers, the distribution of the number of accidents incurred by each during the 10-year period will be Poisson with mean 1.0 in the case of the man, and Poisson with mean 0.5 for the wife and for the daughter. The relevant distributions are shown in tables 9.7.1 and 9.9.1.

The next unused random fraction in table 9.1.1 is 0.907 25 and according to table 9.7.1, the simulated number of accidents for the man in the 10-year period is therefore 2. The random fractions 0.643 64 and 0.089 62 indicate (table 9.9.1) that mother and daughter experience 1 and 0 accidents respectively. In this first simulation, therefore, the man has to pay his wife $1000. The process is now repeated; the calculations are set out in table 9.9.2.

From the figures in table 9.9.2, we estimate that the average amount a husband would have to pay his wife in these circumstances is about

$$\$ \ \frac{10\ 000}{21} = \$476 \ .$$

The actual amount, however, could vary from nothing to several thousand dollars. If an accurate estimate of the distribution of the amount were required, many more simulations would be necessary (exercise 9).

Table 9.9.1. *Poisson distribution with mean 0.5*

j	Probability of j claims $P(j)$	Cumulative distribution P (j or fewer claims)
0	.606 53	.606 53
1	.303 27	.909 80
2	.075 82	.985 62
3	.012 64	.998 26
4	.001 57	.999 83
5	.000 15	.999 98
.	.	.
.	.	.
.	.	.

Table 9.9.2. *Simulation of the male/female accident problem*

Simu-lation num-ber	Husband Random number	Husband Number of accidents	Wife Random number	Wife Number of accidents	Daughter Random number	Daughter Number of accidents	Payment ($)
1	.907 25	2	.643 64	1	.089 62	0	1000
2	.950 12	3	.156 64	0	.164 08	0	3000
3	.186 29	0	.731 15	1	.574 91	0	0
4	.304 05	0	.166 31	0	.967 73	2	0
5	.389 35	1	.316 24	0	.789 19	1	0
6	.150 11	0	.465 73	0	.483 60	0	0
7	.930 93	3	.399 75	0	.069 07	0	3000
8	.729 05	1	.919 77	2	.143 42	0	0
9	.368 57	1	.695 78	1	.409 61	0	0
10	.939 69	3	.611 29	1	.973 36	2	1000
11	.127 65	0	.213 82	0	.540 92	0	0
12	.539 16	1	.976 28	2	.912 45	2	0
13	.584 92	1	.323 63	0	.270 01	0	1000
14	.330 62	0	.722 95	1	.205 91	0	0
15	.573 92	1	.042 13	0	.264 18	0	1000
16	.047 11	0	.698 84	1	.657 95	1	0
17	.579 48	1	.834 73	1	.425 95	0	0
18	.563 49	1	.185 84	0	.896 34	1	0
19	.627 65	1	.075 23	0	.639 76	1	0
20	.282 77	0	.549 14	0	.295 15	0	0
21	.522 10	1	.674 12	1	.003 58	0	0
Total							10000

9.10 When to simulate

Simulation can be a very useful and powerful tool for studying problems in general insurance. It should not, however, be used indiscriminately. There are two main situations in which it may well be the best approach:

1. when the problem cannot be solved exactly mathematically;
2. when an exact mathematical solution is possible but extremely

difficult and/or tedious, and adequate approximate results can be obtained quickly and simply by simulation.

Simulation should *never* be used when a simple, exact mathematical method is available.

Example 9.10.1 demonstrates a situation in which the exact mathematical approach is to be preferred. Later, in section 9.11, we give a complicated example where an exact mathematical solution is possible but somewhat tedious, and simulation may be preferable.

Example 9.10.1. Example 9.1.1 was devised to demonstrate the basic ideas behind simulation. A simple mathematical/arithmetical solution is available, however, which should be used in practice in preference to simulation.

All the possible outcomes to the problem are enumerated in table 9.10.1. The expected payment is obtained exactly by summing the products of columns (3) and (4):

$$0 \times \tfrac{1}{16} + 1 \times \tfrac{2}{16} + 2 \times \tfrac{1}{16} + \ldots + 2 \times \tfrac{2}{16} + 2 \times \tfrac{1}{16} = \$1.375 .$$

Example 9.10.2. The problem described in example 9.9.1 has an infinite number of possible outcomes. It is not possible, therefore, to list all possible outcomes and their respective probabilities. For this reason, the simulation approach may seem preferable.

Table 9.10.1. *Possible outcomes to the problem of example 9.1.1.*

Outcome		Probability	Payment ($)
Number of 'heads' (1)	Number of 'tails' (2)	(3)	(4)
0	0	1/16	0
0	1	2/16	1
0	2	1/16	2
1	0	2/16	1
1	1	4/16	1
1	2	2/16	2
2	0	1/16	2
2	1	2/16	2
2	2	1/16	2
Total		1	—

It is possible, however, to list the more likely outcomes which result in non-zero payments (table 9.10.2). The mean payment is obtained by summing the products of columns (4) and (5). Summing the products for the more likely cases listed in table 9.10.2, we obtain a mean payment of $540.28. The true answer will be slightly larger than this, because possibilities with very small probabilities have been omitted.

Table 9.10.2. *Outcomes to the problem of example 9.1.2 which result in a non-zero payment*

Outcome			Probability	Payment ($)
Husband (1)	Wife (2)	Daughter (3)	(4)	(5)
1	0	0	0.135 34	1000
2	0	0	0.067 67	2000
2	1	0	0.033 83	1000
2	0	1	0.033 83	1000
2	1	1	0.016 92	1000
3	0	0	0.022 55	3000
3	1	0	0.011 28	2000
3	0	1	0.011 28	2000
3	1	1	0.005 64	2000
3	2	0	0.002 82	1000
3	0	2	0.002 82	1000
3	2	2	0.000 35	1000
3	2	1	0.001 41	1000
3	1	2	0.001 41	1000
4	0	0	0.005 64	4000
4	1	0	0.002 82	3000
4	0	1	0.002 82	3000
4	1	1	0.001 41	3000
4	2	0	0.000 70	2000
4	0	2	0.000 70	2000
.	.	.	.	.
.	.	.	.	.
.	.	.	.	.
5	0	0	0.001 13	5000
.	.	.	.	.
.	.	.	.	.
.	.	.	.	.

9.11   Simulation of an NCD system

Example 9.11.1 An insurance company writes motor vehicle business and the basic premium for its damage-only policy is $250 per annum. The following NCD scale is operating:

    0%
    10%
    20%
    30%
    40%
    50%
    60%

and if a policyholder makes a claim, he automatically moves back to the 0% discount category the following year. For each claim-free year, he moves one position forward on the NCD scale.

The 1000 policyholders on the company's books are homogeneous with regards to risk. The number of accidents an individual policyholder has in a given year is a Poisson random variable with mean 0.1, and the distribution of the amount of damage for any given accident is log-normal with parameters $\mu = 6.012$ and $\sigma^2 = 1.792$.

The company wishes to change to a simpler NCD scale:

    0%
    20%
    40%
    60%

and adopt the rule that for each claim, the policyholder moves back one position on the scale, while for each claim-free year he advances one position. The company will also introduce a $75 excess.

Use the method of simulation to assess the effects of the change on the long-term premium income and claim outgo of the company and comment on the results. Ignore the problem of expenses, and assume that all the 1000 policy-holders remain with the company.

If a policyholder in the 0% category makes a claim, his premium the following year (under the original scale) will be $250 instead of $225. It is thus clearly against his own interests to make a claim if the amount involved is less than $25. The reduction of discount in subsequent years might also be taken into account, although there is always the chance of a further accident within a year or so, and it is doubtful whether a policyholder thinks so far ahead (example 8.7.1). Using a time horizon of 1 year as the basis for determining whether a policyholder will claim or not, we obtain the minimum claim amounts (according to level of discount) shown in table 9.11.1.

We are required to assess the effects of the change on the long-term premium income and claim outgo of the insurance company. If we assume that, initially, all the policyholders are in the 0% discount category, it will take several years (slightly more than 6) for the distribution of policyholders in the various discount categories to settle down. Let us therefore simulate the insurer over 20 years under the existing arrangements before examining the effects of the change in the NCD scheme. During the first 10 years, the distribution of policyholders within the various NCD categories will settle down and we should be able to obtain information about the long-term premium income and claim outgo from the second 10 years.

If the change in the NCD system is allowed to take place after the 20th year, a few years will elapse (slightly more than 4) before the distribution within NCD categories again settles down. Let us, therefore, simulate the insurer for a further 20 years under the proposed scale, and use the results for the final 10 years to make a comparison with the long-term income and outgo under the existing scale.

The Poisson distribution with mean 0.1 is exhibited in table 9.11.2. Each year, and for each policyholder, the number of accidents incurred was simulated using the first Poisson method of section 9.7: a random observation U on the

Table 9.11.1. *The decision whether to claim or not. Minimum claim sizes according to NCD level*

Under existing scale		Under proposed scale	
NCD level (%)	Minimum claim size ($)	NCD level (%)	Minimum claim size ($)
0	25	0	125
10	50	20	175
20	75	40	175
30	100	60	125
40	125		
50	150		
60	150		

unit interval was generated; the random observation Y on the Poisson distribution was then obtained as follows:

if $0 \leqslant U \leqslant 0.904\ 837$, Y was set equal to 0 ;

if $0.904\ 837 < U \leqslant 0.995\ 321$, Y was set equal to 1 ;

if $0.995\ 321 < U \leqslant 0.999\ 845$, Y was set equal to 2 ;

if $0.999\ 845 < U \leqslant 0.999\ 996$, Y was set equal to 3 ;

otherwise Y was set equal to 4.

For each accident, the random variable representing the amount of the damage was generated by the log-normal method of section 9.6. The necessary unit normal random variables were generated by the Box–Müller method of section 9.5.

Using these random variables, it was straightforward to simulate the movements of the policyholders among the NCD categories, the premiums received by the insurer and the claim payments made. Losses less than the minima in table 9.11.1 were ignored.

Table 9.11.3 provides a sample of the main output of the computer simulation program. Figure 9.11.1 was drawn using the complete output. The following points should be noted:

(a) During the first 6 or 7 years, as the policyholders distribute themselves in the six NCD categories, the premium income falls rapidly to about 55% of its initial level. It then remains more or less constant for the remainder of the first 20 years.

(b) The premium income falls again immediately after the change in NCD scale, and settles at a level of about 41% of its initial value.

(c) The claim outgo varies widely from year to year. There is some evidence that it falls during the first few years under the original NCD scale as policyholders move into the higher discount categories.

Table 9.11.2. *The Poisson distribution with mean 0.1*

j	Probability of j claims $P(j)$	Cumulative distribution $P(j$ or fewer claims)
0	0.904 837	0.904 837
1	0.090 484	0.995 321
2	0.004 524	0.999 845
3	0.000 151	0.999 996
$\geqslant 4$	0.000 004	1.000 000

Table 9.11.3. *Sample computer output for NCD simulation (example 9.11.1)*

NCD category	Number in group	Number of claims	Number of claimants	Amount of claims	Amount of premiums	Number of losses not claimed	Saving to company
				YEAR 1			
0	1000	108	103	$167 282	$250 000	1	$22
10	0	0	0	$ 0	$ 0	0	$ 0
20	0	0	0	$ 0	$ 0	0	$ 0
30	0	0	0	$ 0	$ 0	0	$ 0
40	0	0	0	$ 0	$ 0	0	$ 0
50	0	0	0	$ 0	$ 0	0	$ 0
60	0	0	0	$ 0	$ 0	0	$ 0
Totals	1000	108	103	$167 282	$250 000	1	$22
				YEAR 2			
0	103	10	8	$ 10 779	$ 25 750	0	$ 00
10	897	89	86	$133 196	$201 825	7	$227
20	0	0	0	$ 0	$ 0	0	$ 0
30	0	0	0	$ 0	$ 0	0	$ 0
40	0	0	0	$ 0	$ 0	0	$ 0
50	0	0	0	$ 0	$ 0	0	$ 0
60	0	0	0	$ 0	$ 0	0	$ 0
Totals	1000	99	94	$143 975	$227 575	7	$227
				YEAR 25			
0	0	0	0	$ 0	$ 0	0	$ 0
20	17	1	1	$ 1 014	$ 3 400	1	$ 0
40	81	5	5	$ 6 321	$ 12 150	0	$ 0
60	902	60	60	$ 70 933	$ 90 200	13	$203
Totals	1000	66	66	$ 78 268	$105 750	14	$203

Table 9.11.4. *Premium income and claim outgo for years 11–20 and 31–40*

Year	Premium income	Claim outgo	Year	Premium income	Claim outgo
11	137 875	71 935	31	105 050	181 341
12	137 150	83 996	32	106 050	105 936
13	136 725	87 303	33	105 850	93 492
14	136 750	63 790	34	105 350	93 303
15	135 300	102 623	35	106 000	68 925
16	135 350	62 027	36	105 050	88 859
17	133 750	73 111	37	105 400	96 705
18	135 200	97 249	38	105 700	112 367
19	136 175	84 763	39	105 850	97 259
20	134 050	93 225	40	104 800	118 458
Totals	1 358 325	820 022	Totals	1 055 100	1 056 645
Average	135 833	82 002	Average	105 510	105 665

(d) The claim outgo continues to vary widely after the change of NCD scale, but at a slightly higher level.

(e) The number of claims varies widely from year to year. After the change in NCD scale, the level is slightly higher.

(f) Premium income falls the year following a small number of claims and rises after a large number of claims.

(g) Whereas the premium income appears to be more than adequate under the original scale, this is not true under the proposed scheme.

(h) The long-term premium income and claim outgo under the original NCD scale (based on the results for years 11–20) are about $136 000 and $82 000 respectively. The long-term income and outgo figures after the change, however, based on years 31–40) are approximately equal at $106 000. (See table 9.11.4.)

(i) If the company wishes to adopt the proposed NCD scale, it will be necessary to increase the basic premium.

(j) The program took less than 39 seconds (29 seconds CPU) to run.

The question asked us to assess the effects of the change of NCD rules on the long-term premium income and claim outgo of the insurer. We did this by study-

Fig. 9.11.1. Summary of NCD simulation.

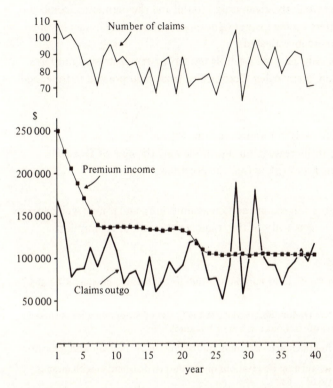

ing a single 40-year realisation of the insurer's operations and comparing the premium income and claim outgo before and after the change in NCD rules. The mean premium receipts and claim payments calculated were based on several observations within the same single 40-year realisation. More reliable estimates could be obtained in either of two ways:

(a) using several realisations of the company's operations over 40 years; or

(b) using a much longer single realisation of the company's operations with a change in NCD rules mid-way.

9.12 Limitations of the model; sensitivity analysis

In our analysis of example 9.11.1, we assumed that the minimum claim size was equal to the excess plus one year's premium discount loss. This rule is somewhat arbitrary.

The sensitivity of the results to variations in the assumptions may be investigated by re-running the program under slightly different assumptions. If, for example, slightly higher minimum claim sizes are adopted, we would expect the number of claims to fall, the claim outgo to fall and the premium income also to fall. The net effect on the insurer (ignoring expenses) may in fact be small, but it does need to be investigated.

We also deliberately adopted a simple model for demonstration purposes. In a practical situation, many other factors need to be incorporated in the model. For example,

> expenses;
> the possible loss of business to competitors;
> the possible increase in business following the new NCD scale;
> heterogeneity of risk within the portfolio;
> etc.

Each of these factors will require certain assumptions, and it may well be necessary to examine the sensitivity of the results to the various assumptions.

9.13 Exercises

1. (Revision). Confirm the Poisson probabilities enumerated in tables 9.7.1 and 9.9.1.

2. Generate five random observations in the Poisson distribution with mean 0.5 by the product-of-fractions method of section 9.7.

3. Generate five random observations on the Poisson distribution with mean 100.

4. Generate ten random observations on the normal distribution with mean $\mu = 2$ and variance $\sigma^2 = 1$.

5. Generate three random observations on the log-normal distribution with parameters $\mu = 2$ and $\sigma^2 = 1$.

6. The following distribution on the non-negative integers is given:

j	$P(j)$	j	$P(j)$
0	.01	5	.19
1	.05	6	.09
2	.10	7	.06
3	.20	8	.03
4	.25	9	.02

Generate five random observations on this distribution.

7. Confirm the first entry in table 9.5.1.

8. Confirm the sample mean and variance quoted in example 9.5.2.

*9. How many simulations are necessary to obtain estimates of the following quantities with the accuracy specified?
(a) The probability that the irate husband in example 9.9.1 does not have to pay anything − accurate to within 10% of the true value with probability 0.95.

(b) The expected payment – accurate to within 10% of the true value with probability 0.99.

10. Calculate the mean and standard deviation of the log-normal distribution assumed in example 9.11.1.

11. You are about to perform the sensitivity analysis outlined in section 9.12. Would you use the same seed as previously for the random number generator? Why?

12. How would you allow for the problem of expenses in the simulation example 9.11.1?

13. How would you include allowances for heterogeneity of risk when studying the effects on the premium income and claim outgo of the NCD changes outlined in example 9.11.1?

10 ESTIMATION OF OUTSTANDING CLAIM PROVISIONS

Summary. Several statistical methods have been devised in recent years to estimate the provisions required for outstanding claims. In this chapter, we describe two of these methods. We also outline a method for estimating incurred but not reported claims (IBNR).

10.1 Delays in claim reporting and claim settlement; run-off

The settlement of claims is always subject to delay, and it is necessary for the insurer to set up provisions for claims in respect of losses which have been incurred by the insured during the period of cover but which have not yet been settled. There are two main types of delay:

1. delay in claim reporting;
2. delay in claim settlement;

and the lengths of the delays vary enormously according to the class of business. In the case of damage-only business for heavy commercial vehicles, claims are notified almost immediately and settled soon after. (A delay of several months would be exceptional.) Many employer liability claims, on the other hand, are not reported until years have elapsed, and the time to settlement of some which are notified almost immediately may be 15 years or more.

The traditional method of estimating provisions for claims which have been reported but not yet settled is for individual estimates to be made in respect of all known outstanding claims at the accounting date. These individual estimates are made by the claims staff who are expected to take into account

1. the severity of the claim;
2. the likely time to settlement;
3. inflation between the accounting date and settlement;
4. trends in claim settlement.

These are difficult factors to assess and incorporate in the estimate of outstanding claims. In liability insurance, for example, the severity of a claim may not emerge for even years after the claim has been reported.

Estimates of provisions for claims which have been incurred but are not yet reported (IBNR) have to be made separately.

Because of the difficulties inherent in the individual claim approach to estimating outstanding claims, *statistical approaches* for dealing with the problem have been developed in recent years. In essence, these methods

> 1. attempt to find a consistent claim run-off pattern which has applied in the past; and
> 2. apply that pattern (with adjustments for anticipated future claim inflation) to estimate the run-off of claims that have been incurred but are still outstanding.

The reader should note, however, that the mechanical application of any statistical method does *not* lead to a 'correct' result, and that the result obtained will often need to be heavily qualified. There may be trends in the settlement pattern, for example, that are difficult or impossible to explain, or there may be some doubt about the likelihood of an existing trend continuing in the future. In such circumstances, a great deal of reliance cannot be placed on the projected future run-off. Or, the settlement patterns of past years may be so erratic that, although a result can be obtained by mechanically applying one of the methods we describe, our confidence in the final result will not be very great.

Even if the past settlement pattern is reasonably stable, the future run-off may be quite uncertain because of doubts that the pattern will continue, and because of claim inflation. The provision to be held will also be affected by assumed investment earnings. In practice, it is seldom possible to do any better than suggest a fairly wide range of not-unreasonable provisions based on different assumptions as to future claim inflation, investment earnings, etc., and possibly on different statistical methodology. Ultimately, however, the company's management is faced with having to adopt one particular figure for the company's accounts. The use of a single method at least has the advantage of consistency from one year to the next.

Further reading: Benjamin [3] 242–3.

10.2 The run-off triangle

The claim experience of an insurer in respect of a particular class of business can be summarised in a run-off triangle exemplified by table 10.2.1. 'Year of origin' is the calendar year (or financial year) in which the incident leading to a claim occurred. In respect of claims originating in 1976, payments totalling $580 222 were made that same year (development year 0), and payments totalling $499 679 were made the following year 1977 (development year 1); the outstanding claim figure for 31 December 1980 in respect of these

Table 10.2.1. *A run-off triangle*

Year of origin	Cumulative payments ($) up to and including development year					Outstanding claim estimate at 31/12/80 ($)	Estimated total liability ($)
	0	1	2	3	4		
1976	580 222	1 079 901	1 319 902	1 453 503	1 508 415	168 987	1 677 402
1977	494 534	993 827	1 186 054	1 345 061			
1978	551 136	1 060 211	1 298 456				
1979	648 031	1 312 219					
1980	746 003						

claims ($168 987) is an estimate, based perhaps on individual estimates of the claims still outstanding or a statistical procedure. Because four years have elapsed, the estimated outstanding claims in respect of 1976 are, however, relatively small compared with total liability in respect of that year.

We need to estimate claim payments after 1980 in respect of years of origin 1977, 1978, 1979 and 1980, in order to deduce the outstanding claim provision required on 31 December 1980 in respect of these years of origin.

10.3 Chain-ladder method without inflation adjustment

The best estimate we can obtain from table 10.2.1. of the ratio of the total claims settled by the end of the second year of development to the claims settled by the end of the first year is

$$m_{1/0} = \frac{1\,079\,901 + 993\,827 + 1\,060\,211 + 1\,312\,219}{580\,222 + 494\,534 + \quad 551\,136 + \quad 648\,031} = 1.955 \ .$$

The best estimates of the ratios of cumulative claim payments in successive periods are calculated similarly:

$$m_{2/1} = \frac{1\,319\,902 + 1\,186\,054 + 1\,298\,456}{1\,079\,901 + \quad 993\,827 + 1\,060\,211} = 1.214 \ ;$$

$$m_{3/2} = \frac{1\,453\,503 + 1\,345\,061}{1\,319\,902 + 1\,186\,054} = 1.117 \ ;$$

$$m_{4/3} = \frac{1\,508\,415}{1\,453\,503} = 1.038 \ ;$$

$$m_{\infty/4} = \frac{1\,677\,402}{1\,508\,415} = 1.112 \ .$$

The best estimate of the total liability at 31 December 1980 in respect of year of origin 1979 is, therefore,

$$1\ 312\ 219 \times 1.214 \times 1.117 \times 1.038 \times 1.112 = \$2\ 053\ 905\ .$$

Ignoring (for the moment) investment earnings on the provision for outstanding claims, the provision required in respect of year of origin 1979 is, therefore,

$$2\ 053\ 905 - 1\ 312\ 219 = \$741\ 686\ .$$

Similarly for the other years of origin. The results may be summarised as follows:

Year of origin	Outstanding claim provision ($)
1976	168 987
1977	207 483
1978	375 648
1979	741 686
1980	1 536 763
Total	3 030 567, say, $3 030 000

If the pattern of delay between an incident giving rise to a claim and the payments made in respect of that claim remains fairly stable over time, inflation is non-existent or at least stable, and the mix of risks in the portfolio is constant, the above chain-ladder method can give reasonable results. The rather sweeping assumptions required by the method are its essential weakness.

It is possible to make allowance for the distortion caused by changes in the rate of inflation using the method of section 8.5.

Further reading: Benjamin [3] 243–7.

10.4   Does the chain-ladder model fit the data?

The investigator can readily check whether the chain-ladder model fits the data by comparing past payments with those predicted by the model. It is important to remember, however, that even if an adequate or good fit is achieved, there is no guarantee that the model is valid for predicting future claim payments in respect of recent past years of origin.

Example 10.4.1. Compare the claim payments in each of the years 1976–80 in respect of the data in table 10.2.1 with the payments predicted by the unadjusted chain-ladder method.

Let us use the observed payments in the zero development years (i.e. years of

Table 10.4.1. *Cumulative claim payments: actual and estimated*

Year of origin		Cumulative payments ($) up to and including year of development					
		0	1	2	3	4	∞
1976	Actual	580 222	1 079 901	1 319 902	1 453 503	1 508 415	1 677 402
	Estimated	580 222	1 i34 334	1 377 081	1 538 199	1 596 651	1 775 475
	(Error)	–	(5%)	(4%)	(6%)	(6%)	(6%)
1977	Actual	494 534	993 827	1 186 054	1 345 061		
	Estimated	494 534	966 814	1 173 712	1 311 036		
	(Error)	–	(-3%)	(-1%)	(-3%)		
1978	Actual	551 136	1 060 211	1 298 456			
	Estimated	551 136	1 077 471	1 308 050			
	(Error)	–	(2%)	(1%)			
1979	Actual	648 031	1 312 219				
	Estimated	648 031	1 266 901				
	(Error)	–	(-3%)				

Table 10.4.2. *Claim payments by year of development: actual and estimated*

Year of origin		Payments ($) in year of development					
		0	1	2	3	4	5–∞
1976	Actual	580 222	499 679	240 001	133 601	54 912	168 987
	Estimated	580 222	554 112	242 747	161 118	58 452	178 824
	(Error)	–	(11%)	(1%)	(21%)	(6%)	(6%)
1977	Actual	494 534	499 293	192 227	159 007		
	Estimated	494 534	472 280	206 898	137 324		
	(Error)	–	(-5%)	(8%)	(-14%)		
1978	Actual	551 136	509 075	238 245			
	Estimated	551 136	526 335	230 579			
	(Error)	–	(3%)	(-3%)			
1979	Actual	648 031	664 188				
	Estimated	648 031	618 870				
	(Error)	–	(-7%)				

origin) and estimate the cumulative payments in subsequent years of development using the *m* ratios of section 10.3. Thus, for example, the estimated cumulative payment by the end of 1979 in respect of year of origin 1977 is

$$494\ 534 \times 1.955 \times 1.214 = \$1\ 173\ 712 \ .$$

The actual cumulative payment (from table 10.2.1) was \$1 186 054, so that the estimate involves an error of 1%. The other actual and estimated cumulative payments in table 10.4.1 were calculated in a similar manner. The percentage errors suggest that the model fits past cumulative payments reasonably adequately.

A more sensitive test is to compare actual and estimated claim payments by year of development. These are obtained by differencing the entries in table 10.4.1, and are shown in table 10.4.2. As we would expect, the errors are larger in percentage terms, but not so large as to suggest the inapplicability of the model.

10.5 Chain-ladder method with inflation adjustment

Let us imagine that the claim inflation rates over the period 1976–1980 were

1 July 1976–1 July 1977	11.3%
1 July 1977–1 July 1978	12.4%
1 July 1978–1 July 1979	14.0%
1 July 1979–1 July 1980	17.3%
1 July 1980–31 December 1980	10.0%

and that the assumed future inflation rate will be a constant 20% per annum.

The data in the run-off triangle table 10.2.1. can be rearranged by year of payment as follows:

Year of origin	Payments (\$) made in development year					
	0	1	2	3	4	5–∞
1976	580 222	499 679	240 001	133 601	54 912	168 987*
1977	494 534	499 293	192 227	159 007		
1978	551 136	509 075	238 245			
1979	648 031	664 188				
1980	746 003					

(*Note:* 238 245 = 1 298 456 – 1 060 211 for example.)

We now express these payments in terms of December 1980 prices. The estimate \$168 987 (indicated by an asterisk) was made at the end of 1980, and is assumed to be assessed at December 1980 prices:

Year of origin	Payment (December 1980 prices) in development year					
	0	1	2	3	4	5—∞
1976	1 067 705	826 139	353 028	172 385	60 403	168 987
1977	817 632	734 431	248 030	174 908		
1978	810 689	656 859	262 070			
1979	836 154	730 607				
1980	820 603					

(*Note:* 734 431 = 499 293 × 1.14 × 1.173 × 1.10 for example)

The cumulative payments (December 1980 prices) are then those shown *above* the stepped line in the following table:

Year of origin	Cumulative payments (December 1980 prices) to development year					
	0	1	2	3	4	∞
1976	1 067 705	1 893 844	2 246 872	2 419 257	2 479 660	2 648 647
1977	817 632	1 552 063	1 800 093	1 975 001	2 024 376	2 162 034
1978	810 689	1 467 548	1 729 618	1 878 365	1 925 324	2 056 246
1979	836 154	1 566 761	1 842 511	2 000 967	2 050 991	2 190 458
1980	820 603	1 505 807	1 770 829	1 923 120	1 971 198	2 105 239

As before, we calculate

$$m_{1/0} = 1.835 ;$$

$$m_{2/1} = 1.176 ;$$

$$m_{3/2} = 1.086 ;$$

$$m_{4/3} = 1.025 ;$$

$$m_{\infty/4} = 1.068 ;$$

and compute the entries *below* the stepped line. For example,

$$2 000 967 = 1 566 761 \times 1.176 \times 1.086 .$$

The next step is to separate the constant-dollar cumulative payments into payments by development year. There is no need to complete the entries above the zig-zag line.

Year of origin	Payments (December 1980 prices) made in development year					
	0	1	2	3	4	5—∞
1976						168 987
1977					49 375	137 658
1978				148 747	46 959	130 922
1979			275 750	158 456	50 024	139 467
1980	685 204	265 022	152 291	48 078	134 041	

(*Note:* 158 456 = 2 000 967 − 1 842 511 for example.)

Finally, we allow for inflation after 31 December 1980. Payments are assumed to be made on average in the middle of the development year, and those in the range 5—∞ in the middle of development year 7. (We assume that information to this effect is available.)

Year of origin	Payments ($) made in development year					
	0	1	2	3	4	5—∞
1976						266 567
1977					54 088	260 577
1978				162 944	61 729	297 391
1979			302 069	208 296	78 910	380 162
1980	750 603	348 380	240 230	91 008	438 446	

(*Note:* 208 296 = 158 456 × $(1.2)^{1.5}$;
260 577 = 137 658 × $(1.2)^{3.5}$.)

Ignoring investment earnings on outstanding claim provisions, the provision required at the end of 1980 in respect of year of origin is

	($)
1976 is 266 567	= 266 567
1977 is 54 088 + 260 577	= 314 665
1978 is 162 944 + 61 729 + 297 391	= 522 064
1979 is 302 069 + 208 296 + 78 910 + 380 162	= 969 437
1980 is 750 603 + 348 380 + 240 230 + 91 008 + 438 446	= 1 868 667
Total	3 941 400

This figure is substantially higher than the outstanding claim provision of $3 030 000 obtained in section 10.3 by the unadjusted chain-ladder method for two main reasons:

1. The outstanding claim estimate of $168 987 in table 10.2.1 is in terms of December 1980 prices. On average, these payments will be made $2\frac{1}{2}$ years later. With anticipated inflation of 20% per annum, a figure of $168\,987 \times (1.2)^{2.5} = 266\,567$ should have been used instead of 168 987 in the unadjusted chain-ladder method. Had this been done, the unadjusted chain-ladder provision would have been approximately $540 000 higher.

2. The anticipated future claim inflation rate of 20% per annum is substantially higher than the inflation experienced in recent years. The unadjusted chain-ladder method, however, assumes that inflation will continue at about the same level as previously.

Example 10.5.1. Estimate the outstanding claim provision required in respect of the above general insurance business assuming that interest is earned on the provision at the rate of 12% per annum.

Our starting point is the fourth unlabelled table of section 10.5, above, which shows the expected payments in future years of claims originating in the period 1976–80 in terms of December 1980 prices. The sum shown as $50 024 and due about the middle of 1983 is expected to grow with inflation to $50\,024 \times (1.2)^{2.5}$. Outstanding claim provisions are expected to earn interest at 12% per annum, however, so that the lesser sum of $[50\,024 \times (1.2)^{2.5}]/(1.12)^{2.5} = \$59\,441$ needs to be set aside at the end of 1980. The complete schedule of provisions is as follows:

Year of origin	Provision required at 31 December 1980 to meet payments due in development year						Totals
	0	1	2	3	4	5—∞	
1976						200 799	200 799
1977					51 108	175 256	226 364
1978				153 968	52 079	178 586	384 633
1979			285 428	175 733	59 441	203 831	724 433
1980		709 254	293 918	180 960	61 209	209 893	1 455 234
Total							2 991 463

(*Note:* $175\,256 = 137\,658 \times (1.2/1.12)^{3.5}$;
$293\,918 = 265\,022 \times (1.2/1.12)^{1.5}$.)

A total provision of about $3 million is required.

Example 10.5.2.[1] The following details have been extracted from the Form 11 returns of an Australian general insurance company:

Year of origin	Payments ($'000) in development year					
	0	1	2	3	4	5
1973	203	318	271	265	105	29
1974	284	385	444	192	110	
1975	330	642	311	212		
1976	420	800	370			
1977	535	941				
1978	640					

All claims are settled by the end of development year 5. Growth in the average payment per claim at each duration may be assumed to be at the same rate as growth in average weekly earnings (AWE), namely:

Year ending 30 June	Growth in AWE (%)
1974	26
1975	14
1976	12½
1977	10
1978	3
6 months to 31.12.1978	3

The company completely revised its administration of outstanding claims at the end of 1975. As a result, 50% of claim payments which would previously have been paid in development year 2 or later, are now being paid, on average, 12 months earlier. Using a chain-ladder method, estimate the necessary provision for outstanding claims at the end of 1978 for this company, assuming that future growth in the average payment per claim will be 15% per annum, while the investment return on the provision will be 10% per annum.

[1] Institute of Actuaries of Australia, examinations, October 1980.

We first express the payments in terms of December 1978 prices:

Year of origin	Payments (December 1978 $'000) in development year					
	0	1	2	3	4	5
1973	383	476	356	309	111	30
1974	425	519	518	204	113	
1975	433	749	330	218		
1976	490	849	381			
1977	568	969				
1978	659					

The cumulative table then takes the form:

Year of origin	Cumulative payments (December 1978 $'000) to development year					
	0	1	2	3	4	5
1973	383√	859	1215	1524√	1635√	1665√
1974	425√	944	1462√	1666√	1779√	
1975	433√	1182√	1512√	1730√		
1976	490√	1339√	1720√			
1977	568√	1537√				
1978	659√					

The ticked cumulative figures follow the new run-off pattern. The remainder follow either the old pattern or a mixture. We shall base our m ratios on ticked values. Thus

$$m_{1/0} = \frac{1182 + 1339 + 1537}{433 + 490 + 568} = 2.722 \; ;$$

$$m_{2/1} = \frac{1512 + 1720}{1182 + 1339} = 1.282 \; ;$$

$$m_{3/2} = \frac{1666 + 1730}{1462 + 1512} = 1.142 \; ;$$

$$m_{4/3} = \frac{1635 + 1779}{1524 + 1666} = 1.070 \; ;$$

$$m_{5/4} = \frac{1665}{1635} = 1.018 \; .$$

The estimated cumulative payments are then as follows:

Year of origin	Cumulative payments (December 1978 $'000) to development year					
	0	1	2	3	4	5
1973						1665
1974					1779	1811
1975				1730	1851	1884
1976			1720	1964	2102	2140
1977		1537	1970	2250	2408	2451
1978	659	1794	2300	2626	2810	2861

The estimated payments are, therefore,

Year of origin	Payments (December 1978 $'000) in development year					
	0	1	2	3	4	5
1973						
1974						32
1975					121	33
1976				244	138	38
1977			433	280	158	43
1978		1135	506	326	184	51

Finally, we allow for 15% per annum claim inflation and 10% investment earnings:

Year of origin	Provision required at 31 December 1978 to meet payments due in development year						Totals
	0	1	2	3	4	5	
1973							
1974						33	33
1975					124	35	159
1976				249	148	42	439
1977			443	299	177	50	969
1978		1162	541	364	214	62	2343
Total							3943

An outstanding claim provision of about $3.95 million is required.

Example 10.5.3. The claim payments data of a general insurance
company by year of origin and year of development are not always in
the form of a full upper triangle. Sometimes the triangle is condensed into a
trapezium like that shown in table 10.5.1. The chain-ladder approach can still
be applied. As an example, let us use the inflation-adjusted chain-ladder method
to estimate the provision required on 31 December 1980 for outstanding claims
in respect of years of origin 1977—80 inclusive. We shall assume a future claim
inflation rate after 31 December 1980 of 15% per annum and an investment
earnings rate of 12% per annum.[2]

A summary of claim inflation over the period 1973—80 is given in table
10.5.2, and it may be assumed that claims settled in development years 4 + are
settled on average in the middle of development year 5.

We start by expressing all payments in terms of December 1980 prices. The
figures are set out in part A of table 10.5.3. The missing figures, indicated by
asterisks, cannot be calculated because we do not know the split-up between
actual payments made and estimated outstanding claims expressed in December

Table 10.5.1. *Claim payments by a general insurance company*

Year of origin	Number of claims (incl. IBNR)	Payments ($'000) in development year				
		0	1	2	3	4+
1973	1032	413	353	208	175	106[a]
1974	1328	606	536	338	251	148[a]
1975	1419	763	722	404	291	171[a]
1976	1480	1003	843	455	331	188[a]
1977	1610	1222	990	540	389	204[b]
1978	1759	1442	1179	637		
1979	1988	1777	1440			
1980	2177	2102				

Notes: (a) actual payments to date, and individual case estimates of outstanding claims
at December 1980 prices;
(b) individual case estimates of outstanding claims at December 1980 prices.

[2] It should be noted, in passing, that the difference between the assumed rate of
investment return and inflation (the *real rate of return*) is far more important
than the absolute value of either.

1980 prices. As a typical calculation, consider the figure 539 for development year 2 following year of origin 1975:

$$539 = 404 \times 1.08 \times 1.09 \times 1.08 \times 1.05 .$$

Part B of table 10.5.3 shows the cumulative payments by development year in December 1980 prices. As a typical calculation, consider the cumulative figure 3 055 for development year 2 following year of origin 1975:

$$3055 = 1437 + 1079 + 539 .$$

The doubly asterisked figures cannot be calculated.

We now compute the usual m ratios and use these to estimate the cumulative payments in part C of table 10.5.3.

$$m_{1/0} = (1832 + \ldots + 3527)/(1047 + \ldots + 2015). = 1.750 ;$$

$$m_{2/1} = (2224 + \ldots + 3788)/(1832 + \ldots + 3119) = 1.214 ;$$

$$m_{3/2} = (2486 + \ldots + 3875)/(2224 + \ldots + 3467) = 1.118 ;$$

$$m_{4+/3} = 4079/3875 \qquad\qquad\qquad = 1.053 .$$

A typical calculation for part C is that of 4787:

$$4787 = 3527 \times 1.214 \times 1.118 .$$

The cumulative payments in parts C and B are differenced in part D to produce payments by development year instead of cumulative payments. For example,

$$755 = 4282 - 3527 ;$$
$$505 = 4787 - 4282 .$$

Table 10.5.2. *Claim inflation 1973–80*

Period	Inflation (%)
July 1973–July 1974	14
July 1974–July 1975	18
July 1975–July 1976	26
July 1976–July 1977	12
July 1977–July 1978	8
July 1978–July 1979	9
July 1979–July 1980	8
July 1980–Dec 1980	5

Table 10.5.3. *Inflation-adjusted chain-ladder calculations for example 10.5.3.*

Year of origin	Development year				
	0	1	2	3	4+
A. Payments (December 1980 prices) ($'000)					
1973	1047	785	392	262	*
1974	1347	1010	505	335	*
1975	1437	1079	539	360	*
1976	1500	1125	562	375	*
1977	1631	1224	612	408	204
1978	1782	1337	669		
1979	2015	1512			
1980	2207				
B. Cumulative payments (December 1980 prices) ($'000)					
1973	1047	1832	2224	2486	**
1974	1347	2357	2862	3197	**
1975	1437	2516	3055	3415	**
1976	1500	2625	3187	3562	**
1977	1631	2855	3467	3875	4079
1978	1782	3119	3788		
1979	2015	3527			
1980	2207				
C. Estimated cumulative payments (December 1980 prices) ($'000)					
1978				4235	4459
1979			4282	4787	5041
1980		3862	4689	5242	5520
D. Estimated payments (December 1980 prices) ($'000)					
1978				447	224
1979			755	505	254
1980		1655	827	553	278
E. Provision at 31 December 1980 ($'000)					
1977					212
1978				453	239
1979			765	525	279
1980		1677	860	591	313

Finally, in part E, we inflate the estimated future payments to allow for inflation at 15% per annum after 31 December 1980 and discount them for future investment earnings at an assumed rate of 12% per annum. For example,

$$860 = 827 \times (1.15/1.12)^{1.5} ;$$
$$239 = 224 \times (1.15/1.12)^{2.5} ;$$
$$212 = 204 \times (1.15/1.12)^{1.5} .$$

Summing the rows of part E, we obtain the following provisions for outstanding claims in respect of years of origin 1977—80:

Year	Provision ($'000)
1977	212
1978	692
1979	1569
1980	3441
Total	5914

A provision of about $5.9 million is required.

Further reading: Benjamin [3] 244—8.

10.6 The separation method (direct future payments approach)

We have seen that the chain-ladder method makes rather sweeping assumptions about inflation, mix of risks, and delay in claim settlement. The method will also be affected by changes in the time to settlement, and, particularly in liability insurance, court settlements. We saw also that a variation of the method with inflation adjustment can be used to overcome the problem of varying levels of inflation.

We now examine another method, the *separation method,* which allows us to separate out the basic settlement delay distribution (assumed stationary) and express the total effects of exogeneous influences, such as inflation, in terms of a portmanteau factor.

The expected run-off triangle is assumed to be of the following form:

Year of origin	Payment in development year				
	0	1	2	$\ldots$	k
0	$N_0 r_0 \lambda_0$	$N_0 r_1 \lambda_1$	$N_0 r_2 \lambda_2$	$\cdots$	$N_0 r_k \lambda_k$
1	$N_1 r_0 \lambda_1$	$N_1 r_1 \lambda_2$	$N_1 r_2 \lambda_3$	$\cdots$	
2	$N_2 r_0 \lambda_2$	$N_2 r_1 \lambda_3$	$N_2 r_2 \lambda_4$	$\cdots$	
.	.	.			
.	.	.			
.	.	.			
k	$N_k r_0 \lambda_k$				

N_i is total expected claims (\$) in respect of year of origin i.

r_j represents the claim payments made in development year j *as a proportion of those made in the first k development years.*

λ_{i+j} is an index of the effect of exogenous influences such as inflation.

Let us denote the expected claim payments in development year j, in respect of year of origin i, by P_{ij}. According to the above expected run-off table then,

- $\qquad P_{ij} = N_i r_j \lambda_{i+j} \, .$ \hfill (10.6.1)

The $\{N_i\}$ are usually unknown and, in practice, the assumption is usually made that the $\{N_i\}$ are proportional to the number of claims $\{n_i\}$ (*including* IBNR). In other words $N_i = c n_i$, where n_i is the estimated total number of claims for year i including IBNR. (A method for estimating the total number of claims including IBNR is given below in section 10.10.) If we divide the $\{P_{ij}\}$ by n_i, we obtain the table

Year of origin	Payment in development year				
	0	1	2	$\ldots$	k
0	$c r_0 \lambda_0$	$c r_1 \lambda_1$	$c r_2 \lambda_2$	$\ldots$	$c r_k \lambda_k$
1	$c r_0 \lambda_1$	$c r_1 \lambda_2$	$c r_2 \lambda_3$	$\ldots$	
2	$c r_0 \lambda_2$	$c r_1 \lambda_3$	$c r_2 \lambda_4$	$\ldots$	
.	.	.			
.	.	.			
.	.	.			
k	$c r_0 \lambda_k$				

We now define the diagonal sums

$$d_0 = cr_0\lambda_0 ;$$
$$d_1 = cr_0\lambda_1 + cr_1\lambda_1 = c(r_0 + r_1)\lambda_1 ;$$
$$d_2 = cr_0\lambda_2 + cr_1\lambda_2 + cr_2\lambda_2 = c(r_0 + r_1 + r_2)\lambda_2 ;$$

$$\begin{array}{cccc} . & . & . & . \\ . & . & . & . \\ . & . & . & . \end{array}$$

$$d_{k-1} = c(r_0 + r_1 + \ldots + r_{k-1})\lambda_{k-1} ;$$

and

$$d_k = c(r_0 + r_1 + \ldots + r_k)\lambda_k = c\lambda_k$$

(since the sum of all the $\{r_i\}$ is 1, by definition).

If the *observed* claim payments in development year j, in respect of year of origin i are denoted by P^*_{ij}, and these are divided by the number of claims n_i, *observed* diagonal sums $d^*_0, d^*_1, \ldots, d^*_k$ can be calculated from the data. Estimates of the unknown parameters $\{c\lambda_{i+j}\}$ and $\{r_j\}$ can then be calculated as follows (circumflexes have been used to denote estimates).

- $\quad c\hat{\lambda}_k = d^*_k ;$
- $\quad \hat{r}_k = P^*_{0,\ k}/(c\lambda_k) ;$
- $\quad c\hat{\lambda}_{k-1} = d^*_{k-1}/(1 - \hat{r}_k) ;$ $\qquad\qquad (10.6.2)$
- $\quad \hat{r}_{k-1} = (P^*_{0,\ k-1} + P^*_{1,\ k-1})/(c\hat{\lambda}_k + c\hat{\lambda}_{k-1}) ;$

  etc.

We are now in a position to estimate the lower triangle of the run-off table. The payment in development year 2 of year of origin k, for example, is given by

$$\hat{P}^*_{k,\ 2} = n_k r_2 c\lambda_{k+2}$$
$$= n_k r_2 (c\lambda_k)(1 + f)^2 , \qquad\qquad (10.6.3)$$

where f is the assumed rate of inflation over the next two years. Each of the quantities in this formula is known. Thus, with suitable assumptions as to future inflation, the outstanding claim payments in each development year (up to development year k) can be estimated for each year of origin.

The problem of the claim payments $\{P_{i,\ k+}\}$ after development year k remains, however. Provided these are only a small proportion of the total liability, it is sufficiently accurate, in view of the uncertainty surrounding future inflation, to take as an estimate of the outstanding liability

- $\quad \hat{P}_{i,\ k+} = (n_i/n_0) (\lambda_{k+i+1}/\lambda_{k+1}) \hat{P}_{0,\ k+} . \qquad\qquad (10.6.4)$

Example 10.6.1. Use the separation method to estimate the outstanding claim payments for the experience summarised in table 10.2.1. You are told that the estimated numbers of claims in respect of 1976, 1977, 1978, 1979 and 1980 (*including* IBNR) are as follows:

Year	Number of claims (incl. IBNR)
1976	48 298
1977	43 430
1978	41 454
1979	41 674
1980	39 265

Furthermore, future claim inflation is expected to be 20% per annum.

Dividing the claim payments in table 10.2.1 by the numbers of claims shown above, we obtain the average payment per claim by year of origin and development year:

Year of origin i	Average payment made in development year j				
	0	1	2	3	4
0	12.01	10.35	4.97	2.77	1.14
1	11.39	11.50	4.43	3.66	
2	13.29	12.28	5.75		
3	15.55	15.94			
4	19.00				

(*Note:* 12.01 = 580 222 ÷ 48 298, for example.)

The calculations are then as follows:

d_0^* = 12.01 ;

d_1^* = 11.39 + 10.35 = 21.74 ;

d_2^* = 13.29 + 11.50 + 4.97 = 29.76 ;

d_3^* = 15.55 + 12.28 + 4.43 + 2.77 = 35.03 ;

d_4^* = 19.00 + 15.94 + 5.75 + 3.66 + 1.14 = 45.49 ;

$c\hat{\lambda}_4$ = 45.49 ;

$\hat{r}_4$ = 1.14/45.49 = 0.025 060 4 = 0.025, say ;

$c\hat{\lambda}_3 = 35.03/(1 - 0.025\ 060\ 4) = 35.93$;

$\hat{r}_3\ \ = (2.77 + 3.66)/(45.49 + 35.93) = 0.079$;

$c\hat{\lambda}_2 = 29.76/(1 - 0.025 - 0.079) = 33.21$;

$\hat{r}_2\ \ = (4.97 + 4.43 + 5.75)/(45.49 + 35.93 + 33.21) = 0.132$;

$c\hat{\lambda}_1 = 21.74/(1 - 0.025 - 0.079 - 0.132) = 28.45$;

$\hat{r}_1\ \ = (10.35 + \ldots + 15.94)/(45.49 + \ldots + 28.45) = 0.350$;

$c\hat{\lambda}_0 = 12.01/(1 - 0.025 - 0.079 - 0.132 - 0.350) = 29.01$;

$\hat{r}_0\ \ = (12.01 + \ldots + 19.00)/(45.49 + \ldots + 29.01) = 0.414$.

Check:

.414
.350
.132
.079
.025

———

$1.000\ \checkmark$

We now complete the table of payments made according to year of origin and year of development. In the case of year of origin 3 development year 4, for example, the calculation is

$$\hat{n}_3\ \hat{r}_4\ (c\hat{\lambda}_7) = \hat{n}_3\ \hat{r}_4\ (c\hat{\lambda}_4)\ (1.2)^3$$

$$= 41\ 674 \times 0.025 \times 45.49 \times (1.2)^3$$

$$= 81\ 896 .$$

Year of origin	Expected payments made in development year				
	0	1	2	3	4
0 (1976)					
1 (1977)					59 269
2 (1978)				178 770	67 888
3 (1979)			300 286	215 660	81 896
4 (1980)	750 196	339 518	243 835	92 596	

The estimate of $168 987 for claims outstanding at the end of 1980 in respect of year of origin 1976 (table 10.2.1) takes no account of future inflation for on average 2.5 years. It is necessary, therefore, to increase the estimate to $168 987 × $(1.2)^{2.5}$ = $266 567. Then

$$P_{0, 4+} = 266\ 567\ ;$$
$$P_{1, 4+} = (43\ 430/48\ 298) \times 1.2 \times 266\ 567 = 287\ 639\ ;$$
$$P_{2, 4+} = (41\ 454/48\ 298) \times (1.2)^2 \times 266\ 567 = 329\ 463\ ;$$
$$P_{3, 4+} = (41\ 674/48\ 298) \times (1.2)^3 \times 266\ 567 = 397\ 453\ ;$$
$$P_{4, 4+} = (39\ 265/48\ 298) \times (1.2)^4 \times 266\ 567 = 449\ 374\ .$$

The outstanding claim payments are, therefore, as follows:

Year of origin	Outstanding claim payments ($)	
1976	266 567	= 266 567
1977	287 639 + 59 269	= 346 908
1978	329 463 + 67 888 + 178 770	= 576 121
1979	397 453 + 81 896 + 215 661 + 300 286	= 995 295
1980	449 374 + 92 596 + 243 835 + 339 518 + 750 196 = 1 875 519	
Total		4 060 410

The total $4.06 million is broadly consistent with the figure obtained by the inflation-adjusted chain-ladder method in section 10.5 ($3.94 million).

Example 10.6.2. Estimate the outstanding claim provision required in respect of the above general insurance business assuming that interest is earned on the outstanding claim provision at the rate of 12% per annum.

The approach is similar to that of example 10.5.1. The sum shown as $287 639, in the solution to example 10.6.1, will be paid about the middle of 1984. The provision which needs to be set aside on 31 December 1980, in order to be able to pay this sum, is

$$287\ 639 \div (1.12)^{3.5} = \$193\ 457\ .$$

Similarly for the other payments, which are scheduled below:

Year of origin	Provision required at 31 December 1980 to meet payments due in development year						Totals
	0	1	2	3	4	5—∞	
1976						200 799	200 799
1977					56 004	193 457	249 461
1978				169 922	57 275	197 845	425 042
1979			283 744	181 946	61 690	213 102	740 482
1980		708 869	286 441	183 675	62 277	215 125	1 456 387
Total							3 072 171

(*Note:* $181\,946 = 215\,660 \div (1.12)^{1 \cdot 5}$;
$193\,457 = 287\,639 \div (1.12)^{3 \cdot 5}$.)

A provision of about \$3.07 million is required, which is broadly consistent with the answer to Example 10.5.1.

Example 10.6.3. The separation approach can also be used when the run-off data are in the form of a trapezium like that in Table 10.5.1. If anything, the computations are slightly simpler, as the following solution to the problem of example 10.5.3 will show.

We begin, as usual, by dividing the payments in table 10.5.1 by the numbers of claims. The results are shown in part A of table 10.6.1. The λ-values and r-values are then calculated. Using a slightly different, but obvious, notation, we have

$$\hat{\lambda}_{80} = 965 + \ldots + 242 = 2293 ;$$
$$\hat{\lambda}_{79} = 894 + \ldots + 224 = 2123 ;$$
$$\hat{\lambda}_{78} = 820 + \ldots + 205 = 1947 ;$$
$$\hat{\lambda}_{77} = 759 + \ldots + 189 = 1803 ;$$
$$\hat{\lambda}_{76} = 678 + \ldots + 170 = 1612 .$$

$$\hat{\lambda}_{76} + \ldots + \hat{\lambda}_{80} = 9778 .$$

$$\hat{r}_3 = (170 + \ldots + 242)/9778 = 0.1053 ;$$
$$\hat{r}_2 = (255 + \ldots + 362)/9778 = 0.1579 ;$$
$$\hat{r}_1 = (509 + \ldots + 724)/9778 = 0.3158 ;$$
$$\hat{r}_0 = (678 + \ldots + 965)/9778 = 0.4209 .$$

The estimated payments in part B of table 10.6.1 are then calculated using these λ-values and *r*-values and the number of claims shown in table 10.5.1. It should be noted that inflation from July 1980 to December 1980 is known (5%). Thereafter, we assume 15% per annum. Consequently,

$$\hat{\lambda}_{81} = 2293 \times (1.05) \times (1.15)^{\frac{1}{2}} = 2582 \, ;$$
$$\hat{\lambda}_{82} = 2582 \times (1.15) = 2969 \, ;$$
$$\hat{\lambda}_{83} = 2969 \times 1.15 = 3415 \, ;$$
etc.

Table 10.6.1. *Calculations for the separation approach to the solution of example 10.5.3 (example 10.6.3)*

Year of origin	Development year				
	0	1	2	3	4+
A. Payments divided by numbers of claims					
1973	400	342	202	170	103
1974	456	404	255	189	111
1975	538	509	285	205	121
1976	678	570	307	224	127
1977	759	615	335	242	127
1978	820	670	362		
1979	894	724			
1980	965				
B. Estimated payments ($'000)					
1977					252
1978				478	317
1979			811	622	411
1980		1775	1021	783	518
C. Provision at 31 December 1980 ($'000)					
1977					213
1978				452	239
1979			766	524	276
1980		1677	861	590	311

The following are typical calculations for part B of table 10.61.:

$$1021 = (2177 \times 2969 \times 0.1579)/1000 ;$$
$$252 = [1610 \times 127 \times (1.15)^{1.5}]/1000 ;$$
$$317 = 252 \times (1759/1610) \times 1.15 .$$

Finally, in part C, the estimated payments of part B are discounted at 12% per annum, to 31 December 1980, to produce the figures shown. Typical examples of the discounting are:

$$861 = 1021/(1.12)^{1.5} ;$$
$$276 = 411/(1.12)^{3.5} .$$

Summing the rows of part C, we obtain

Year	Provision ($'000)
1977	213
1978	691
1979	1566
1980	3439
Total	5909

The total provision of $5.9 million is surprisingly close to the figure obtained by the inflation-adjusted chain-ladder method.

*10.7 The separation method (two other approaches)

In the 'direct future payments' approach to the separation method in section 10.6, estimates of the parameters $\{c\lambda_{i+j}\}$ and $\{r_j\}$ were obtained and these were used to estimate, directly, expected future payments in respect of outstanding claims. The estimated parameters can also be used to estimate the payments which might have been expected in the past, and if this is done, two further variants of the separation method are possible: the *ratio method* and the *total payments method.*

The philosophy behind the 'ratio' method is that if past actual payments have exceeded past expected payments, expected future payments should be adjusted upwards in the same ratio and, conversely, if past expected payments have exceeded past actual payments. The philosophy behind the 'total payments' method, on the other hand, is that the total expected payments (past and future) are fixed. If past actual payments have been higher than expected, future actual payments will be less than expected; and conversely, if past expected payments were higher than the actual payments.

The direct future payments method and the ratio method are both quite popular. The total payments method, however, has not found much support.

Example 10.7.1. Use the ratio method to estimate the claims outstanding on 31 December 1980 in respect of the data in table 10.2.1. Inflation after 31 December 1980 is expected to be 20% per annum.

We begin by completing the upper expected run-off triangle using the estimated parameters $\{c\lambda_{i+j}\}$ and $\{r_j\}$ from section 10.6. The triangle turns out to be:

Year of origin	Expected payments made in development year					Total
	0	1	2	3	4	
0 (1976)	580 066	480 927	211 724	137 092	54 927	1 464 736
1 (1977)	511 532	504 809	205 978	156 075		1 378 394
2 (1978)	569 949	521 305	248 918			1 340 172
3 (1979)	619 902	663 513				1 283 415
4 (1980)	739 472					739 472
Total						6 206 189

The remaining calculations are set out in table 10.7.1, and an outstanding claim figure of $4.08 million emerges.

Table 10.7.1. *'Ratio' method adjustment of outstanding claims estimates*

Year of origin	Payments prior to 31 Dec. 1980			Expected future payments	Adjusted future payments
	Actual	Expected	Ratio (2)/(3)		(5) × (4)
(1)	(2)	(3)	(4)	(5)	(6)
1976	1 508 415	1 464 736	1.0298	266 567	274 511
1977	1 345 061	1 378 394	0.9758	346 908	338 513
1978	1 298 456	1 340 172	0.9689	576 121	558 204
1979	1 312 219	1 283 415	1.0224	995 295	1 017 590
1980	746 003	739 472	1.0088	1 875 519	1 892 024
Total					4 080 842

Sources: column (2) – from table 10.2.1;
column (3) – calculated above (example 10.7.1);
column (5) – from the final calculation of example 10.6.1.

Table 10.7.2. *'Total payments' method for estimating outstanding claims*

Year of origin	Expected payments			Actual payments to	Estimated outstanding claims
	Prior to 31 Dec. 80	After 31 Dec. 80	Total (2) + (3)	31 Dec. 80	(4) – (5)
(1)	(2)	(3)	(4)	(5)	(6)
1976	1 464 736	266 567	1 731 303	1 508 415	222 888
1977	1 378 394	346 908	1 725 302	1 345 061	380 241
1978	1 340 172	576 121	1 916 293	1 298 456	617 837
1979	1 283 415	995 295	2 278 710	1 312 219	966 491
1980	739 472	1 875 519	2 614 991	746 003	1 868 988
Total					4 056 445

Sources: column (2) – calculated above (example 10.7.1);
column (3) – from the final calculations of example 10.6.1;
column (5) – from table 10.2.1.

Example 10.7.2. Use the total payments method to estimate the claims outstanding on 31 December 1980 in respect of the data in table 10.2.1. Inflation after 31 December 1980 is expected to be 20% per annum.

The calculations are set out in table 10.7.2, and an outstanding claim figure of $4.06 million emerges.

Further reading: Benjamin [3] 248–51; van Eeghen [29] 77–85.

10.8 IBNR, and the chain-ladder and separation methods

It should be noted that provided 'year of origin' refers to the year in which the incident occurred which gave rise to the claim, and the run-off includes payments in respect of late-reported claims, both methods automatically include provisions for IBNR claims. The separation method, as described in sections 10.6 and 10.7, does require, however, estimates of the numbers of incurred but not reported claims, by year of origin. A method for doing this is described in section 10.10.

Further reading: Benjamin [3] 254.

10.9   Alternative methods of assessing outstanding claim provisions

At this stage there is no general agreement as to which is the 'best' method. The methods we have described and others are all used. Because none has proved itself to be superior in all circumstances, most workers prefer to use several methods and compare the results before reaching any conclusion about the appropriate level of outstanding claim provisions.

Before any method is applied, one needs to study the figures closely (including those for numbers of claims) to check whether trends and other features exist in the data which might conflict with the stability assumptions necessary for the application of the method. Large claims settled in late development years, may, in particular, cause large distortions. Past changes in reinsurance arrangements can have a disruptive effect on settlement patterns for net claim payments. It is usually better, therefore, to work on a gross basis throughout, and make a final adjustment for the anticipated effect of reinsurance on projected future payments.

> *Further reading:* van Eeghen [29] 3–29.

10.10   Estimation of IBNR claim provisions

Let us define $u(j, t)$ to be the proportion of claims incurred in calendar month j, reported within t months of their incidence. A smoothed function $u(t)$ (the proportion of claims notified within t months of the month of incidence) can be obtained by smoothing $u(j, t)$ over several months of incidence j (fig. 10.10.1). For most classes of business of a direct-writing insurer, $u(t)$

Fig. 10.10.1. Delay function $u(t)$ showing the proportion of claims notified within t months of incidence.

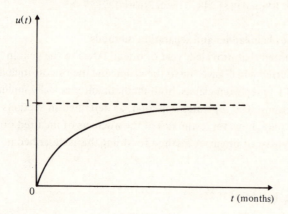

approaches 1 rapidly as t increases. The notable exception is liability insurance.

At the account date, the total number of claims, in respect of the month t months earlier, is estimated by multiplying the claims already notified in respect of that month by $1/u(t)$. The products are then summed to provide an estimate of the total number of incurred, but not reported, claims for the year (example 10.10.1).

We noted above, in section 10.8, that the chain-ladder and separation methods for estimating outstanding claim provisions usually automatically include provisions for IBNR claims. Occasions do arise, however, when separate IBNR provisions are required. The basis for calculating IBNR claim provisions is then as follows:

- $$\text{IBNR provision} = \left(\begin{array}{l} \text{Expected no. of late-} \\ \text{reported claims} \end{array} \right) \times \left(\begin{array}{l} \text{average cost} \\ \text{per claim} \end{array} \right). \quad (10.10.1)$$

If investment earnings at rate i per annum are taken into account in setting the IBNR provision, and average time to the payment of an IBNR claim is r years, the IBNR provision figure becomes

- $$\text{IBNR provision} = \left(\begin{array}{l} \text{Expected no.} \\ \text{of late-reported} \\ \text{claims} \end{array} \right) \times \left(\begin{array}{l} \text{average} \\ \text{cost per} \\ \text{claim} \end{array} \right) \times (1+i)^{-r}. \quad (10.10.2)$$

The average cost of an IBNR claim often differs from that of a currently reported claim, so that it is advisable to develop and monitor a ratio

$$\frac{\text{average cost of an IBNR claim}}{\text{average cost of a reported claim}}. \qquad (10.10.3)$$

Outstanding claim provisions are usually calculated some time after the valuation date and a substantial number of IBNR claims will then be known (but not their amount). Part of the provision for an unknown number of claims of unknown amounts can be converted, therefore, to a reserve for a known number of claims but still of unknown amounts.

The reader should note that it is important to keep a sense of proportion in the statistical work. We must be prepared, for example, to make special allowances in the IBNR reserve if a catastrophe occurs in the closing days of the accounting period.

Example 10.10.1. Use the delay table 10.10.1 and the data in table 10.10.2 to estimate the total number of claims in respect of 1980 for the portfolio involved.

Claims occurring in June 1980 will have occurred on average about 6½

Table 10.10.1. *A delay table*

Delay t	Proportion notified by time t u(t)
0	0.000
1	0.556
2	0.840
3	0.893
4	0.930
5	0.958
6	0.973
7	0.983
8	0.990
9	0.996
10	1.000

Table 10.10.2. *Claims reported by 31 December 1980 in respect of 1980 by month of incidence*

Month of occurrence	Number reported by 31 December 1980
January	974
February	964
March	955
April	1040
May	1023
June	969
July	937
August	989
September	965
October	893
November	880
December	535

months before 31 December 1980, and we therefore need to interpolate in
table 10.10.1 to obtain u (6.5) = 0.978. Similarly for the other months.

The calculations of the estimated numbers of claims for the various months
are set out in table 10.10.3. Note, for example, that the estimated total
number of claims for June is 969/0.978 = 991. The estimated total number of
claims for 1980 is 12 546 compared with 10 924 reported by 31 December 1980.

Further reading: Benjamin [3] 254–6.

Table 10.10.3. *Estimation of total number of claims for 1980*

Month of occurrence (1)	Number reported by 31 Dec. 1980 (2)	t (months) (3)	$u(t)$ (4)	Estimated total number of claims (2)/(4) (5)
January	974	11.5	1.000	974
February	964	10.5	1.000	964
March	955	9.5	0.998	957
April	1040	8.5	0.993	1047
May	1023	7.5	0.986	1038
June	969	6.5	0.978	991
July	937	5.5	0.965	971
August	989	4.5	0.944	1048
September	965	3.5	0.911	1059
October	893	2.5	0.866	1031
November	880	1.5	0.698	1261
December	335	0.5	0.278	1205
Total	10 924			12 546

10.11   Exercises

1. The following details are given concerning the claims on a general insurance company over the period 1975–80:

Year	Number of claims (incl. IBNR)	Payments ($'000) in development year					
		0	1	2	3	4	5
1975	6203	192	251	153	145	98	0
1976	6372	205	280	195	150	102	
1977	6505	230	345	230	212		
1978	6512	288	410	275			
1979	7523	398	563				
1980	8250	530					

Assuming you have no further information, use the chain-ladder method to estimate the outstanding claim provision required at the end of 1980, making no allowance for investment earnings.

2. Use the data in question 1 and the separation method to estimate the outstanding claim provision required at the end of 1980. Assume an inflation rate of 18% per annum after 1980 and investment earnings on the funds of 10% per annum.

3. Assuming inflation to have been constant at 10% per annum over the period 1975–80, use the chain-ladder method with inflation adjustment and the data of question 1 to calculate the outstanding claim provision required at the end of 1980. Inflation is expected to be 10% per annum after 1980. Compare your answer with that obtained in question 1 and comment.

4. The general insurer of examples 10.6.1 and 10.6.2 expects future claim inflation to be 10% per annum, and investment earnings on the provisions for outstanding claims to be 10% per annum also. Estimate the provision which should be set aside at the end of 1980 using the figures calculated in example 10.6.1 as far as practicable.

5. How would your answer to question 4 be affected if future inflation and investment earnings were both assumed to be 8% per annum?

6. The average time to settlement of IBNR claims, in respect of a general insurance portfolio, is known to be 8.2 years from the incident which led to the claim. The IBNR provision in the accounts is to include specific allowances for claim inflation and investment earnings on the provision. Is it correct to use the average time to settlement of 8.2 years in the calculations? Why?

*7.[3] The following data relate to a particular class of insurance of an Australian general insurance company. The claim payment figures include expenses associated with the settlement of claims.

Year	Average number of policies in force	Number of claims (incl. IBNR)	Claim payments ($'000) in development year					
			0	1	2	3	4	5 +
1976	10 123	1012	810	173	39	15	17	17*
1977	10 073	1108	1010	218	50	19		
1978	9936	1093	1146	247	56			
1979	9567	1148	1384	290				
1980	9762	1269	1714					

(*This figure is based on individual case estimates, and assumes a future claim inflation rate of 15% per annum.)

(a) Assuming a future claim inflation rate of 15% per annum, a net investment return of 10% per annum on technical provisions, and a risk loading of 5% of the risk premium, and that 20% of the office premium is consumed by expenses, calculate the premium the insurer should charge for this class of business during 1982. Explain clearly what you are doing, and why.

(b) Does the assumption of a future claim inflation rate of 15% per annum appear reasonable in the light of the company's recent experience? Give your reasons.

[3] Macquarie University, examinations, 1981.

11 ELEMENTARY RISK THEORY

Summary: In this chapter we develop some relationships between reserves, premiums, risk loadings and retention levels that are useful to the general insurer. The relationships are based on some of the statistical tools developed in the earlier chapters.

11.1 Introduction

Conventional actuarial and insurance techniques are based on a simplified model of an insurance portfolio in which random variables are replaced by their mean values. De Moivre, a French mathematician, proved as early as 1700 that an insurance business would eventually be ruined if it failed to include a margin in its favour in the price it charged for its contingent payments: in other words, the insurer must include a safety loading in his premium to guard against losses due to random fluctuations.

Studies of the random fluctuations (stochastic variations) which occur in accumulated claim amounts constitute the branch of actuarial mathematics termed the *theory of risk*. The theory is useful as a guide to the relationship between reserves, retentions and the level of risk, and the general order of magnitude of these quantities.

Example 11.1.1. Consider three insurance contracts. Under the first, the only possible claim amount is $10; only one claim is possible during the year the policy is in force, and the probability of a claim is 1.0. The other two contracts are of the same form, but with claim sizes $100 and $1000 respectively, and claim probabilities 0.1 and 0.01 respectively

The risk premium is the same for all three contracts, namely, $10 (section 7.1). Under the first contract, the insurer is certain to pay out exactly the same amount as he receives in risk premium, no more, no less. The contract is riskless as far as he is concerned.

Under the second contract, there is the possibility that the insurer will have to pay out ten times as much as he receives as risk premium income. In other words, he runs the risk that his premium income will be insufficient to meet his claim liabilities. For running this risk he ought to charge an additional premium. This is usually implemented by adding a safety loading to the basic risk premium.

The third contract is even riskier than the second because of the possibility of an even larger loss, and this ought to be reflected in the premium.

It is convenient to measure the risk inherent in an insurance portfolio by the *standard deviation* (section 4.2) of the accumulated claim amount. In the case of a portfolio consisting of exactly one contract of the first type, the standard deviation of the claim outgo is

$$\sqrt{[10^2 \times 1.0 - (10 \times 1.0)^2]} = 0.$$

The portfolio is riskless and the standard deviation is zero.

If the single contract in the portfolio were of type 2 or type 3, the standard deviation of the claim outgo would be

$$\sqrt{[100^2 \times 0.1 - (100 \times 0.1)^2]} = 30.0 \qquad \text{(type 2)},$$

or

$$\sqrt{[1000^2 \times 0.01 - (1000 \times 0.01)^2]} = 99.5 \qquad \text{(type 3)}.$$

According to this measure of risk, the third contract is more than three times riskier than the second.

Example 11.1.2. Three insurance contracts were described in example 11.1.1. An insurer with reserves of $1000 writes 1000 contracts of type 2 and charges a premium for each policy of $10.50. There are no other contracts. Ignoring the problem of expenses, calculate the probability that the insurer will be unable to meet his claim liabilities.

Let us use C to denote the random variable representing the total claim payout in respect of these contracts. The expected value of C is

$$1000 \times 0.1 \times 100 = 10\ 000.$$

We assume that the contracts are independent, in which case the variance of C will be

$$1000 \times 30^2 = 900\ 000,$$

using the standard deviation calculated in example 11.1.1, and the additive rule for the variance of the sum of independent random variables (section 4.2). The standard deviation of C is, therefore, 949.

The random variable C is the sum of 1000 independent identically distributed random variables. The Central Limit Theorem (section 5.2) tells us, therefore, that $Z = (C - 10\ 000)/(949)$ is approximately a normal random variable with zero mean and unit variance.

The premium income and reserves of the insurer amount to

$$1000 \times 10.50 + 1000 = \$11\ 500.$$

We require

$$P(C > 11\ 500);$$

i.e.

$$P\left(\frac{C - 10\ 000}{949} > \frac{11\ 500 - 10\ 000}{949}\right),$$

or

$$P(Z > 1.58).$$

As Z is a unit normal random variable, we can obtain this probability directly from table 5.1.1 (0.057 05). The probability that the insurer will be unable to meet his claim liabilities is thus about one in seventeen.

Further reading: Beard *et al*. [2] 1–10.

11.2   Portfolio with constant (fixed) claim size

We have already given a simple example of this type of insurance portfolio (example 11.1.2). The example was artificially simple, however, in that only one claim per contract was possible during the year. We now relax this assumption. We assume

1. all claims are for the same amount X;
2. the total number of claims in respect of the insurance portfolio follows the Poisson distribution with mean n (section 5.6).

If K denotes the total number of policies in the portfolio and q the claim frequency rate (per policy), then $n = Kq$.

Let N denote the number of claims during the year in respect of the portfolio. According to assumption (2) then,

$$P(N = r) = e^{-n}\ n^r/r! \tag{11.2.1}$$

$(r = 0, 1, 2, \ldots)$. The expectation and variance of N are both n (section 5.6). If n is reasonably large (greater than 10, say) the normal approximation to the Poisson can be used (section 5.7), and

$$P(N \leqslant x) \doteqdot \Phi\ ((x - n)/\sqrt{n}), \tag{11.2.2}$$

where $\Phi\ (z)$ denotes the area under the unit normal curve to the left of z. The random variable $Z = (N - n)/\sqrt{n}$ will have the unit normal distribution (equation (5.7.3)).

Let us assume that the free reserves of the insurer amount to U at the beginning of the year and that all contracts are issued on the first day of the year. The total risk premium for the portfolio will be

$$P = KqX = nX, \tag{11.2.3}$$

and if a safety loading of λ is included in the premium, the actual premium receipts will amount to

$$P' = nX(1 + \lambda). \tag{11.2.4}$$

The total claim outgo during the year will be

$$C = XN. \tag{11.2.5}$$

The insurer's funds will be augmented by the premium income during the year and depleted by the claim outgo. The free reserves of the insurer at the end of the year will amount to

$$U_1 = U + nX(1 + \lambda) - XN. \tag{11.2.6}$$

The free reserve U_1 must be non-negative if the insurer is to be able to meet his liabilities. It is important, therefore, that the probability that U_1 is negative be small (ϵ say). In symbols,

$$P(U_1 < 0) = \epsilon. \tag{11.2.7}$$

In view of (11.2.6), equation (11.2.7) may be re-written

$$P[(U + nX(1 + \lambda) - XN) < 0] = \epsilon.$$

That is,

$$P[N > (U/X) + n(1 + \lambda)] = \epsilon,$$

or

$$P\left[\frac{N-n}{\sqrt{n}} > \frac{U}{X\sqrt{n}} + \lambda\sqrt{n} \right] = \epsilon.$$

But $(N - n)/\sqrt{n}$ is approximately a unit normal random variable. It follows, therefore, that

$$\frac{U}{X\sqrt{n}} + \lambda\sqrt{n} = z_\epsilon, \tag{11.2.8}$$

where z_ϵ is the point such that the area under the unit normal curve to the *right* of it is ϵ (fig. 11.2.1). Re-arranging (11.2.8) we obtain

■ $$U = z_\epsilon X\sqrt{n} - \lambda nX. \tag{11.2.9}$$

We can now make several observations.

1. Reserve requirements and risk loadings are inter-related. The higher the risk loading, the smaller the required reserve. The higher the reserve, the smaller the risk loading.

2. If the risk loading λ is zero, the reserve required is directly

proportional to $X\sqrt{n}$ (the standard deviation of the total claim amount, and the measure of risk indicated in section 11.1).

3. No reserve is required if the right-hand side of (11.2.9) is negative. In this situation

$$\lambda > z_\epsilon/\sqrt{n}, \tag{11.2.10}$$

or

$$n > (z_\epsilon/\lambda)^2. \tag{11.2.11}$$

Example 11.2.1. A portfolio consists of 1000 contracts. The sum insured is fixed for each at \$500. The claim frequency rate for each contract is 0.01 and the safety loading is $\lambda = 0.1$. How large a security reserve U should the company have to be sure, at a 99% probability level, that after a one-year period the balance does not show a deficit.

Here $n = 1000 \times 0.01 = 10$, $X = 500$, $\epsilon = 0.01$ and from table 5.1.1, $z_{0.01} = 2.33$.

Applying equation (11.2.9), we have

$$U = 2.33 \times 500 \times \sqrt{(10)} - 0.1 \times 10 \times 500$$
$$= \$3184.$$

Example 11.2.2. How many contracts should the portfolio, in the above example, have for no security reserve to be necessary under the conditions mentioned?

Let K represent the total number of contracts. The expected number of claims is then $n = 0.01\,K$. According to (11.2.11), we need to have

$$0.01\,K > (2.33/0.1)^2,$$

which means K must be greater than 54 289.

Further reading: Beard et al. [2] 10–17.

Fig. 11.2.1. The area to the right of z_ϵ under the unit normal curve.

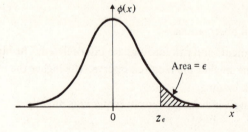

11.3 Variable claim size

We now remove the restriction that the claim size be fixed, and allow it to vary. We shall denote the random variable representing the claim amount for claim i by X_i and suppose that $X_1, X_2, \ldots, X_N$ are all independent and that N (the number of claims) is also independent of each X_i. The random variable representing the total claim amount is

$$C = X_1 + X_2 + \ldots + X_N. \tag{11.3.1}$$

(This expression reduces to (11.2.5) when the individual claim amounts are all fixed at exactly the same amount X.)

As before, the expected number of claims is given by $n = Kq$. The actual number of claims is a Poisson random variable with this mean; its distribution is given by (11.2.1).

The claim amounts $X_1, X_2, \ldots, X_N$ are assumed to be identically distributed, each with mean m and second moment *about the origin* α_2 (section 4.2). Using the conditional formulae (4.4.3) and (4.5.2) we can deduce that the expectation and variance of C are given by

$$E\,(C) = nm; \tag{11.3.2}$$
$$\text{Var}\,(C) = n\alpha_2. \tag{11.3.3}$$

The proof is given in section 11.4.

As before, we shall assume that the free reserves of the insurer amount to U at the beginning of the year and that all contracts are issued on the first day of the year. The total risk premium for the portfolio will be

$$P = Kqm = nm, \tag{11.3.4}$$

and if a safety loading of λ is included in the premium, the actual premium receipts will amount to

$$P' = nm\,(1 + \lambda). \tag{11.3.5}$$

The insurer's funds will be augmented by the premium income during the year and depleted by the claim outgo. The free reserves at the end of the year will amount to

$$U_1 = U + nm\,(1 + \lambda) - C. \tag{11.3.6}$$

If the insurer is to be able to meet his liabilities, U_1 cannot be less than zero. The probability ϵ that U_1 is negative must, therefore, be small. Substituting (11.3.6) for U_1, we have

$$P[U + nm\,(1 + \lambda) - C < 0] = \epsilon.$$

That is,

$$P[C > U + nm\,(1 + \lambda)] = \epsilon,$$

or

$$P\left[\frac{C - nm}{\sqrt{(n\alpha_2)}} > \frac{U + nm\lambda}{\sqrt{(n\alpha_2)}}\right] = \epsilon.$$

The exact distribution of the random variable C is usually very complicated. We do know, however, that its mean is nm and its variance is $n\alpha_2$. In the case of a large portfolio, the distribution of C tends to be approximately normal, provided the claim size distribution of the $\{X_i\}$ is not too skew. The distribution of $(C - nm)/\sqrt{(n\alpha_2)}$ is then unit normal, and we can write

$$\frac{U + nm\lambda}{\sqrt{(n\alpha_2)}} = z_\epsilon$$

(fig. 11.2.1). Re-arranging this formula, we obtain

■ $\quad U = z_\epsilon\sqrt{(n\alpha_2)} - nm\lambda.$ (11.3.7)

Note that this formula reduces to (11.2.9) if each claim is of a constant fixed size X, for then $m = X$ and $\alpha_2 = X^2$.

Example 11.3.1. Table 11.3.1 shows the observed claim size distribution of a certain general insurance portfolio. Estimate the moments m and α_2 of this distribution. Estimate also the moments m and α_2 of the retained liability when the retention limit under an excess of loss treaty[1] is (a) \$1200, (b) \$1400, (c) \$1600 and (d) \$2000.

Without reinsurance, estimates $\hat{m}$ and $\hat{\alpha}_2$ of the underlying moments m and α_2 are calculated as follows:

$\hat{m}$ = $100 \times 0.014 + 300 \times 0.067 + \ldots + 2300 \times 0.007 = 971.00$;
$\hat{\alpha}_2$ = $100^2 \times 0.014 + 300^2 \times 0.067 + \ldots + 2300 \times 0.007 = 1\,148\,400$.

The effect of a \$1200 retention is to modify the calculation as follows:

$\hat{m}$ = $100 \times 0.014 + 300 \times 0.067 + \ldots + 1100 \times 0.144 + 1200 \times 0.291$
= 870.90;

$\hat{\alpha}_2$ = $100^2 \times 0.014 + 300^2 \times 0.067 + \ldots + 1100^2 \times 0.144$
$+ 1200^2 \times 0.291$.
= $853\,250$.

This is because 29.1% of claims exceed \$1200, but these claims result in only \$1200 liability to the direct insurer.

The results for the other retentions are shown in table 11.3.2.

Example 11.3.2. The general insurer of example 11.3.1 has free reserves of \$12 000, and expects to write 1000 policies. The premium charged includes a safety loading of 5% of the risk premium, and the claim frequency

[1] section 7.5.

Table 11.3.1. *Observed claim size distribution of a general insurance portfolio*

Claim size		Percentage of claims in given range
Range ($)	Mid-point of range ($)	
0–200	100	1.4
200–400	300	6.7
400–600	500	14.8
600–800	700	17.3
800–1000	900	16.3
1000–1200	1100	14.4
1200–1400	1300	11.5
1400–1600	1500	7.7
1600–1800	1700	4.8
1800–2000	1900	2.9
2000–2200	2100	1.5
2200–2400	2300	0.7
2400+	–	0.0
Total	–	100.0

Table 11.3.2. *Moments of the retained liability in respect of the general insurance portfolio with the observed claim size distribution shown in table 11.3.1*

Retention ($)	Moments	
	$\hat{m}$	$\hat{\alpha}_2$
1200	870.90	853 250
1400	917.60	973 520
1600	945.10	1 055 250
2000	967.40	1 133 220
∞	971.00	1 148 400

rate is estimated to be 3.5%. What is the maximum possible retention if the insurer wishes to be 99% sure of being able to meet his liabilities?

The expected number of claims n is $1000 \times 0.035 = 35$, and we are told that the risk loading $\lambda = 0.05$. According to table 5.1.1, the area under the unit normal curve to the right of 2.33 is 0.01. We can, therefore, use (11.3.7) with $z_\epsilon = 2.33$ to calculate the free reserves required corresponding to the various retentions shown in table 11.3.2. The results are given in table 11.3.3, and it is clear that a maximum retention of slightly more than (but say) $1400 is required.

Example 11.3.3. The general insurer of example 11.3.2 arranges an excess of loss treaty with a retention of $2000. How many policies may be written if the insurer is to be 99% sure of being able to meet his liabilities under these contracts?

Again, we can use (11.3.7). We know $U = 12\,000$, $\lambda = 0.05$, $\hat{m} = 967.40$, $\hat{\alpha}_2 = 1\,133\,220$ and $z_\epsilon = 2.33$. The unknown is n. Substituting the known values into (11.3.7), we obtain

$$12\,000 = 2480.3502\,\sqrt{n} - 48.37\,n. \qquad (11.3.8)$$

If x^2 is written instead of n, we need to solve the quadratic equation

$$48.37\,x^2 - 2480.3502\,x + 12\,000 = 0.$$

This equation has two solutions: $x = 5.408$ and $x = 45.870$, corresponding to $n = 29.3$ and $n = 2104.1$. Which is the relevant solution to our problem? To answer this we go back to equation (11.3.8), which applies to the limiting value of n, and may be re-written in the form

$$48.37\,n - 2480.3502\,\sqrt{n} + 12\,000 = 0.$$

Table 11.3.3. *Free reserve requirements corresponding to various retention limits (example 11.3.2)*

Retention ($)	Free reserve requirement ($)
1200	11 209
1400	11 995
1600	12 506
2000	12 981
∞	13 073

All permissible values of n must satisfy the inequality

$$g(n) = 48.37n - 2480.3502 \sqrt{n} + 12000 \geqslant 0 . \qquad (11.3.9)$$

The graph of the left-hand side of this inequality $g(n)$ is given as fig. 11.3.1. From this graph, we deduce that n must either be less than 29.3 or else greater than 2104.1. The claim frequency rate is 0.035; the number of policies written should, therefore, be either less than 837 or else greater than 60 117.

The insurer's free reserves of $12 000, and the 5% loading in the premiums, together provide for adverse fluctuations in the claim experience. If the number of policies written is small, the overall contribution of the 5% premium loading is small, and most of the security is provided by the insurer's free reserves. If, on the other hand, the number of policies written is very large, the contribution to security of the insurer's free reserves is relatively minor, and the 5% margin in the premium rate will be sufficient to provide the required security.

Example 11.3.4. The general insurer of example 11.3.2 arranges an excess of loss reinsurance treaty whereby the excess over $1400 of any claim is paid by the reinsurer. An excess of $600 will also be introduced, and the insurer anticipates writing 1000 contracts as before. Estimate

(a) the new reduced risk premium following the introduction of the excess;

Fig. 11.3.1. Graph of $g(n)$, the function on the left-hand side of inequality (11.3.9).

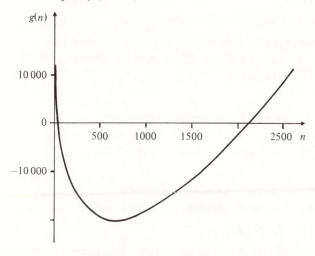

(b) the proportion of the risk premium retained by the direct insurer; and

(c) the probability that the direct insurer will not be able to meet his claim liabilities.

(a) the average liability of the insurer and reinsurer together, in respect of a loss (including losses which involve them in no payment), is

$$0 \times 0.229 + (700 - 600) \times 0.173 + (900 - 600) \times 0.163 + \ldots$$
$$+ (2300 - 600) \times 0.007 = \$412.90.$$

The loss frequency rate (as distinct from the claim frequency rate) is 0.035, so that the risk premium for each contract is $0.035 \times 412.90 = \$14.45$. This figure does not include the safety loading.

(b) The average liability of the direct insurer in respect of a loss is

$$100 \times 0.173 + \ldots + 700 \times 0.115 + 800 \times 0.176 = \$359.50.$$

The risk premium retained by the direct insurer is, therefore, $0.035 \times 359.50 = \$12.58$, or 87% of the overall risk premium. Again, these figures take no account of the safety loading.

(c) This part of the question can be answered independently of (a) and (b). The moments of the direct insurer's liability in respect of a loss need to be estimated as follows:

$$\hat{m} = 100 \times 0.173 + \ldots + 700 \times 0.115 + 800 \times 0.176 = 359.50;$$
$$\hat{\alpha}_2 = 100^2 \times 0.173 + \ldots + 700^2 \times 0.115 + 800^2 \times 0.176 = 221\,390.$$

Substituting these moments and the parameters $U = 12\,000$, $n = 35$ and $\lambda = 0.05$ into (11.3.7), we obtain

$$12\,000 = z_\epsilon \sqrt{(35 \times 221\,390)} - 35 \times 359.50 \times 0.05,$$

whence $z_\epsilon = 4.54$. This value lies outside the range of table 5.1.1, indicating that the probability that the insurer will be unable to meet his liabilities is less than about 0.000 01, which is negligible.

Example 11.3.5. How would your answers to example 11.3.4 be altered if the reinsurance treaty provided for 90% of the excess over \$1400 of any one loss to be met by the reinsurer, and the remaining 10% by the direct insurer?

(a) The total risk premium would be unchanged at \$14.45.

(b) The risk premium retained by the direct insurer would become

$$12.58 + 0.1 \times (14.45 - 12.58) = \$12.77,$$

so that the direct insurer would retain 88% of the overall risk premium.

(c) We first need to calculate the liabilities of the direct insurer in respect of losses of various sizes. These are set out in table 11.3.4, and are obtained as follows:

The average loss in the range $1800–$2000, for example, will be about $1900. The insured meets the first $600 of this himself. The direct insurer is then liable for the next $800 plus 10% of the remaining $500. The remainder is met by the reinsurer. The total liability of the direct insurer is, therefore, $850. Similarly for the other ranges of loss (table 11.3.4).

The moments of the direct insurer's liability are then estimated as follows:

$$\hat{m} = 100 \times 0.173 + 300 \times 0.163 + \ldots + 890 \times 0.007 = 364.84;$$
$$\hat{\alpha}_2 = 100^2 \times 0.173 + 300^2 \times 0.163 + \ldots + 890^2 \times 0.007 = 230\,188.$$

Substituting these moments and the parameters $U = 12\,000$, $n = 35$ and $\lambda = 0.05$ into (11.3.7), we obtain

$$12\,000 = z_\epsilon \sqrt{(35 \times 230\,188)} - 35 \times 364.84 \times 0.05,$$

Table 11.3.4. *Liabilities of direct insurer in respect of losses of various sizes (example 11.3.5)*

Size of loss ($)	Liability of direct insurer ($)	Percentage of losses in given range
0–200	–	1.4
200–400	–	6.7
400–600	–	14.8
600–800	100	17.3
800–1000	300	16.3
1000–1200	500	14.4
1200–1400	700	11.5
1400–1600	810	7.7
1600–1800	830	4.8
1800–2000	850	2.9
2000–2200	870	1.5
2200–2400	890	0.7
2400+	–	0.0
Total	–	100.0

whence $z_\epsilon = 4.45$. The probability that the direct insurer will be unable to meet his liabilities is greater than previously, but still negligible (table 5.1.1).

Further reading: Beard *et al.* [2] 18–24, 41–2, 52–63.

**11.4   The expectation and variance of C

The expectation and variance of C were quoted in sections 8.3 and 11.3 without proof. We now give the proofs which rely on (4.4.3) and (4.5.2). By definition,

$$C = X_1 + \ldots + X_N.$$

It follows that

$$E(C) = \underset{N}{E}[E(C|N)] \qquad \text{from (4.4.3)}$$

$$= \underset{N}{E}[NE(X_i)] \qquad \text{from (4.1.5)}$$

$$= \underset{N}{E}(Nm)$$

$$= m\underset{N}{E}(N) \qquad \text{from (4.1.4)}$$

$$= mn.$$

$$\mathrm{Var}\,(C) = \underset{N}{\mathrm{Var}}[E(C|N)] + \underset{N}{E}[\mathrm{Var}(C|N)] \qquad \text{from (4.5.2)}$$

$$= \underset{N}{\mathrm{Var}}[NE(X_i)] + \underset{N}{E}[N\,\mathrm{Var}\,(X_i)] \qquad \text{from (4.1.5) and (4.2.7)}$$

$$= \underset{N}{\mathrm{Var}}(Nm) + \underset{N}{E}[N(\alpha_2 - m^2)]$$

$$= m^2\,\underset{N}{\mathrm{Var}}(N) + (\alpha_2 - m^2)\,\underset{N}{E}(N) \qquad \text{from (4.2.5) and (4.1.4)}$$

$$= nm^2 + (\alpha_2 - m^2)n$$

$$= n\alpha_2.$$

Further reading: Beard *et al.* [2] 41–55; Parzen [24] 54–5.

11.5   The assumption of normality

Throughout section 11.3, we assumed that the distribution of the total claim amount C was normal. This is the classical approach to the problem, and it is usually quite satisfactory provided the number of policies in the portfolio is large and the likely claim amounts are of similar size.

The reader is warned, however, that there are situations in which the assumption of normality may be quite wrong, and even dangerous. For example,

1. when the distribution of claim size is markedly skew, and the portfolio is not very large; or

2. when the portfolio is heterogeneous in the sense that, in addition to a

large number of 'standard' policies, it also contains a small number of policies under which much larger claim amounts are likely.

Methods for dealing with problem (1) are described by Beard *et al.* [2] 41–51. The following example demonstrates problem (2).

Example 11.5.1. A general insurer with free reserves of $250 000 has a large portfolio of policies of comparable size. The expected number of claims n, in respect of these policies, is 1000. The mean claim size m = $2036.36, and the second moment about the origin α_2 = 5 017 600. The insurer has been asked to underwrite a different type of policy, under which the claim amount is fixed at $500 000. Only one claim is possible under the policy, and the probability of a claim is assessed as 0.1. The insurer loads all risk premiums 5% 'for contingencies', and will do the same with this single special policy.

What is the maximum net retention M for this policy if the insurer is to be 99% certain of being able to meet his liabilities?

Without the single large policy, the distribution of the total claim liability would be normal (fig. 11.5.1(a)) with

mean	= 2036.36 × 1000 = 2 036 360;
variance	= 5 017 600 × 1000 = 5.0176 × 10^9;
standard deviation	= $\sqrt{(5.0176 \times 10^9)}$ = 70 835.

The effect of the single large policy with net retention M is to make the distribution of the total claim amount markedly non-normal. The distribution is in fact bimodal[2] (fig. 11.5.1(b)). The first peak is centred at $2 036 360, and corresponds to the situation when there is no claim under the large special policy. The second is centred at $(2 036 360 + M), corresponding to a claim under the special policy. The first hump is almost identical to the normal distribution, with mean 2 036 360 and standard deviation 70 835, but scaled down by the factor 0.9. The second smaller hump is almost identical to the normal distribution, with mean (2 036 360 + M) and standard deviation 70 835, but scaled down by the factor 0.1.

The free reserves and retained risk premium income (including contingency loadings) of the insurer amount to

$$250 000 + 2036.36 \times 1000 \times 1.05 + 1.05 \times 0.1 \times M$$

dollars, i.e. $(2 388 178 + 0.105 M). We need to choose M so that the area under the bimodal distribution density curve to the right of (2 388 178 + 0.105 M) is equal to 0.01.

We concentrate on the smaller hump, which is almost identical to the normal curve with mean 2 036 360 + M and standard deviation 70 835, but scaled down

[2] has two peaks.

by the factor 0.1. The total area under this hump will be 0.1, instead of the usual 1.0. The area to the right of 2.33 'standard deviations' from the mean of the hump will be $0.1 \times 0.01 = 0.001$, instead of 0.01 the figure we require. The area to the right of 1.28 'standard deviations' from the mean (table 5.1.1), on the other hand, will be $0.1 \times 0.1 = 0.01$ as we require. It follows that we must have

$$(2\,388\,178 + 0.105\,M) - (2\,036\,360 + M) \geqslant 1.28 \times 70\,835,$$

whence

$$M \leqslant 291\,787.$$

A maximum retention of $290 000 is required.

An incorrect assumption of normality for the total claim amount would result in a grossly exaggerated retention limit: $448 000 (exercise 4).

Further reading: Beard *et al.* [2] 41–51, 76–97, 98–102.

11.6   Summary and further reading

The fundamental expression (11.3.7) can be used as a device for relating net retentions to reserves, as in examples 11.3.1–11.3.5. Additional mathematical analysis (Beard *et al.* [2] 58–65) leads to the formula

$$U \fallingdotseq 2.5\,\sqrt{(PM)} - \lambda P, \qquad\qquad (11.6.1)$$

Fig. 11.5.1. Distribution of total claim amount: (a) special policy not included; (b) special policy included.

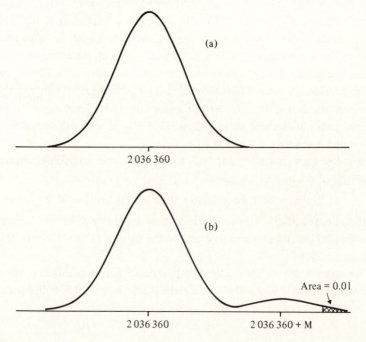

where

> P is the total risk premium;
> M is the net retention; and
> λ is the safety loading.

Formula (11.6.1) suggests some practical rules of thumb.

> 1. If premiums increase without any increase in reserves then the retention limit must fall.
>
> 2. If the reserves and premiums are correspondingly increased in the same ratio the retention limit can rise.

The formula may also be re-written in the form

$$M/U = 0.16 \, (1 + \lambda P/U)^2 /(P/U). \qquad (11.6.2)$$

When M/U is plotted against P/U for fixed λ, the curve shows remarkably little variation over quite a wide range of realistic values for P/U (fig. 11.6.1). Varying the value of the safety loading λ, on the other hand, has a marked effect on the height of the curve. For a given value of λ, the height of the M/U curve is approximately

$$M \fallingdotseq 0.64 \, \lambda U. \qquad (11.6.3)$$

We deduce, therefore, another rule of thumb:

> 3. The net retention of a general insurer should be a percentage of the reserve U which the insurer is willing to lose by way of covering losses during the year. The percentage is about two thirds of the safety loading percentage.

Fig. 11.6.1. Plot of M/U against P/U for various values of λ. (Reproduced with permission from R. E. Beard, T. Pentikäinen and E. Pesonen (1977), *Risk Theory*, page 64, Chapman and Hall, London.)

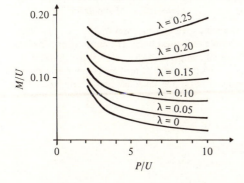

'Rule' 3 is often used in practice by reinsurers. Note, however, that it conflicts with a common (but not generally satisfactory) practice of selecting the retention M as a certain percentage of the premium income, or of total sums insured.

Further reading: Beard *et al*. [2] 58–65; Benjamin [3] 223–7.

11.7   Exercises

1. An observed claim size distribution is given in table 5.3.1. Calculate the (sample) moments $\hat{m}$ and $\hat{\alpha}_2$ of this distribution. Calculate also the moments $\hat{m}$ and $\hat{\alpha}_2$ of the retained liability when the retention under an excess of loss treaty is $2000.

2. How are the moments $\hat{m}$ and $\hat{\alpha}_2$ in the second part of question 1 changed when an excess of $400 is introduced?

3. A general insurer writes 1500 policies. The loss frequency rate for each of these contracts is 0.015, and the loss size distribution is that given in table 5.3.1. The insurer's net retention is $2000, and the policies include an excess of $400. The insurer includes a safety loading $\lambda = 0.05$ in his premium. How large should the free reserves of the insurer be if he is to be 99.9% sure of being able to meet his claim liabilities in respect of these policies?

*4. (a) Show that the mean and variance of the total liability in example 11.5.1 are $(2\,036\,360 + 0.1\,M)$ and $(5.0176 \times 10^9 + 0.09\,M^2)$ respectively. M is the retention for the special large policy
(b) Prove that, if the incorrect assumption of normality for the total liability is made, a maximum retention of $448\,000 for the special large policy is obtained.

*5. Show that the reserves needed by two merged insurance companies are always less than those of the two separate companies if the level of security $(1 - \epsilon)$ in both the sample companies is to be maintained in the merged organisation. (*Hint*: Use equation (11.3.7) with suffix A for company A and suffix B for company B, and recall the inequality $\sqrt{x} + \sqrt{y} > \sqrt{(x + y)}$ for all positive values of x and y.)

6. The claim size distribution for a certain class of policy is log-normal with mean $8500 and standard deviation $38\,600. The claim frequency rate is 0.015, and a small insurer has 200 of these contracts on its books. The insurer has free reserves of $10\,000 and includes a safety loading of 5% of the risk premium in its rates. Describe in some detail the simulation experiment you would perform to estimate the probability that the insurer will not be able to meet its liabilities. The net retention after reinsurance is $25\,000. Do you think the normal approach of section 11.3 would produce an accurate answer in lieu of simulation?

*7. There are r insurance companies with premium incomes $P_1, P_2, \ldots, P_r$. The companies exchange reinsurance on a reciprocal basis. The contract provides that company i takes from each risk of all companies a share P_i/P, where $P = P_1 + P_2 + \ldots + P_r$. Prove that the total reserve funds required in these companies is the same as if the companies were incorporated into one single company.' (Beard *et al*. [2] 63.)

8. Explain (11.3.9).

REFERENCES

[1] Backhouse, J.K., Houldsworth, S.P.T., Cooper, B.E.D. (1966). *Pure Mathematics: A Second Course.* Longmans, Green.

[2] Beard, R.E., Pentikäinen, T., Pesonen, E. (1969). *Risk Theory.* Methuen.

[3] Benjamin, B. (1977). *General Insurance.* Heinemann.

[4] Campbell, R.C. (1974). *Statistics for Biologists* (second edition). Cambridge University Press.

[5] Chemical Rubber Publishing Company (1963). *Standard Mathematical Tables.* (C.D. Hodgman, Editor).

[6] Croucher, J.S. (1980). *Operations Research: A First Course.* Pergamon Press.

[7] De Vylder, F. (1975). *Introduction to the Actuarial Theory of Credibility.* English translation by C.A. Hachemeister. Office des Assurers de Belgique.

[8] Dolciani, M.P., Beckenbach, E.F., Donnelly, A.J., Jurgensen, R.C., Wooton, W. (1970). *Modern Introductory Analysis.* Houghton Mifflin.

[9] Feller, W. (1968). *An Introduction of Probability Theory and its Applications,* vol. 1 (third edition). Wiley.

[10] Freund, J.E. (1965). *Mathematical Statistics.* Prentice-Hall.

[11] Green, S.L. (1966). *Advanced Level Pure Mathematics* (third edition). University Tutorial Press.

[12] Hammersley, J.M. & Handscomb, D.C. (1965). *Monte Carlo Methods.* Methuen.

[13] Hoel, P.G. (1971). *Elementary Statistics* (third edition). Wiley.

[14] Hoel, P.G. (1971). *Introduction to Mathematical Statistics* (fourth edition). Wiley.

[15] Johnson, P.D. & Hey, G.B. (1971). Statistical Studies in Motor Insurance. *J. Institute of Actuaries,* vol. 97, parts II and III.

[16] Johnson, N.L. & Kotz, S. (1969). *Distributions in Statistics. Discrete Distributions.* Houghton Mifflin.

[17] Johnson, N.L. & Kotz, S. (1970). *Distributions in Statistics. Continuous Univariate Distributions* − 1. Houghton Mifflin.

[18] Johnson, N.L. & Kotz, S. (1970). *Distributions in Statistics. Continuous Univariate Distributions* − 2. Houghton Mifflin.

[19] Kendall, M.G. & Stuart, A. (1963). *The Advanced Theory of Statistics,* vol. 1 (second edition). Griffin.

[20] Kendall, M.G. & Stuart, A. (1967). *The Advanced Theory of Statistics,* vol. 2 (second edition). Griffin.

[21] Mendenhall, W. & Scheaffer, R.L. (1973). *Mathematical Statistics with Applications.* Duxbury.

[22] Mode, E.B. (1961). *Elements of Statistics* (third edition). Prentice-Hall.

[23] Mood, A.M. & Graybill, F.A. (1963). *Introduction to the Theory of Statistics* (third edition). McGraw-Hill.

[24] Parzen, E. (1962). *Stochastic Processes.* Holden-Day.
[25] Pollard, J.H. (1973). *Mathematical Models for the Growth of Human Populations.* Cambridge University Press.
[26] Pollard, J.H. (1979). *A Handbook of Numerical and Statistical Techniques.* Cambridge University Press.
[27] Reichmann, W.J. (1969). *Calculus Explained.* Methuen.
[28] Tranter, C.J. & Lambe, C.G. (1970). *Advanced Level Mathematics* (*Pure and Applied*) (second edition). The English Universities Press.
[29] van Eeghen, J. (1981). *Loss Reserving Methods.* Surveys of Actuarial Studies Nr. 1 (G.W. de Wit, Editor). Publication of Nationale-Nederlanden N.V.
[30] Yamane, T. (1964). *Statistics, An Introductory Analysis.* Harper and Row.

SOLUTIONS TO EXERCISES

Chapter 1

1. 55.
2. 385.
3. ln 1.1 = 0.095 31.
4. $\binom{6}{3} = 20$.
5. 6.
6. 1.414; 1.260; 1.189; 1.072; 1.007.
7. 0.837; 0.888; 0.915; 0.965; 0.996.
8. For any positive constant k, the limit as n approaches infinity, of $k^{1/n}$ equals 1.
9. 0.90; 0.82; 0.74; 0.67; 0.61; 0.55; 0.50; 0.45; 0.41; 0.37.
10. -0.06 approximately.
11. $-0.1\,e^{-0.5} = -0.061$.
13. ln 3 = ln 1.103 639 + ln e = 1.098 61.
14.

x	$(x-1)!$	Stirling approximation	% error
1	1	0.9221	7.8
2	1	0.9595	4.1
3	2	1.9454	2.7
5	24	23.6038	1.7
8	5 040	4 987.7994	1.0

Chapter 2

1. $\frac{5}{36}$; $\frac{6}{36}$; $\frac{1}{36}$; $\frac{10}{36}$; $\frac{1}{6}$; $\frac{1}{5}$.
2. (a) $1 - P(A)$; (b) $P(B|A)$; (c) $1 - P(A|B)$.
3. $\frac{1}{2}$.
4. The probability of obtaining any specified sequence of 'heads' and 'tails' in four tosses of an unbiased coin (e.g. $HHTH$) is $\frac{1}{2} \times \frac{1}{2} \times \frac{1}{2} \times \frac{1}{2} = \frac{1}{16}$. There are $4 = \binom{4}{3}$ possible sequences which yield three 'heads' and one 'tail' ($THHH, HTHH, HHTH$ and $HHHT$). We deduce that the probability of obtaining three 'heads' is $\frac{4}{16}$. The other probabilities are calculated similarly.

5. (a) $\frac{1}{16}$; (b) $\frac{1}{2}$; (c) $\frac{5}{16}$; (d) 0; (e) 0; (f) $\frac{1}{5}$; (g) 1; (h) $\frac{4}{5}$; (i) $\frac{1}{2}$.

Chapter 3

1. $P(2) = \frac{1}{36}$; $P(3) = \frac{2}{36}$; $P(4) = \frac{3}{36}$; $P(5) = \frac{4}{36}$; $P(6) = \frac{5}{36}$; $P(7) = \frac{6}{36}$; $P(8) = \frac{5}{36}$;

   $P(9) = \frac{4}{36}$; $P(10) = \frac{3}{36}$; $P(11) = \frac{2}{36}$; $P(12) = \frac{1}{36}$.

2. 49/60.

3. (a) $F(50) = 1728/7821 = 0.22$;
   $F(100) = (1728 + 1346)/7821 = 0.39$;
   $F(200) = 0.63; F(400) = 0.86$;
   $F(800) = 0.98; F(\infty) = 1.00$.

   (b) $F(500) \doteq 0.89$ so the probability of a claim being greater than \$500 is approximately 0.11.

4. The probability that at least one of two claims exceeds \$500 is equal to 1 − the probability that neither claim exceeds \$500.

   $\doteq 1 - (0.89)^2 \doteq 0.21$.

6. $f(x) = \begin{cases} 0 & x < 0 \\ 1 & 0 < x < 1 \\ 0 & x > 1 \end{cases}$ $F(x) = \begin{cases} 0 & x < 0 \\ x & 0 < x < 1 \\ 1 & x > 1 \end{cases}$

7. approximately one in five.

Chapter 4

1. \$332.65 ; \$428.59.

2. (a) $(25 \times 1728 + 75 \times 1346 + \ldots + 1200 \times 149)/7821 = \$216.61$;

   (b) $(25^2 \times 1728 + 75^2 \times 1346 + \ldots + 1200^2 \times 149)/7821 - (216.61)^2$
   $= 49\,712.73$.

   Note: It has been assumed that payments in excess of \$800 are concentrated at \$1200.

4. (a) $f(x)$ is a proper probability density function because

   (i) $f(x) \geqslant 0$ for all $x \geqslant 0$,

   (ii) $\int_0^\infty f(x)\,dx = 1$;

   (b) mean $= r + 1$; variance $= r + 1$.

6. See note in solution to question 2.

   $\alpha_3 = (25^3 \times 1728 + 75^3 \times 1346 + \ldots + 1200^3 \times 149)/7821 = 65\,142\,656$.

   $\mu_3 = 65\,142\,656 - 3 \times 216.61\,(49\,712.73 + 216.61^2) + 2 \times 216.61^3 = 22\,674\,514$.

   From question 2, standard deviation $s = \sqrt{(49\,712.73)} = 222.96$. Estimate of $\sqrt{\beta_1}$ is therefore

   $\dfrac{22\,674\,514}{(222.96)^3} = 2.05$.

Chapter 5

1. (a) 0.980 77;
   (b) 0.049 47;
   (c) 1.15;
   (d) −0.18.

2. $\Phi\left(\dfrac{x-120}{15}\right) = \dfrac{8}{15}$ from which $x = 121.3$;

   $\Phi\left(\dfrac{100-120}{15}\right) = 0.0918$ so the expected number of claims is 1500×0.0918
   $= 138$.

3. $\exp\left(\mu + \frac{1}{2}\sigma^2\right) = 120$ and $\exp\left(2\mu + \sigma^2\right)\left[\exp\left(\sigma^2\right) - 1\right] = 225$, from which
   $\mu = 4.7797$ and $\sigma = 0.1245$.

4. $\Phi\left(\dfrac{\ln x - 4.7797}{0.1245}\right) = \dfrac{8}{15}$ from which $x = 120.3$.
   The estimated number of claims less than \$100
   $= 1500\,\Phi\left(\dfrac{\ln 100 - 4.7797}{0.1245}\right) = 121.$

5. $P(X = 1) = \dfrac{q\,e^{-q}}{1!} = \dfrac{q^2\,e^{-q}}{2!}$ from which $q = 2$ and the required probability $= 0.27$.

6. The claim frequency rate per policy per annum, q, $= 0.12$, so that the probability of a single policy having more than two claims equals 0.000 263 3. The expected number of policies having more than two claims each, from a portfolio of 80 000 policies, is $80\,000 \times 0.000\,263\,3 = 21$.

7. Assuming independence, the claim frequency rate for the new type of policy may be taken as 0.13 per annum per policy. So for 1000 similar policies, the total number of claims X will be a Poisson random variable with mean 130 and standard deviation $\sqrt{(130)}$. According to the normal approximation to the Poisson, the probability that X is greater than 140 is
   $1 - \Phi\left(\dfrac{140.5 - 130}{\sqrt{(130)}}\right) = 0.179.$

8. $\Phi\left(\dfrac{\ln 5000 - 5}{1.2}\right) - \Phi\left(\dfrac{\ln 50 - 5}{1.2}\right) = 0.817.$

9. $1 - \Phi\left(\dfrac{180\,000 - 310 \times 520}{420\,\sqrt{(520)}}\right) = 0.025.$

Chapter 6

1. variance = 293 552.

2. $\mu + \frac{1}{2}\sigma^2 = \ln 230.79$,

   $2\mu + 2\sigma^2 = \ln (293\,552 + 230.79^2)$,

   from which $\mu = 4.504\,75$ and $\sigma = 1.368\,77$.

Actual numbers	Fitted numbers
168	333
474	311
329	222
205	164
367	372
241	341
80	131
84	72
2	4
1950	1950

   The fit is poor.

3. mean = 0.125 461 3; variance = 0.129 959 9.

Number of claims in a year	Observed frequency	Poisson ($q = 0.125\,461\,3$)	Negative binomial $k = 3.498\,985\,8$ $p = 0.965\,384\,7$
0	565 664	564 493	565 735
1	68 714	70 822	68 521
2	5177	4443	5336
3	365	186	339
4	24	6	19
5	6	–	–
6	–	–	–
	639 950	639 950	639 950

4. $L = \binom{n}{X} p^X \left(1 - p\right)^{n-X}$;

   $\ln L = \ln \binom{n}{X} + X \ln p + (n - X) \ln (1 - p)$;

   $\dfrac{d \ln L}{dp} = \dfrac{X}{p} - \dfrac{n - X}{1 - p} = 0$ when $p = \dfrac{X}{n}$.

   So $\hat{p} = X/n$.

   From table 5.9.1 $X = 11\,415$ and $n = 100\,000$; so $\hat{p} = 0.114\,15$.

5. $0.114\,15 \pm 0.001\,97$.

7. Equate the Pareto mean (5.4.3) to the calculated mean of 230.79 and the Pareto variance (5.4.4) to the calculated variance of 293 552 (question 1) to obtain $\alpha = 2.0869$, $\beta = 120.2024$. The fit is unsatisfactory because the Pareto distribution with this β value allows no claim under $120.

Chapter 7

1. Table 7.2.2 becomes

Date of termination	Assumed renewal date	Reduction in exposure	Date of termination	Assumed renewal date	Reduction in exposure
4. 1.78	15 May	0	18. 1.79	15 August	209
12. 2.78	15 November	0	13. 2.79	15 November	275
19. 2.78	15 May	0	10. 3.79	14 February	296
17. 3.78	15 August	0	17. 3.79	15 November	243
5. 4.78	15 August	0	21. 4.79	15 November	208
24. 4.78	15 November	0	30. 4.79	15 November	199
1. 5.78	14 February	45	17. 5.79	15 November	182
4. 6.78	14 February	45	6. 6.79	15 November	162
7. 7.78	14 February	45	14. 7.79	15 August	32
29. 7.78	15 November	0	20. 8.79	15 May	133
3. 9.78	15 August	227	5. 9.79	15 May	117
16. 9.78	15 May	135	30. 9.79	15 November	46
1.10.78	15 May	135	3.10.79	15 May	89
5.11.78	15 August	227	18.11.79	15 August	43
19.11.78	14 February	45	Total reduction (days)		3138

The reduction in example 7.2.1 was 3006 days. A further reduction of 132 days or 0.4 years is therefore called for. A point estimate of the claim frequency rate is $18/322.5 = 0.056$, and the remainder of the solution is the same as in example 7.2.1.

2. Exposure $\doteq \frac{1}{2}(2560 + 2977) = 2768.5$. There were 364 claims, so that the claim frequency rate = $364/2768.5 = 0.131$.

3. For 1980 year of origin, 1000 claims will be settled in 1980 at a cost of $\$100\,000$ and 1000 claims will be settled in 1981 at a cost of $\$500\,000$. The average claim size settled in 1980 will be $(\$375\,000 + \$100\,000)/1750 = \$271$, while the average claim size for year of origin 1980 will be $(\$100\,000 + \$500\,000)/2000 = \$300$.

4. 0.134 ± 0.014.

6. Using the normal approximation to the Poisson, the probability is

$$\Phi\left(\frac{108.5 - 115}{\sqrt{(115)}}\right) = 0.272.$$

7. Equating the mean 980 to the log-normal mean (5.3.1) and the variance $(1560)^2$ to the log-normal variance (5.3.2) yields $\mu = 6.256\,34$ and $\sigma = 1.123\,57$. These values are substituted into (7.5.5) with $A = 2000$ to obtain a mean payment per claim by the direct-writing insurer of $\$749.82$, implying an average payment per claim by the reinsurer (averaged over *all* claims) of $\$230.18$. The reinsurance risk premium in respect of 1500 policies is therefore

$$1500 \times 0.05 \times 230.18 = \$17\,264.$$

8. The reduction in insurance payout in respect of a loss of under $\$500$ will be under $\$500$, and the reduction in respect of a loss over $\$500$ will be exactly $\$500$. The average reduction will therefore be less than $\$500$ i.e. less than 50% of the average loss of $\$1000$.

10. If X is a random variable having the log-normal distribution with parameters μ and σ^2,

$(\ln X - \mu)/\sigma$

is a unit normal random variable. It follows that

$1 - F(A) = P(X > A)$

$$= P\left(\frac{\ln X - \mu}{\sigma} > \frac{\ln A - \mu}{\sigma}\right)$$

$$= 1 - \Phi\left(\frac{\ln A - \mu}{\sigma}\right).$$

Substituting this expression into the second part of (7.5.2) and (5.3.3) into the first part, we obtain

$$\int_A^\infty \frac{1}{\sigma\sqrt{(2\pi)}} \exp\left[-\frac{1}{2}\left(\frac{\ln x - \mu}{\sigma}\right)^2\right] dx - A\left[1 - \Phi\left(\frac{\ln A - \mu}{\sigma}\right)\right].$$

The transformation $y = (\ln x - \mu - \sigma^2)/\sigma$ is now made, and on simplification, this yields

$$\exp\left(\mu + \frac{1}{2}\sigma^2\right)\left[1 - \Phi\left(\frac{\ln A - \mu - \sigma^2}{\sigma}\right)\right] - A\left[1 - \Phi\left(\frac{\ln A - \mu}{\sigma}\right)\right]$$

for the mean amount paid by the insurer when there is an excess of A. The mean amount paid by the insured himself (7.5.5) is obtained by subtracting the above expression from the mean loss $\exp(\mu + \frac{1}{2}\sigma^2)$.

Chapter 8

1. Fitted numbers are as follows (actual numbers are shown in brackets):

Number of claims	25+ family sedan	25+ high performance	<25 family sedan	<25 high performance
0	5018 (5019)	1067 (1068)	2906 (2907)	1231 (1232)
1	740 (738)	184 (182)	594 (592)	336 (334)
2	63 (65)	26 (27)	64 (66)	49 (50)
3	4 (4)	3 (4)	5 (5)	5 (6)
4	0 (0)	0 (0)	0 (0)	0 (0)

The fit is good.

3. $Z = \sqrt{(0.015 \times 5000/1363)} = 0.23$.
   Total risk premium $= 0.77 \times 95\,000 + 0.23 \times 88\,200$
   $\qquad\qquad\qquad\quad = 93\,426$.
   Premium per contract $= 93\,426/5000 = \$18.69$.

5. $P(D = U | L = U) = \dfrac{0.9 \times 0.8}{0.9 \times 0.8 + 0.15 \times 0.2} = 0.96$.

8. (a) If x_0, x_1, x_2 are the numbers in the 0%, 30%, 50% categories respectively, and p_0 is the probability of a claim-free year, then

$x_0 = 10\,000\,(1 - p_0)$

$x_1 = x_0\,p_0$

$x_2 = (x_1 + x_2)\,p_0$;

(b) (i) $x_0 = 952; x_1 = 861; x_2 = 8187$,

   (ii) $x_0 = 1813; x_1 = 1484; x_2 = 6703$;

(c) Only marginally better. The average poor risk will pay about 10% more for his insurance than the average good risk;

(d)

time t	q = 0.1 0%	30%	50%	q = 0.2 0%	30%	50%
0	10000	–	–	10000	–	–
1	952	9048	–	1813	8187	–
2	952	861	8187	1813	1484	6703
3	952	861	8187	1813	1484	6703
4	952	861	8187	1813	1484	6703
5	952	861	8187	1813	1484	6703

9. The transition matrix would become

	0%	30%	50%
0%	0.0952	0.9048	–
30%	0.0952	–	0.9048
50%	–	0.0952	0.9048

The proportions in the respective categories would be, in the steady state, 0.0099, 0.0943, 0.8958.

Chapter 9

2. The next unused random fraction in table 9.1.1 is 0.683 79 and $e^{-0.5} = 0.606\,53$. Random values X on the Poisson distribution with mean 0.5 are obtained as follows using successive random fractions:

$e^{-0.5} < 0.683\,79$,

$e^{-0.5} > 0.683\,79 \times 0.104\,93$; So $X = 1$.

$e^{-0.5} < 0.818\,99 \times 0.819\,53$,

$e^{-0.5} > 0.818\,99 \times 0.819\,53 \times 0.351\,01$; So $X = 2$.

$e^{-0.5} > 0.167\,03$; So $X = 0$.

$e^{-0.5} < 0.839\,46$,

$e^{-0.5} > 0.839\,46 \times 0.350\,06$; So $X = 1$.

$e^{-0.5} > 0.202\,06$; So $X = 0$.

3. The next unused random fraction in table 9.1.1 is 0.642 02. Random Poisson values are obtained as follows:

Random fraction	Random unit normal value	Random Poisson value
0.642 02	0.36	104
0.763 84	0.72	107
0.194 74	−0.86	91
0.015 36	−2.16	78
0.255 95	−0.66	93

4. The next unused random fraction in table 9.1.1 is 0.225 27. The corresponding unit normal random value is −0.75. The resultant normal value with mean 2 and variance 1 is therefore 1.25. Subsequent values are 0.47, 2.91, 0.77, 2.16, 0.40, 2.35, 2.08, 3.19 and 1.96.

5. The next unused random fraction in table 9.1.1 is 0.526 36.

Random fraction	Random unit normal variable	Random normal variable	Random log-normal variable
0.526 36	0.07	2.07	7.92
0.875 29	1.15	3.15	23.34
0.710 48	0.55	2.55	12.81

6. The cumulative distribution is as follows:

j	0	1	2	3	4	5	6	7	8	9
$P(X \leqslant j)$	0.01	0.06	0.16	0.36	0.61	0.80	0.89	0.95	0.98	1.00

The next unused random fraction in table 9.1.1 is 0.518 21

Random fraction	Random observation
0.518 21	4
0.524 04	4
0.333 62	3
0.463 69	4
0.337 87	3

9. (a) Assume n simulations and probability p of no payment. Number X of outcomes resulting in no payment will be binomial with mean np and variance $np(1 - p)$. We require

$$P\left(0.9p < \frac{X}{n} < 1.1p\right) = 0.95$$

which may be written

$$P\left\{ \frac{-0.1\, np}{\sqrt{[np(1 - p)]}} < \frac{(X - np)}{\sqrt{[np(1 - p)]}} < \frac{0.1\, np}{\sqrt{[np(1 - p)]}} \right\} = 0.95.$$

Using the normal approximation to the binomial distribution we have

$$\frac{0.1\, np}{\sqrt{[np(1 - p)]}} = 1.96,$$

whence $n = 384\,(1 - p)/p$.

The parameter p is unknown. An estimate $\hat{p} = \frac{15}{21}$ is available from the pilot simulation in table 9.9.2. We deduce that $n \doteqdot 154$.

(b) Assume n simulations, and at each trial a random payment with mean μ and variance σ^2. Total payment X in n simulations will be normal (Central Limit Theorem) with mean $n\mu$ and variance $n\sigma^2$. We require

$$P\left(0.9\mu < \frac{X}{n} < 1.1\mu\right) = 0.99$$

which may be written

$$P\left\{\frac{-0.1\,n\mu}{\sqrt{(n\sigma^2)}} < \frac{X - n\mu}{\sqrt{(n\sigma^2)}} < \frac{0.1\,n\mu}{\sqrt{(n\sigma^2)}}\right\} = 0.99.$$

From the normal table 5.1.1 therefore

$$\frac{0.1\,n\mu}{\sqrt{(n\sigma^2)}} = 2.58,$$

whence $n = 666\,(\sigma/\mu)^2$.

The parameters μ and σ are not known. Estimates $\hat{\mu} = 476.2$ and $\hat{\sigma} = 906.0$ can be calculated from the results of the pilot simulation, and we deduce that $n \doteqdot 2404$.

10. \$1000.24; \$2236.94.

Chapter 10

1. Outstanding claims provisions in respect of claims arising

Year	\$(thousands)
1975	0
1976	0
1977	129
1978	391
1979	909
1980	1954
Total	3383

2.

t	$c\hat{\lambda}_t$	r_t
0	114	0.273
1	120	0.328
2	132	0.186
3	163	0.137
4	191	0.076
5	230	0.000

Outstanding claims provisions in respect of claims arising:

Year	\$(thousands)
1975	0
1976	0
1977	130
1978	365
1979	817
1980	1668
Total	2980

3. Outstanding claims provisions in respect of claims arising:

Year	$ (thousands)
1975	0
1976	0
1977	130
1978	390
1979	983
1980	2047
Total	3550

4. Outstanding claims provisions in respect of claims arising:

Year	$ (thousands)
1976	168 987
1977	203 756
1978	350 733
1979	615 045
1980	1 235 161
Total	2 573 682

5. Very little. In the case of the payment due in development year 3 in respect of year of origin 1979, for example, the exercise 4 figure needs to be multiplied by the factor

$$\frac{(1.10)^{1.5}}{(1.10)^2} \times \frac{(1.08)^2}{(1.08)^{1.5}} = \sqrt{\left(\frac{1.08}{1.10}\right)} = 0.991.$$

The same adjustment factor $\sqrt{(1.08/1.10)}$ is used for all years of origin and all development years up to and including development year 4. In the case of year of origin 1979 and the development period 4+, the adjustment factor is

$$\frac{(1.10)^{6.5}}{(1.10)^{6.5}} \times \frac{(1.08)^{6.5}}{(1.08)^{6.5}} = 1.$$

All the figures for the 4+ development periods in fact require no adjustment.

A total provision of $2 557 017 is required.

The only reason the payments for development years 0, 1, 2, 3 and 4 require the small adjustment of $\sqrt{(1.08/1.10)}$ is that these payments are projected forward from *mid*-1980 (λ_4) and then discounted back to the *end* of 1980 at the same rate. If the inflation index $\lambda_{4.5}$ at the *end* of 1980 were known, and projections for development years 0, 1, 2, 3 and 4 were made from the *end* of 1980, no adjustment whatsoever would be needed.

The generalisation to any equal inflation/investment earnings situation should be evident.

6. The average time to settlement of claims can be calculated in (at least) two ways, depending upon whether the weighting used is by number of claims or by size of claims. For the calculation required in question 6, neither gives the correct theoretical answer, although the latter may come close and is therefore often used.

As an example consider 3 claims, one settled after exactly one year for $1000, the second settled after exactly two years for $ 2000, and the third settled after exactly six years for $10 000. The mean times to settlement by the two methods are respectively

$$(1 \times 1 + 2 \times 1 + 6 \times 1)/3 = 3 \text{ years,}$$

and

$$(1 \times 1000 + 2 \times 2000 + 6 \times 10\,000)/13\,000 = 5 \text{ years.}$$

If one third of IBNR claims were of the first type, one third were of the second type and one third were of the third type, and future inflation and investment earnings were 10% per annum and 8% per annum respectively, the correct provision for each estimated IBNR claim would be

$$\tfrac{1}{3} \times 1000 \times \frac{1.10}{1.08} + \tfrac{1}{3} \times 2000 \times \left(\frac{1.10}{1.08}\right)^2 + \tfrac{1}{3} \times 10\,000 \times \left(\frac{1.10}{1.08}\right)^6 = \$4752$$

Using a mean time to settlement of 3 years and the mean claim size of $4,333.33, a provision of

$$4333.33 \times \left(\frac{1.10}{1.08}\right)^3 = \$4579$$

is obtained. A mean time to settlement of 5 years, on the other hand yields a figure close to the correct value:

$$4333.33 \times \left(\frac{1.10}{1.08}\right)^5 = 4750.$$

7. (a)

t	$c\hat{\lambda}_t$	$\hat{r}_t$
0	1000	0.800
1	1140	0.150
2	1310	0.030
3	1507	0.010
4	1689	0.010

Development year payments for single claim incurred in the middle of 1982:

	Payment in development year					
Year	0	1	2	3	4	4+
1982	1787	385	89	34	39	39

Discounting these payments to 1 January 1982 at 10% per annum we obtain a discounted future payments figure of

$$\frac{1787}{(1.1)^{\frac{1}{2}}} + \frac{385}{(1.1)^{\frac{3}{2}}} + \frac{89}{(1.1)^{\frac{5}{2}}} + \cdots + \frac{39}{(1.1)^{\frac{11}{2}}} = \$2180.52.$$

The claim frequency rates for 1976 policies, 1977 policies, ... 1980 policies are seen to be 0.10, 0.11, 0.11, 0.12, 0.13 respectively. Assuming a claim frequency rate of 0.15 for 1982 policies, the office premium for policies taken out over the calendar year of 1982

$$= \frac{0.15 \times 2180.52 \times 1.05}{0.80} \times (1.15)^{\frac{1}{2}} = \$460.36.$$

(b) From the $c\hat{\lambda}$ values we see that recent claim inflation rates were

1976–7	14.0%
1977–8	14.9%
1978–9	15.0%
1979–80	12.1%

The assumed future rate of 15% is higher than the 1979–80 rate, but is in line with other recent years.

Chapter 11

1. 1216 ; 1 841 600 ; 1162 ; 1 582 800.

2. 766, 812 400.

3. $12 349.

8. According to (11.3.7) we must have

$$12\,000 \geqslant 2.33 \sqrt{(n\alpha_2)} - \lambda mn.$$

Substitution of numerical values and rearrangement yields (11.3.9).

AUTHOR INDEX

SUBJECT INDEX